S0-BSK-014

MARTIN LUTHER KING, JR.
AND THE CIVIL RIGHTS MOVEMENT

Edited by David J. Garrow

A CARLSON PUBLISHING SERIES

St. Augustine, Florida, 1963-1964

MASS PROTEST AND RACIAL VIOLENCE

Edited with a Preface by David J. Garrow

INTRODUCTION BY
DAVID R. COLBURN

CARLSON
Publishing Inc

BROOKLYN, NEW YORK, 1989

Library of Congress Cataloging-in Publication Data

St. Augustine, Florida, 1963-1964 : mass protest and racial violence /
   edited with a preface by David J. Garrow ; introduction by David R.
   Colburn.
        p.   cm.   — (Martin Luther King, Jr. and the Civil Rights
   Movement ; 10)
      Includes bibliographies and index.
      1.   Civil rights demonstrations—Florida—St. Augustine–
   –History—20th century. 2. Saint Augustine (Fla.)—Race relations.
   3. Afro-Americans—Civil rights—Florida—Saint Augustine–
   –History—20th century.   I. Garrow, David J., 1953-   .
   II. Series
   F319.S2S15   1989   89-22230
   975.9'18—dc20
   ISBN 0-926019-06-6 (alk. paper)

Typographic design: Julian Waters

Typeface: Bitstream ITC Galliard

The index to this book was created using NL Cindex, a scholarly indexing program from the Newberry Library.

For a complete listing of the volumes in this series, please see the back of this book.

Printed on acid-free, 250-year-life paper.

Manufactured in the United States of America.

Contents

Series Editor's Preface

St. Augustine, Florida, is one of the significant but not unduly famous chapters of the black freedom struggle in the South during the 1950s and 1960s. Occurring in the peak years of the southern movement, 1963 and 1964, and centrally involving the most notable single figure in the southern struggle, Dr. Martin Luther King, Jr., the St. Augustine movement additionally offers an important case study in each of the three sets of dynamics that can be witnessed in each chapter of the southern struggle: the relationships between local white leaders and local black activists, between those local black activists and outside civil rights organizations whose assistance was summoned, such as the NAACP and Dr. King's Southern Christian Leadership Conference (SCLC), and between the civil rights activists and the ambivalent federal government.

St. Augustine is perhaps most justifiably notable in the annals of southern movement struggles for the unmatched intensity of resistance that its white community offered to local civil rights initiatives. While much of the explanation for that intensity, and the accompanying level of white violence, can be attributed to the strength of local Ku Klux Klan elements, the very strong and rigid conservatism of city officials and businessmen was an equally important part of the picture. Even when some seemingly "moderate" whites did conclude that desegregation negotiations with the black activists were inescapable, Klan-style whites turned their tactics of violent intimidation against these perceived turncoats, and with some success.

The brunt of the white violence, however, was born by local blacks, who had requested the assistance of Dr. King and SCLC after learning the hard way that the national office of the NAACP would not enthusiastically support the style of aggressive, direct action efforts that some of St. Augustine's leading black activists, particularly dentist Dr. Robert B. Hayling, were intent upon pursuing. Hayling's unflinching dedication was central to the strength of the black community's efforts and to the recruitment of

SCLC's involvement, but his unapologetically *local* orientation—the improvement of life for black St. Augustinians—sometimes placed him apart from the nationally-oriented media strategy that was the first concern of some SCLC staffers, as David Colburn notes in his introduction to this volume.

Thirdly, the St. Augustine movement witnessed a fundamentally ambivalent and noncommittal response on the part of the federal government and particularly President Lyndon B. Johnson, a response that both troubled and somewhat surprised the local black community as well as Dr. King. Despite sustained black protest and dramatic white violence against peaceful demonstrators, the White House took a basically hands-off approach to the crisis, and encouraged and allowed Florida Senator George Smathers and Florida Governor Farris Bryant to be the principal behind-the-scenes actors working for some settlement or accord.

Professor Colburn's 1985 book, *Racial Change and Community Crisis* (Columbia University Press), provides a significant scholarly overview of the St. Augustine events of 1963 and 1964. My own *Bearing the Cross: Martin Luther King, Jr., and the Southern Christian Leadership Conference* (1986), treats the St. Augustine movement more briefly (pp. 316-341) and from the perspective of Dr. King and SCLC's involvement, but places particular emphasis upon how King and SCLC used Governor Bryant's announcement of a spurious biracial local negotiating committee as an opportunity and excuse for pulling out of a local movement situation which they no longer felt could continue serving any significant national agenda purpose. As Professor Colburn's work has emphasized, SCLC's departure from St. Augustine left the local black community in general, and Dr. Hayling in particular, disappointed and at times embittered that more significant local gains had not been achieved during the actual life of the direct action protest campaign.

Each of the four works presented in this volume offers a significant contribution to a full understanding of the St. Augustine story. Robert Hartley's previously unpublished 1972 master's thesis is the one other full treatment of the St. Augustine campaign in addition to Professor Colburn's book and has been of valuable use to a number of scholars who have written on the subject. Edward Kallal's previously unpublished 1976 bachelor's thesis on the Ku Klux Klan in St. Augustine, written under Professor Colburn's direction at the University of Florida, provides a unique and important picture of the radical white opposition to the movement. Klan-style opponents of the movement have so far received extremely little serious academic attention from scholars, and Kallal's essay will be instructive reading for any scholar or student interested in this important but under-studied aspect of the movement's history.

The 1965 Florida Legislative Investigation Committee "report" on the St. Augustine campaign offers an informative and instructive picture of the blinders and biases that limited even state-level officials' understanding of the initially indigenous black activism that appeared in St. Augustine and in scores of other southern towns. Lastly, Professor Colburn's own 1982 analysis of St. Augustine's white business leadership again stresses the degree to which potentially "moderate" whites, faced with a strong Klan presence, fundamentally abdicated any principled or courageous role in solving their community's crisis and beginning the elimination of formal, overt segregation from St. Augustine's public life.

I am very pleased that Carlson Publishing's series of volumes on *Martin Luther King, Jr., and the Civil Rights Movement* is able to bring this group of significant papers on St. Augustine to a broader audience of readers, and I trust that their wider availability, in conjunction with Professor Colburn's own scholarship, will help draw greater attention to the useful lessons and conclusions that emerge from the St. Augustine story.

David. J Garrow

The Oldest Segregated City in America: St. Augustine, Florida, 1963-1964

DAVID R. COLBURN

In 1964 the Southern Christian Leadership Conference decided to bring its nonviolent army into the nation's oldest city to assist local black leaders in their effort to break down the walls of segregation. This historic community, established by the Spanish in 1565, had shown little understanding or appreciation of its multicultural heritage as it pursued legal and extralegal steps to block the desegregation process in the post-*Brown* era. It was in this context that the Reverend Martin Luther King, Jr. and his advisers decided to enter St. Augustine in March of 1964, making it the third city—after Albany, Georgia, and Birmingham, Alabama—targeted by the organization in the 1960s. Following as it did on the heels of the Birmingham crisis, St. Augustine became a media event for several months as the drama of the civil rights movement unfolded on the city's streets and in its courtrooms.

St. Augustine was one of several communities that confronted the racial traditions of its past in the sixties. It was, no doubt, more celebrated than most because it confronted the SCLC and its remarkable leader, the Reverend King. Like New Orleans, Savannah, Charleston, and Jackson, however, it confronted more than this civil rights leader and his organization.

The community also faced the racial and historic traditions of its celebrated past. As such, it was not likely to embrace change very quickly. Indeed, like New Orleans, Charleston, and Jackson, St. Augustine had a respect for tradition, for a pattern of interpersonal arrangements, and for a social hierarchy that did not lend itself to change. As with many southern communities, St. Augustine did not see itself as an extremist community; indeed, most white residents perceived themselves as enlightened and characterized race relations as harmonious and designed to promote good will. It was in this context that racial change unfolded in the 1960s, and it was these traditions and perceptions that made St. Augustine a very difficult community to reform.

As King and his advisers prepared for the long, hot summer of 1964 in St. Augustine, they felt the need for a clearcut victory in their struggle to desegregate the South. In fact, the organization had wrestled at considerable length with its plans for 1964. Although SCLC had not earned a reputation as an organization that gave much attention to detail, this certainly was not the case in late 1963 and 1964. Indeed, the leaders of the organization discussed a number of possibilities for civil rights demonstrations as they sought to maintain pressure on Congress in order to insure the passage of the Civil Rights Bill of 1964.

Discussions among the leaders of SCLC centered on Birmingham and Montgomery, Alabama as possible target sites for 1964, with James Bevel in particular championing the idea of a statewide mass movement in Alabama. Most agreed that it would be difficult to generate interest among supporters if the organization returned to Birmingham and that the political defeat of Public Safety Commissioner Eugene "Bull" Connor had removed the biggest obstacle to racial advancement in the city.

The debate within SCLC pointed out that this was no ordinary group of civil rights activists by 1964. The experience of Albany and Birmingham had welded SCLC and its ministerial leaders into a sophisticated and skillful group of political activists. Weighing carefully the pros and cons of the options, SCLC sent two representatives to St. Augustine to assess both the local white and black leadership and to recommend a strategy, before the organization committed itself fully to involvement in this historic community.

Another critical factor in selecting St. Augustine for SCLC was its news worthiness. The organization depended on the television and print media to circulate its message to the nation and to Congress, especially in 1964. Without adequate coverage of the civil rights effort, SCLC's efforts would be severely circumscribed. St. Augustine offered certain features that satisfied this concern, the most important of which was that it was about to celebrate its 400th anniversary in 1965 and was already the focus of considerable national attention. Using this as its focal point, King announced in March 1964 that SCLC would use its non-violent army to desegregate the "Oldest Segregated City in America."

The campaign in St. Augustine proved more difficult than King or his aides had anticipated. Despite a highly successful economic boycott of the community that SCLC organized, the white leadership refused to seek a compromise. Heavily influenced by members of the John Birch Society and the Ku Klux Klan, St. Augustine's civic leaders opted to batten down the hatches as the storm worsened. Moreover, the Klan and other white militant groups sent in many of their leading spokesmen in an effort to derail SCLC and prevent further desegregation in the South. Working closely with police officials in the city and county, the Klan operated without restraint, attacking civil rights demonstrators at will and bombing King's rental home. As happened in many southern communities, white moderates found that their pleas for a racial compromise were ignored and they were isolated by white friends if they persisted in supporting negotiations. As the crisis deepened, white moderates virtually disappeared as a voice of reason. St. Augustine thus became a war zone in which the civil rights forces and white militants prepared to do battle.

Despite the sophisticated nature of SCLC's operation, the demonstrations in St. Augustine also revealed that there were sharp divisions within the black community over the need for a boycott and widespread protests. Generally speaking, older black residents in St. Augustine and in other southern communities refrained from participating in the demonstrations and attempted to discourage their children from participating. Pressured by white employees, these black residents faced the loss of their jobs and potential economic ruin if they engaged in demonstrations. Moreover, most had lived their entire lives in St. Augustine and, while not pleased with race relations, they considered them better than most communities in Florida and the South generally. Complacency and opposition proved to be a serious problem for SCLC, and the organization was forced to call upon substantial outside assistance and the support of the city's black youth to conduct its protests.

During the course of the St. Augustine demonstrations, King and his aides kept one eye on Washington as they planned their local tactics. The movement's leaders had a very good understanding of what it took to obtain national attention and support for their efforts. SCLC was hence sometimes criticized by local black residents for not being sufficiently concerned about their local problems as distinct from national considerations. In part this was true; King firmly believed that he was engaged in a national struggle to remove the barriers of freedom for black Americans, and, as a consequence, St. Augustine occasionally took a back seat to events elsewhere. As noted previously, in developing and implementing strategy, the organization gave substantial consideration to media coverage, so that the protests would receive national exposure. Thus, despite repeated warnings from state and federal agents that nighttime demonstrations would almost surely result in massive violence, SCLC conducted nighttime marches and occasionally did so without informing police of the path of the march. The consequence was that these marches deteriorated into bloodbaths but, in the process, attracted the interest of the national media. Were King and SCLC consciously Machiavellian in their approach to events in St. Augustine? Perhaps. The evidence suggests that their primary concern was indeed the passage of the Civil Rights Bill and only secondarily race relations in St. Augustine. Whenever media interest and thus national attention to the racial protests in St. Augustine flagged, King and his top aides developed alternative tactics to resuscitate such coverage. These tactics included having King arrested, undertaking the evening marches, and conducting protests at the ocean beaches. Moreover, King acknowledged subsequently that the role of the protesters in St. Augustine was to remind Congress that the South was unrepentant and that without federal legislation, black Americans would be unable to enjoy the liberties guaranteed by the Constitution. King observed later that a few communities like St. Augustine occasionally had to pay the price so that all black Americans would benefit.

When King and his advisers arrived in St. Augustine, they assumed direction of the movement, quickly superceding the local leadership formerly provided by Dr. Robert B. Hayling and other black residents. Hayling and his supporters were pleased to have SCLC's involvement in the community, but at times they were disappointed that they were no longer calling the shots. King's advisers questioned Hayling's commitment to nonviolence, and, in part, this accounted for their action. SCLC's staff also thought that the local leadership could not on its own plan and coordinate this new, large-scale movement. They were right on both scores, but SCLC's usurpation of leadership would have a profound effect on local developments after its departure.

Although St. Augustinians took pride in their community's historic past, they often viewed it through the lens of tourism and economic development. This is not to suggest that the residents of the community did not take great pride in being the oldest community in the nation and in reminding people of its rich Spanish heritage. Still, day to day life in the community focused on business and economic development. Business leaders dominated local politics to the point that city commissioners rarely took action without seeking the support of bankers and businessmen. Political and economic leaders perceived tourism as the stimulus for the community's prosperity and they recognized that it was the community's rich history that attracted so many tourists to the city.

Strategists for SCLC realized early on that tourism was the Achilles heel of the community, and the one area that would be certain to attract the attention of local leaders. St. Augustine was dependent on favorable national publicity to attract tourists. Moreover, with the 400th anniversary only a year away, civic leaders had begun the process of publicizing the community's anniversary to the nation. During the first stage of its protests, SCLC invited Mrs. Malcolm Peabody, the mother of the Governor of Massachusetts to participate in the demonstrations. Their arrests during sit-ins attracted widespread national attention and had a profound impact on the local economy. Suddenly motel and hotel owners found themselves with cancellations and empty hotel rooms. Only those few motels that accommodated television and newspaper reporters had any occupants. Within two months, the community's summer tourist trade was devastated and millions of dollars in local revenue were lost. Still, however, local white leaders did not move to end the crisis.

In the aftermath of the crisis, when SCLC withdrew its forces following passage of the Civil Rights Bill, local black residents found themselves in a very precarious position. No longer able to look to SCLC for assistance, local blacks confronted a hostile white community that blamed them for the racial confrontation and St. Augustine's economic collapse. Dr. Hayling saw his dental practice erode and virtually collapse as whites boycotted his office, and as some black residents blamed him for the aftermath of the crisis in the community. In 1966 he left St. Augustine for another Florida town. Other black leaders and residents encountered economic reprisals that led to the loss of jobs and lack of funding for public facilities in the black community. Many black residents thought that race relations had never been worse in the community. Thus, despite the passage of the Civil Rights Act and the prominent role played by St. Augustine in securing its passage, blacks saw conditions worsen locally.

The story of St. Augustine and its confrontation with the aspirations of its black residents is a dramatic story that was told and retold in other communities throughout the South during the 1960s. No community had exactly the same experiences; indeed some communities accepted the inevitability of change and quietly went about the process of providing equal access and integrated schools. St. Augustine was different from most, of course, because it became the target of Reverend Martin Luther King, Jr. and SCLC. The desegregation story in this community unfolded before the eyes of the nation on nightly television and on the front pages of the nation's major newspapers. Because events in the community took place before a national audience, they made it more difficult for a compromise to be achieved. King and SCLC were not interested in ending the demonstrations until they could be sure that the Civil Rights Bill was to become law, and local white leaders were not interested in compromise as long as their community continued to be portrayed as the oldest segregated community in the nation. Although St. Augustine went through a traumatic period that left many wondering whether the civil rights crisis had, in fact, worsened race relations, the community, under pressure from the federal courts and the federal government, gradually removed its racial barriers and integrated its schools. Moreover, without the demonstrations conducted by civil rights activists and the passage of the Civil Rights Act, the community would not have taken such steps voluntarily.

The racial developments in St. Augustine represent one of the major episodes of the civil rights era. Events there offer an instructive lesson in the dynamics of race in American society. Three of the four accounts included in this volume have not been readily available previously. The first piece is a substantial 1972 master's thesis on the St. Augustine protests by Robert Hartley, a former resident of St. Augustine, who was able to interview local white residents who were not available to subsequent scholars. Hartley's study examines the period from late 1963 through 1964 in considerable detail. According to his analysis, the civil rights demonstrations led to a significant change in the attitudes of black residents and set the stage for subsequent racial change in the community.

The second piece, Edward Kallal's essay on the Ku Klux Klan, was an honors thesis written at the University of Florida. During the course of his research, Kallal interviewed J. B. Stoner, head of the National States Rights

Party, Hoss Manucy, a local Klan leader in St. Augustine, and Sheriff L. O. Davis. These are among the few or only interviews that have been conducted with these three men who served as leading spokesmen for the white militant cause in St. Augustine. Kallal's study also points out the extent of the influence of the Klan and other white militant organizations in St. Augustine and the adjacent communities.

The 1965 Report of the Florida Legislative Investigation Committee chronicles the events that occurred in St. Augustine in 1963 and 1964. The Commission places most of the blame for the crisis on the black community and on what it refers to as militant civil rights activists like Dr. Hayling and Dr. King. In the process, however, the study provides a number of important documents that are attached to the body of the report and that would otherwise be unavailable to scholars.

Lastly, my own "Southern Businessmen and Desegregation" examines the role of business in the process of desegregation. A number of historical essays have argued that businessmen often became central figures in the desegregation process, because the social disruption initiated by civil rights leaders threatened the profitability of their operations. This essay, however, argues that businessmen in St. Augustine opposed racial change because they were part of the fabric of a very traditional and conservative society that regarded change of almost any kind as counterproductive. Moreover, many shared the views and ideology of the John Birch Society, which opposed any modification of segregation.

All in all, these four papers each make a substantive contribution to a full scholarly understanding of both the local and national elements that played significant roles in the St. Augustine civil rights crisis of 1964.

David R. Colburn
University of Florida
May, 1989

St. Augustine, Florida

1963-1964

A Long, Hot Summer: The St. Augustine Racial Disorders of 1964

ROBERT W. HARTLEY

Contents

Preface

During the summer of 1964 the city of St. Augustine, Florida found itself in the throes of an agonizing racial dilemma. A long history of discrimination and intolerance exploded during the "long, hot summer" promised by Dr. Martin Luther King, Jr. Hundreds of demonstrators marched nightly for five consecutive weeks during June and July in unsuccessful attempts to force the nation's oldest city to desegregate its public facilities. The demonstrations continued up to the signing of the 1964 Civil Rights Act; an inglorious reminder to the nation of the need for such a law.

The St. Augustine demonstrations marked the end of one phase of the civil rights movement of the early 1960s. That violent summer signaled the end of massive demonstrations to desegregate public accommodations. The Civil Rights Act which took effect in July, 1964, successfully destroyed the legal basis for segregated public facilities. After St Augustine, the movement turned its attention to the Northern ghetto. The emphasis shifted from public accommodations to voting rights and a vast array of economic and social problems.

The "long, hot summer" also marked the end of an era punctuated by unbridled and often naive optimism. During the 1950's and early 1960's many white liberals and blacks felt the answer to America's racial dilemma required only systematic destruction of the legal supports of segregation. Watts, Newark, Detroit and dozens of other riots destroyed this optimism and alienated much of the movement's white support. But the movement of the early 1960's expressed confidence in the future of America's race relations. "We shall overcome . . . Black and White together . . ." reached its peak in St. Augustine during the summer of 1964.

A study of the St. Augustine demonstrations is both worthwhile and important. From a historical standpoint, the demonstrations mark a watershed in the national civil rights movement. But "the long, hot summer" also provides a useful case study of racism in America. The St. Augustine confrontations graphically illustrate the inherent dangers of America's persistent racism. The greatest danger is a lack of communication between the two races. St. Augustine's interracial communications consisted of time honored "understandings." Negroes stayed "in their places," and the city boasted of "excellent race relations." The analysis of subsequent events makes abundantly clear the fact that there can be no real communication between the races in such a situation.

So long as such "understandings" were the basis for racial harmony in St. Augustine, the threat of violence remained a very real possibility. When violence took over the city, it was difficult to distinguish winners from losers. Negroes won their battle over public accommodations, but neither court orders, laws, nor bi-racial committees succeeded in improving the city's race relations. The violent struggle in St. Augustine destroyed many of the old "understandings," but it failed to attack the real problems of communication. When such a lack of communication between the races persists in American society, other cities may one day face "a long, hot summer."

My research for this paper followed three closely related and interlocking avenues. I first collected a large volume of newspaper and magazine articles. These articles provided a chronology of events and formed the basis for the organization of the paper. I used five newspapers in my early research, and I tried to balance my selections. *The St. Augustine Record* and *The Florida Times Union* usually presented events in a conservative, pro-St. Augustine light. *The Miami Herald*, *The New York Times* and *The Daytona Beach Morning Journal* usually presented events in a more liberal, pro-civil rights fashion.

The second phase of my research consisted of gathering pertinent documents. The transcripts of numerous court cases, Grand Jury presentments, background information on St. Augustine and its power structure, and manuscript collections occupied the second phase of research. The most valuable manuscript collection and scrapbooks were those of the St. Augustine Historical Society Library, Mr. and Mrs. Henry Twine (local NAACP officials), Dr. Robert B. Hayling, Reverend Charles Seymour, and Mr. Dana Swan (a former SCLC field worker).

The final phase of research consisted of private interviews. The interviews provided invaluable information, but they also contained two basic weaknesses. One weakness concerned primary source materials, e. g., letters, telegrams, and unpublished reports. Several interviews yielded valuable collections of such materials, but I did not have time to properly evaluate the material during the interview. Several questions later arose concerning this material. A second weakness of the interviews involved the reluctance and unavailability of several people. I interviewed Juvenile Counselor Fred

Brinkoff, Frank Upchurch, Sr., State Senator Verle Pope, Reverend Seymour, and I talked with Mayor Shelley and School Superintendent W. Douglas Hartley. H. E. Wolfe was ill at the time, and I failed to interview him. Sheriff Davis and Halstead Manucy failed to reply to my requests for interviews. On the integrationist side, I interviewed several local NAACP officials, local black moderates, Dr. Robert B. Hayling, Dr. David M. Chalmers and Ronald Messina, a local businessman. I also talked informally with many white and Negro citizens, and I tried to recall my own experiences. I lived through "the long, hot summer."

Introduction

"Save Our Republic: Impeach Earl Warren," glared the faded red, white and blue letters. The large billboard, located several miles south of St. Augustine on U. S. Highway One, seemed strangely out of place. Compared to other states in 1963, Florida appeared urban, cosmopolitan and relatively sophisticated. The state weathered the civil rights controversies of the late 1950's, and Miami Beach seemed far removed from battlegrounds like Birmingham and Little Rock. Governor Farris Bryant seemed moderate in comparison to some deep South demagogues, and the state's politicians counted few radical rabble-rousers in their ranks. On the surface at least, the "sunshine state" appeared to be the tropical, palm-shaded tourist mecca promoted by its Chamber of Commerce.

While parts of Florida appeared urban and moderate, the northern portion of the peninsula remained essentially rural and very conservative. North Florida controlled the state legislature through the infamous "pork-chop gang," a small group of senators and representatives with influence, power, and seniority. Politically conservative and geographically rural, the state's northern portion resembled its Georgia and Alabama neighbors far more than it resembled south Florida.

An integral part of conservative north Florida is the small tourist mecca of St. Augustine (See Appendix A). Founded by Don Pedro Menendez de Aviles in 1565, the city is the oldest permanent settlement in the United States. St. Augustine skillfully uses its history to support itself, and the tourist dollar is the life-blood of the community. Estimates of the importance of tourism vary, but most city officials agree that at least 70 per cent of the town's income comes from tourism.

The remainder of the town's economy is dependent upon several small industries, including an aircraft repair facility, a shrimp boat building firm, and a variety of small businesses. The city also benefits from surrounding agricultural areas. Timber, cattle, potatoes, and cabbage from Hastings, Spuds, and Elkton all add to the economy of the nation's oldest city.

Despite its agriculture, tourism, and small industries, however, the city was not wealthy. The median income in 1962 ($4,149) was not high, and 35 per cent of the city's residents earned under $3,000 per year.[1] Nearly 60 per cent of the city's 14,734 residents earned less than $5,000 per year.[2]

St. Augustine was one of the most conservative cities in the United States in the early 1960's, even by north Florida and southern standards. The city boasted an active John Birch Society, a White Citizens Council, and the St. John's County Coalition of Patriotic Societies. During the early 1960's these groups kept a steady stream of right-wing propaganda and speakers flowing through the community. Led by the Reverend Billy James Hargis and others, these speakers peddled the usual anti-communist line. They went to great lengths to equate the early civil rights movement with communism. Full page news paper advertisements and pictures allegedly showing Dr. Martin Luther King at a meeting with communists appeared on handbills and in the local newspapers. These allegations went uncontested and served to place civil rights demonstrations in an extremely unfavorable light. Early sit-ins and freedom rides became part of an international communist plot.

A powerful, well-entrenched power structure added to the town's conservatism. This powerful group of men presided over the nation's oldest city in such a way as to discourage any progress which threatened their power or threatened the uniqueness of the city. They de-emphasized industry, and worked diligently to preserve the older areas of the city.

Herbert E. Wolfe presided over St. Augustine's power structure. Wolfe owned several banks, a large ranch, and a construction company. He had considerable influence in the national Democratic party organization, and prominent democrats such as U. S. Senator George Smathers frequently visited Wolfe for weekend hunting trips at his ranch. Wolfe took a more moderate, compromising position on civil rights than many others in the power structure. He worked diligently for nearly a half million dollars in federal funds to restore part of the city along the lines of such places as Williamsburg, Virginia. The possibility of losing funds for a favorite project finally made Wolfe willing to at least negotiate Negro demands.

Frank D. Upchurch, Sr. occupied a position only slightly behind that of his close friend, H. E. Wolfe. Upchurch presided over a local, family-run law firm, which also handled Wolfe's legal affairs. While Wolfe's influence centered in national politics, Upchurch exercised considerable influence in state and local politics. Any candidate for a state office interested in carrying St. Johns County came to Upchurch. On at least one occasion a delegation of local Negroes asked Upchurch for permission to register to vote, and he benevolently granted it. Upchurch, unlike Wolfe, saw no need for compromise on any Negro demands.

Sheriff L. O. Davis also held an important and powerful position in the local power structure. Known affably to every one as "L. O.," Davis had been in office for nearly twenty years. An ex-railroad detective and football coach, he enjoyed more popularity than any other elected official. He consistently garnered more votes than any other candidate in St. Johns County, including presidential candidates. Davis remained intransigent on civil rights. Before his primary election in 1964, he gave some indication of his position in a speech to local Negroes.

> . . . I went out to Elk's Rest to talk with those Niggers. Niggers. That's what I called them. I told them I didn't want a single nigger vote, because I didn't want to beholden to them for any election.[3]

State Senator Verle Pope, "the Lion of the Florida Senate," found himself in an increasingly uncomfortable position during the racial disorders. He became the most outspoken member of the power structure for moderation and negotiation. Despite his best efforts, his real estate office became a target for local vandals, and cranks threatened his life on several occasions.

Dr. Joseph Shelley, a general practitioner and mayor of St. Augustine, played an important role as the city's racial drama unfolded. Despite his position as a symbolic figure under the city's manager-commission form of government, Mayor Shelly became the spokesmen for a city commission which followed an increasingly hard line with respect to the racial disorder.

County Judge Charles C. Mathis had the responsibility of meting out punishment of those arrested during demonstrations. Mathis began impartially, but his sentences eventually reflected the biases of the white community, as well as those of the majority of the power structure.

Clearly outside of the regular power structure, Halstead "Hoss" Manucy rose to new heights of glory during the demonstrations. As a convicted felon, moonshine runner, and special deputy sheriff, Manucy became somewhat of a folk hero. Appearing in the newspapers and on national television, he became the spokesman for the town. Newspaper and magazine articles claimed he led over one thousand whites knows as "Manucy's Raiders," and Manucy himself carefully cultivated his newly won prestige. His outspoken defense of white racism and his flamboyant manner prompted one writer to describe him as a "Hollywood director's dream."[4]

13

Besides Manucy, St. Augustine's formal power structure appeared strong, vigorous, and extremely well entrenched.[5] Many of its central figures served in their present positions for several decades or more. Wolfe, Upchurch, Davis, and Mathis were all in their sixties. They possessed nearly absolute control of the available power in St. Augustine. They protected their power from outside influence by emphasizing tourism and keeping large industries away from the area. Large industries meant large money and a potential influx of people into the area. (Both of which could threaten the power structure.) A stable population also protected the power structure from within. The city actually lost population between 1950 and 1970; a rare occurrence in a rapidly growing state like Florida. While no figures are available as to the age of those who left, many young, college-educated individuals probably headed the list. Unable to find employment in a tourist economy, they did not long remain in the area. Nearly 60 per cent of the population over the age of twenty-five did not complete high school, the median year of completed school being 10.5.[6]

The city's right-wing elements and its power structure remained secure, as well as omnipresent. The small size of the city meant relatively few people served in a variety of functions. Businessmen's groups, civic clubs, the Chamber of Commerce, the local Historical Society, and the United Fund all had remarkably homogeneous memberships. This control over a variety of community groups proved to be invaluable for those elements who controlled these various organizations. Dissent from views of the power structure and right-wing elements had little chance of succeeding when the only effective vehicles for dissent (including the only newspaper) were already committed to a particular point of view.

St. Augustine's power structure looked with pride upon many of the city's accomplishments, including its race relations. Mayor Shelley never tired of pointing out that city-owned facilities were open to members of both races; twenty-nine Negroes worked for the city; Negroes registered and voted freely and Negroes served in both city and county law enforcement agencies.[7] State Senator Verle Pope stated, "I felt that the relationship between colored and white in St. Augustine for many years had been excellent."[8]

Despite the official "line" on race relations, inconsistencies abounded. The city hastily desegregated its facilities in 1963 before a visit by Vice-President Lyndon B. Johnson. Negroes still refused to use the library or beaches for fear of reprisal by whites. While the city employed a number of blacks, they occupied very menial positions. None held management positions, and the two Negro law enforcement officers confined their activities largely to the Negro community. Negroes registered and voted freely, but they exerted little political muscle. They comprised only about one-fourth of the city's population. The Negro's situation in St. Augustine reflected prevailing national conditions of poor housing, few jobs, inadequate schools, blatant discrimination, and the ever-present fear of an omnipotent white society. St. Augustine's race relations were in fact no better or worse than those of most other cities across the country.

An ominous preview of the city's coming racial catastrophe occurred during the spring of 1960. Caught up in the wave of lunch counter sit-ins sweeping the country, a group of six black college students staged a sit-in at Woolworth's variety store on March 15, 1960. The students attended the local Florida Memorial College, and their sit-in took the town by complete surprise. Police arrested the youths and led them from the store.

The students tried unsuccessfully for three days to get service at the dime store's lunch counter. Violence exploded on the third day as the Negroes began their sit-in. Employees and customers alike cleared the store as the Negroes sat down at the lunch counter. A white mob gathered outside the front entrance and finally entered the store. Other whites locked the outside doors to keep police out while their friends tormented the trapped Negroes. The panic-stricken Negroes bore the brunt of a furious assault with clubs, fists, and chains. Police finally forced their way into the store and rescued the now badly beaten Negro students. Police arrested the blacks and led them through a hostile crowd of whites. An exasperated police chief, Virgil Stuart, finally had to threaten the mob with arrest in order to get the Negroes safely away.[9]

The day after the last demonstration city officials and Negroes met to discuss the sit-ins. They declared a moratorium on further sit-ins. They also announced that a biracial committee would be named at the next meeting of the City Commission on March 28, but no such committee was ever formed. The city's racial problems receded quietly into oblivion for the next few years.

Although the 1960 sit-ins failed, they revealed a distinct pattern which manifested itself during the "long, hot summer" of 1964. Peaceful, non-violent demonstrations by Negroes led to violent reprisals by white toughs. The power structure then turned deaf ears to Negro demands, and attempts at negotiations failed. Pressures continued to build and finally exploded in the streets. These pressures failed to explode in 1960, but 1963 dawned with the situation somewhat altered. The ingredients for a racial explosion changed little between 1960 and 1963, but the catalyst necessary for a racial confrontation emerged in the spring of 1963 in the person of Dr. Robert B. Hayling.

ONE

"Don't Forget Us
Mr. Vice-President"

Dr. Robert B. Hayling was born in Tallahassee, Florida on November 20, 1929. The son of a college professor and the second of four children, Hayling grew up in Tallahassee and attended Florida A & M University. He served as a lieutenant in the United States Air Force and later attended dental school in Tennessee. Hayling graduated from dental school in 1960 and began his practice in St. Augustine that same year.[1] His practice grew rapidly, and he became popular with whites, as well as blacks. Whites constituted about 50 per cent of his practice, and he treated the county's prisoners in addition to his own patients.

Hayling joined the local chapter of the National Association for the Advancement of Colored People (NAACP) and became advisor to the group's Youth Council in 1963. His activist approach to civil rights quickly pushed him into the vanguard of local civil rights activity and earned him the vituperation of both whites and blacks. Local whites considered him an irresponsible militant, and many local blacks feared his outspoken condemnation of St. Augustine's influential power structure and his militant rhetoric. His main source of support came from his Youth Council and a handful of adults in the local NAACP.

During the winter of 1963, the racial issue again surfaced in St. Augustine. The city sought some $400,000 in federal funds for the restoration and preservation of its downtown area in preparation for its four hundredth birthday in 1965. The city worked diligently to secure these funds, and the project moved ahead steadily under the leadership of Herbert E. Wolfe. Wolfe's influence brought about the appointment of a national Quadricentennial Commission to promote the project, and Vice-President Lyndon B. Johnson planned an Easter visit to the city to give federal endorsement to the project.

When news of the Vice-President's planned trip became publicly known in February, the local NAACP quickly advised Johnson of the racial problems in the town. They also protested that a planned banquet and program for Johnson excluded local blacks.

> How could you come into a city where every fifth or sixth person was a black and not invite the blacks? How could you have any celebration representing the city of St. Augustine and not invite the blacks?[2]

Johnson then sent his press secretary, George Reedy, to St. Augustine to make sure no racial trouble took place during his visit. The Vice-President also made it clear that he would not participate in any segregated event.[3]

Reedy arrived in St. Augustine and found himself cast in the role of mediator between the local NAACP and a group of local officials headed by Wolfe. Hayling threatened demonstrations unless local Negroes participated in activities during Johnson's visit. Wolfe's group wanted the Vice-President's visit, but negotiations with Hayling's group had not transpired. Reedy acted as mediator. He met first with one group and then with the other. The national president of the NAACP, Roy Wilkins, exerted pressure on Hayling to compromise.

> Roy Wilkins called from New York to try to tell me that tangible results were going to be gained. What would we gain from blocking the Vice-President from participating? They were also afraid that with the Spanish Ambassador being there, an international incident was a possibility.[4]

The pressure and assurances from Wilkins convinced Hayling to compromise. The city agreed to desegregate all city-owned facilities in the face of Johnson's threatened refusal to participate. They also agreed to include Negroes in activities during Johnson's visit, and they promised Hayling a meeting to discuss Negro grievances after Johnson's visit.

> If you let us have our banquet and other activities with no protests, then we will meet with your leadership tomorrow at 9:30 A.M. George Reedy promised us that the Vice-President was interested and would leave people there from Washington.[5]

Wolfe's group then moved to implement its part of the agreement. The city desegregated its public facilities, which included a library, park, several buildings, a miniature golf course, and the beaches. White Only signs disappeared from restrooms and water fountains in city-owned buildings. One of the city's two black policemen had previously been confined to the Negro section without a police car or uniform. He now appeared in the downtown area with a new uniform and car. All activities during Johnson's visit now included Negroes, including the Easter parade review stand and the banquet highlighting Johnson's visit.

Johnson arrived Easter weekend amid much fanfare and no hint of racial trouble. His visit went smoothly, and a banquet at the Ponce De Leon Hotel concluded his stay. The banquet prompted some heated negotiations between Wolfe's group and the NAACP.

> They wanted to give some of us blacks tickets, but we said "No." We wanted to buy ours. So they took two tables and put them off to the side. They put George Reedy and some secret service men at our tables.
>
> But it so happened that we sat right along the aisle where the dignitaries had to pass, and as Johnson came by I shook his hand and said, "Don't forget us Mr. Vice-President."[6]

Johnson's group left the following day for Washington, and local Negroes prepared for their promised meeting with federal, state, and local officials. Hayling and his group arrived at 9:30 A. M. The federal, state, and local officials consisted of City Manager Barrier, his secretary, and a tape recorder. Hayling immediately realized his mistake. He lost his leverage (the threat of demonstrations) when Johnson left town. He forced city officials to negotiate with him out of fear before Johnson's visit. Now he could not force them to negotiate at all. He surrendered his only weapon for a promise, but he never again made such a mistake.

Hayling and the local NAACP tried throughout the spring of 1963 to bring local officials into meaningful negotiations. But every attempt to meet with the city commission failed. Hayling viewed these refusals to negotiate with dismay. He also looked with some apprehension upon the election of Dr. Joseph Shelley as mayor on June 4, 1963. With Shelley heading an already intransigent city commission, Hayling saw no chance for negotiations.

> Mayor Shelly and others were well indoctrinated in John Birch Society techniques, and one of their major themes is, "Never Negotiate!" We never had a chance to meet these fellows face-to-face. They had evasive actions all the time.[7]

Hayling now decided on a two-pronged course of action. He continued to pressure the city commission to negotiate. He also moved to gain new leverage by picketing local businesses which refused service to Negroes. Pickets appeared during the first week in June at selected locations in the downtown area. Hayling also continued to write letters to the city commission asking for a meeting.

After two weeks of picketing and letters, the city commission agreed to meet with a delegation of local Negroes on June 20. Local Negroes arrived at the appointed time for the promised meeting. Only two members of the city commission bothered to attend, however, and the meeting adjourned for lack of a quorum. The commission scheduled a new meeting for June 28.

NAACP pickets now expanded their activities to the local Chamber of Commerce and other businesses. They also appealed again to the city commission for a meaningful dialogue. They also made public a rather modest list of demands they hoped to negotiate with the city commission.

1. Fair employment in city government.
2. Complete desegregation of all city-owned facilities.
3. Assurance from the City Fathers that picketing within the code of the city will be allowed with adequate police protection.
4. A blanket statement from the Mayor and City Commission making their position known to all about desegregation.
5. The establishment of a bi-racial committee.
6. We are asking the Commissioners to use their influence to get the White and Colored Religious leaders of the city together so that their Wisdom and Christian training might be brought to bear in attempting to achieve racial harmony in the City of St. Augustine, Florida.[8]

The long awaited meeting between Negroes and the city commission finally occurred on June 28. The results proved disappointing and anti-climactic. Hayling and other Negro leaders presented their demands. The city commission listened politely, and Mayor Shelley later issued a statement in which he rejected every demand. He specifically rejected a bi-racial committee, and later in the summer he further explained his opposition.

A bi-racial commission defeats the very purpose for which it was formed. It polarities the White race and the Negro race and begins with the assumption there is a difference.[9]

The civil rights struggle in St. Augustine might well have withered away at this point. Hayling finally had his meeting with the city commission which produced no results. His picketing helped produce the meeting, but it now appeared that further demonstrations could accomplish little. But Hayling received help from an unexpected source. A group of militant whites attacked his home with shotgun fire and effectively kept Hayling and his movement from collapsing.

Hayling received numerous phone calls threatening his life after Vice-President Johnson left town. He referred these calls to the Federal Bureau of Investigation, and they referred him to local police officials. Hayling expected no protection from local authorities, and he formed his own police force of young Negroes. He bought guns for his group and trained these young blacks in their use.[10] He then stationed his "troops" at strategic locations in the Negro sections of town.

Melvin Thomas and his wife borrowed Hayling's compact car for a trip into town on July 1, 1963. They stopped at a red light, and another car bumped them from behind. Thomas glanced in his rear-view mirror and noticed a group of laughing white youths in the car behind. They continued to bump the Thomas car until the light changed, and Thomas quickly returned to Hayling's house with the whites in pursuit. He pulled into the driveway, and the whites stopped in front of the house. As Thomas and his wife left their car, the whites got out of their car and threw a brick at the fleeing couple. Simultaneously, someone fired a shot at the brick throwers, who then piled into their car and fled.

The white youths fled only far enough to arm themselves with shotguns. They returned to the Hayling home, now being guarded by four young Negroes sitting on the front porch. Several rounds of shotgun fire shattered the still summer evening, and all four Negroes received slight wounds. Police arrested the whites, as well as the wounded Negroes. The gun used in the shooting belonged to one of the white youths, but the county later dropped all charges against both groups for lack of evidence.[11]

An enraged Hayling angrily promised, "we are not going to die like Medgar Evers. I and others of the NAACP have armed ourselves and we will shoot first and ask questions later."[12] These angry statements also pointed up a growing schism in the local civil rights' movement. Hayling's Youth Council did not reflect the views of the older members of the local organization. His militant rhetoric prompted another phone call from Roy Wilkins.

> Roy Wilkins called and wanted to know what was going on and who was running the show down there. The NAACP doesn't engage in this kind of dialogue . . . I let him know that I was trained by this country as an Air Force officer to defend democracy, and I certainly knew that if I could defend a

country that didn't give me my rights, I could use the same techniques to defend my own life.[13]

The shooting incident at Hayling's home gave new impetus to the local civil right's movement. Hayling gained new stature in the Negro community, and he now had fresh ammunition to use on the power structure. Surely the threat of a shooting war between Negroes and whites would force the power structure into meaningful negotiations.

The moderate wing of the power structure moved cautiously into action. Hayling called Senator Verle Pope and asked him to call in the governor. Frank Harrold, a local bank president, also called Pope and suggested a committee of himself, Pope and Wolfe. Pope considered such a committee political suicide, but he finally agreed to serve.[14] Wolfe refused to serve, however, and St. Augustine lost one of many golden opportunities to solve its racial problems at the conference table.

Despite the failure of the power structure to act, several elements of the white community voiced concern over the possibility of further violence. A. H. Tebault, editor of the local *St. Augustine Record*, fired off a strong front page editorial. He called for tough penalties for the youths involved in the shooting incidents. He also admonished the city to solve its racial problems, and he closed his editorial with a remarkable bit of insight. "The responsibility for any further racial violence rests with us all."[15]

Mayor Shelley then demonstrated his total misunderstanding of the situation in a curious editorial the following day. He recognized that racial tensions existed in the community, but he blamed these tensions on the "radical fringe in both races."

> Use prudence and reason so that we might avoid the pitfalls that can destroy the respect and friendships which are the foundation of the good race relations that exist in our community.[16]

Unfortunately for Mayor Shelley, Hayling saw very little in the way of good race relations. He redoubled his efforts and increased the picketing. The national NAACP and the Southern Christian Leadership Conference (SCLC) also appealed to Vice-President Johnson for help in St Augustine.[17] The renewed picketing and pressure on Johnson produced no results, and Hayling again faced a critical decision. He could continue his present course and hope for a breakthrough, or he could up the ante.

Hayling decided on the latter course of action. Confined to picket lines by Hayling, young Negroes now engaged in sit-ins at several drug store lunch counters. The sit-ins began on July 18 and 19, and police quickly moved into action. Police and sheriff's deputies used electric cattle prods and dogs on those demonstrators who offered any form of resistance. The sit-ins lasted four days and resulted in dozens of arrests.

On July 23, County Judge Charles Mathis banned picketing and participation in demonstrations by juveniles. He ordered any juvenile caught picketing to be taken to his parents, and he required both parents and children to appear in juvenile court. If the juvenile refused to cease picketing or demonstrating, police turned him over to Juvenile Counselor Fred Brinkoff, for prosecution.[18] Mathis' order reached a mass meeting of angry Negroes at a local Negro church. The meeting concerned one of the most bizarre incidents in the history of the city's racial disorders.

During the first few days of sit-in demonstrations, police arrested seven juveniles and turned them over to Brinkoff. Judge Mathis held a hearing for the seven Negroes and their parents. He offered to release the children to their parents if the parents promised to keep the children out of further demonstrations. The parents refused, but three of the parents reconsidered and asked for another meeting with Mathis. These three parents agreed to keep their children out of further demonstrations, and Mathis released three of the seven children. He then sentenced the remaining four juveniles to reform school! Local authorities put the youths in the local county jail, as no juvenile facilities existed in the county.

Mathis' actions enraged the Negro community. For the first time since Johnson's visit, the Negro community united behind Hayling. Three hundred angry Negroes converged on the county jail on the night of July 25 to protest the sentencing of the four youths. They surrounded the jail and began singing and chanting. They pressed toward the front door of the jail, demanding the release of the four children.

The only person on duty at the jail was Mrs. Louis Cook, wife of the jailor. Seeing the group of Negroes at the jail door, Mrs. Cook became enraged. She foolishly walked out the front door into the mass of Negroes, expecting them to wilt before her onslaught. Several angry exchanges followed and Mrs. Cook found herself on the ground. Several trustees then came to her rescue and took her back inside. The badly shaken Mrs. Cook managed to call Sheriff Davis and Brinkoff, both of whom soon arrived on the scene.

Davis and Brinkoff arrived at the besieged jail and agreed to meet with a delegation of Negroes. The delegation demanded the release of the youths, but Brinkoff called Mathis, who refused to budge. "We weren't going to submit to mob rule."[19] Stalemated by white officials, the Negroes maintained their singing and praying vigil far into the night. They finally began to disperse around midnight, and the four children remained behind bars.

City officials transferred the children to Jacksonville the following day and later to the state reform schools at Mariana and Ocala. Local Negroes then began a long court fight to secure the release of the children with the aid of the NAACP Legal Defense Fund. Judge Mathis agreed to release the children on several occasions if the juveniles met an 8:30 P. M. curfew; refrained from participation in any demonstrations; and remained on probation until age twenty-one.[20] The State Cabinet, which had jurisdiction over state prisons, finally broke the stalemate on January 14, 1964. They ordered the four youths released without any conditions, and thus ended a six month nightmare for the youths.

Tension continued to mount after the jail demonstration. Police arrested four Negroes for handing out handbills in a fashionable white neighborhood. The handbills contained a copy of a newspaper editorial criticizing St. Augustine officials for their handling of racial incidents in the city. The editorial appeared in the *Daytona Beach Morning Journal*. Police charged the youths with disturbing the peace, and Judge Weinberg sentenced the youths to sixty days in jail or a $100 fine.[21]

The hearings and trials of other arrested demonstrators continued and several of them brightened an otherwise gloomy summer. On August 1, Justice of the Peace, Marvin Greer, sentenced six Negro youths to pay $100 fines or serve forty-five days in jail. The courtroom, packed with Negroes, hooted derisively at Greer's sentence. Greer angrily threatened to clear the court, and the gallery finally quieted down. At that point Sheriff Davis burst into the courtroom and shouted, "Who's got my letter?"

Davis had earlier passed a letter around the courtroom he received from Ocala, concerning that city's racial troubles. The letter fell into Hayling's hands, and Davis walked over to Hayling and demanded his letter. A Negro near Hayling returned the letter to Davis, who then angrily cleared the noisy courtroom. A thoroughly shocked Greer managed to call a recess, as Davis stalked out of court.[22] Davis later said, "That was a personal letter and I didn't want it read by any niggers!"[23]

Deeply troubled by the deteriorating situation, Hayling again appealed to Vice-President Johnson. He wrote the Vice-President a long letter in which he reviewed his struggle in St. Augustine.[24] Unfortunately for Hayling and St. Augustine, however, the Vice-President probably had more pressing civil rights business. For some 250,000 people staged an unprecedented march on Washington at the same time Hayling sent his plea. All eyes were on Washington, not St. Augustine, in August, 1963.

Hayling finally persuaded the Florida Advisory Committee to the United States Commission on Civil Rights to hold a hearing in St. Augustine on August 16, 1963. The Advisory Committee invited members of both races to appear, but the local power structure boycotted the meeting entirely. After a day of testimony by local Negroes the Advisory Committee made public the following conclusions and recommendations.

Conclusions:

1. The Committee found a deep-seated and wide spread feeling of discontent among the Negro citizens of St. Augustine . . . civil rights conditions are considerably worse than in most if not all other cities in the state.
2. There are no lines of communication between the Negro and white communities in St. Augustine.
3. Negroes have no choice but to make their grievances known by means of demonstrations.
4. The atmosphere in St. Augustine is repressive. Negro employees at Fairchild Stratos Corporation were warned not to participate in demonstrations on pain of dismissal.

Recommendations:

1. The United States Commission on Civil Rights should schedule early hearings in St. Augustine.
2. The Federal Government should closely scrutinize any expenditure of federal funds . . . ($400,000)
3. The President's Committee on Equal Opportunity, as well as the Departments of the Army and Air Force, should launch an investigation to determine whether the Fairchild Stratos Corporation is complying with the spirit and the Letter of Executive Order 10925.[25]

The city's power structure ignored both the Advisory Committee and its report. Another chance for meaningful negotiations between Negroes and the power structure passed, and St. Augustine's racial situation continued to deteriorate. A member of the Advisory Commission warned, "St. Augustine is a segregated superbomb aimed at the heart of Florida's economy and political integrity—the fuse is short."[26]

TWO

"Don't Tread on Grandmother Peabody"[1]

Mary Parkman Peabody grew up in Back Bay, a quiet elegant section of Boston. After her debut in 1910, she and a girl friend took a trip around the world. During this trip she met a young teacher named Malcolm Peabody, whom she later married. Malcolm Peabody followed his famous father Endicott, into the Episcopal church. Mrs. Peabody's son, Endicott, Jr., served as governor of Massachusetts, and her other children held such prominent positions as minister, teacher, representative to the United Nations, and urban affairs expert. During the spring of 1964, however, Mrs. Peabody left her comfortable Boston surroundings. Following in the footsteps of the old New England abolitionist, Mrs. Peabody joined the civil rights crusade. Before she arrived in St. Augustine, Dr. Hayling and his followers succeeded in stirring up a nest of white-robed hornets known as the Ku Klux Klan.

During the early 1960's, the Ku Klux Klan enjoyed a resurgence across the South. The lunch counter sit-ins and freedom rides offered an impetus and occasion for the type of direct violence in which the Klan excelled.[2] Hayling's activities in St. Augustine also led to increased activity in north Florida. Hoping to boost its membership rolls and appeal, the Klan moved into St. Augustine in force shortly after the Advisory Commission issued its report.

The Klan quickly demonstrated its power of coercion in trying to find a suitable site for its rallies. They sought out Ron Messina, the owner of the Hi-Nabor market, a small curb market located just outside the city limits. Messina's father owned a large tract of land which the Klan wanted to use for their meeting. Messina refused to allow the use of his land, and the Klan found another section of land for its rallies. Messina soon felt the full wrath of the Klan. His children were harassed at school; vandals smashed his store and car windows; and a Klan speaker, Reverend Connie Lynch, cost Messina nearly eight thousand dollars during the next three months.

Everybody here knows that blond-haired bastard who runs this market down the street is a nigger lover. I don't want anybody to shop at his place.[3]

The presence of the Klan added one more volatile ingredient to the St. Augustine pressure cooker. The other ingredient, Dr. Hayling, continued his campaign in the face of growing city commission intransigence. The Advisory Commission report brought only denials and inaction from the city commission. Hayling resolved to force the issue by continuing the sit-ins, and local police continued to arrest and jail the demonstrators. Police used cattle prods and dogs to arrest twelve demonstrators on August 31.[4]

St. Augustine's gloomy racial picture brightened a little with the opening of public schools in the county. For the first time since Reconstruction six Negro youths attended previously all-white schools. The decision to integrate the schools came from a federal court case begun in 1962 by several local Negroes. The integration of the schools under a federal court order, however, provided only a one-week lull in the city's racial dilemma.

Hayling continued his campaign with a Labor Day rally in the Slave Market.[5] As Negro speakers began to explain their grievances to the growing crowd, police interrupted the proceedings. They used cattle prods to move reluctant Negroes, and they arrested twenty-seven people for violating a 1928 ordinance which prohibited a public meeting in a city park without a permit.[6]

St. Augustine was now primed for a major confrontation. Two volatile elements like Hayling and the Klan occupied the city with no authority willing to exert influence on either force. The city commission remained intransigent, the power structure was divided and ineffectual without Wolfe's influence; and the business community refused to act in the face of real and implied intimidation. Dr. Hayling, as usual, provided the necessary spark when he visited a Klan rally in his honor.

One of the most bizarre episodes of the long civil rights campaign began on the evening of September 18. A strong wind blew off the Atlantic Ocean, scattering hundreds of Klan distributed handbills throughout the downtown area. The handbills announced another Klan meeting and urged all white people to attend.[7] The Klan scheduled the meeting near a bowling alley south of the city on United States Highway One. The actual meeting occurred about a half mile off the highway in a large clearing. The only access to the meeting was a narrow dirt road.

Klansmen stood on the main highway and the dirt road, directing cars to the meeting. Children also lined the road, selling Confederate flags and automobile tags. By 6.30 P.M., about three hundred people congregated around a large cross in the middle of the clearing. Klansmen in red, white, and black hooded robes mingled with a large number of local curiosity seekers. A robed Klansman finally stepped forward to light the twenty foot cross, and the burlap-wrapped cross burst into flames. Robed Klansmen and Klanswomen walked in a circle around the cross, giving a rather sloppy, left-handed sign of obedience. Unfortunately for the Klan, large chunks of flaming burlap began blowing into the woods. Several small fires started, and several men finally toppled the cross and extinguished the flames.[8]

A robed Klansman now called the meeting to order, and Brother Gene F. gave the invocation. The main speaker of the evening was introduced as Reverend Connie Lee of Alabama. But Connie Lee turned out to be Conley Lynch, a professional agitator from California. He arrived in St. Augustine in August, 1963, and promptly paid Ron Messina a visit. Lynch later arranged the boycott of Messina's store.[9] Lynch also played a vital role during the "long, hot summer" of 1964.

Lynch quickly captured the spirit of the evening and whipped the crowd into a frenzy. His interpretation of the Birmingham church bombings, Dr. King, and Dr. Hayling proved particularly enlightening.

> Not long ago, a man from the F. B. I. came by to talk with me. They came by and said, 'Now you don't advocate violence, do you?'
> And I said, 'The hell you say. The niggers has declared all out war on the plan of God and on God's family, the white man, and in war you shoot.'
> . . . But I'll tell you people here tonight, if they can find those fellows (the church bombers), they ought to pin medals on them.
> . . . You've got a Nigger in St. Augustine that ought not to live . . . that burr-headed bastard of a dentist. He ought to wake up tomorrow morning with a bullet between his eyes.
> . . . Martin Luther Coon? . . . I heard him on TV the other night saying, 'The NEEEgro is not satisfied.' Well, he never will be, because before they are satisfied they all will be six feet under the ground.[10]

While Lynch poured out his vituperation, Hayling and three companions parked their car on the main highway. Armed with a tape recorder, they hoped to record the proceedings. They had recorded Klan meetings in Jacksonville, using the same procedure.[11] They felt sure of their safety as long as they stayed on a main federal highway, despite the fact that Klansmen directed traffic all around them.

29

The Klansmen soon grew suspicious of the Hayling car, and a car full of Klansmen pulled up behind Hayling. James Houser, the driver of the Hayling car, quickly drove away. Houser thought he knew the area, but be made a fatal mistake as he turned down a dirt road. He now headed straight for the Klan meeting with several cars in hot pursuit The dirt road dead ended at the meeting, and several robed Klansmen stepped out from behind trees. Armed with shotguns and rifles, the men dragged Hayling and his companions from the car and hauled them before the meeting.

The Klan meeting came to an abrupt halt as shouts of "Nigger! Nigger!" filled the air. Guns, knives, and clubs appeared from beneath robes, as the Negroes marched through the crowd.

"Boy, what y'all doing out here?" questioned one Klansman.

"We just came out to run our fish lines," replied Hayling.

"Dressed in a shirt and tie?" snarled the Klansman.[12]

A search of the Negroes produced Hayling's NAACP identification card, and the beating began. Several burly white men held each Negro as fists and clubs pounded the helpless blacks. The women in the crowd screamed hysterically, "Castrate the bastards! Kick their balls out. Come on, do something!"[13] At this point Reverend Cheney made his way slowly to his car and went for help. He managed to find a phone booth, and he called the F. B. I. and local police.

Hayling and his friends lost consciousness from the beatings, but he remembered someone saying, "Work on his right hand. He's a right-handed dentist."[14] The Klansmen clearly intended to murder the Negroes. They piled the unconscious Negroes on top of each other, and sent a man for some gasoline. At this point Sheriff L. O. Davis arrived on the scene, and the dwindling crowd began to disperse. Davis arrested four Jacksonville Klansmen and took Hayling and his companions to the hospital.

Events now began to take a strange twist. Police found a gun in the glove compartment of Hayling's demolished car, and the Klansmen claimed that Hayling had threatened them. Davis then arrested the Negroes and charged them with assault and battery! Three of the Negroes required hospital treatment and Hayling's injured hand kept him from his practice for two weeks. Yet, the Negroes and Klansmen stood trial for the same alleged crimes.

One week later Hayling filed a petition in federal court. The petition asked the court to stop St. Augustine officials from interfering in racial demonstrations.[15] The NAACP also called for federal and state investigations of the Klan meeting. Hayling and the other beaten Negroes meanwhile pleaded not guilty to the assault charges against them. The pleas helped little, however, as a white jury convicted Hayling of assault and battery. The same jury also acquitted the four Klansmen.

The Florida Advisory Committee to the United States Commission on Civil Rights again issued a stern warning to the city. The Committee urged the Justice Department to investigate renewed Ku Klux Klan activities in the state and called upon the U. S. Commission on Civil Rights to hold meetings in St. Augustine. "Civil rights conditions in St. Augustine were considerably worse than in most if not all other cities in the state."[16] Unfortunately, the Committee's warnings again went unheeded.

On the night of October 25, the city's fragile racial peace again cracked under pressure. William Kinard, a white shrimp boat crewman, and three other white men drove slowly through the Negro section of town. The whites were all armed with shotguns, and Kinard's gun rested on his lap. Several shots fired by unknown assailants struck Kinard in the head. The shotgun on his lap discharged through the floor of the car. The men with Kinard charged that the shots came from the front porch of Goldie Eubanks, a local NAACP official. Kinard's companions also said that four or five Negroes ran from the front porch of the Eubanks home.[17] Police indicted Eubanks and three other Negroes for second degree murder, but they were later released for lack of evidence.

White segregationists retaliated for Kinard's murder four nights later. Two carloads of whites roared through the Negro section of the city. Two Negro homes, a grocery store, and two nightclubs were hit by gunfire. Whites also threw a hand grenade at one of the nightclubs, but it failed to explode. One Negro suffered a hand wound in the raid, but no other injuries were reported. The morning after the incident police arrested Hayling at the scene of one of the shootings. Sheriff Davis arrived and found Hayling conducting his own investigation. After an angry exchange of words, Davis charged him with interfering with an official police investigation.[18]

On the same day of Hayling's arrest, a home owned by a white family near the Negro section bore the brunt of a sniper attack. The rifle fire injured no one, but St. Augustine moved ever closer to a possible race war. Governor Farris Bryant ordered a dozen more state police to St. Augustine, and local officials hurriedly canceled a high school homecoming parade and curtailed Halloween activities.

The city's racial dilemma seemed to cool, however, as abruptly as it heated up. On November 15, federal Judge William McRae ruled on Hayling's September petition. He found St. Augustine officials acted within the law, had not used unnecessary force; and did not prohibit the use of parade permits. He also accused Hayling of displaying a lack of restraint, common sense, and good judgment.[19] McRae's ruling exonerated the city and seemed to take some of the steam out of the local civil rights movement.

The day after McRae's ruling a local Grand Jury convened to study the racial situation in St. Augustine. The Jury consisted of sixteen whites and two blacks, but the people most directly involved in the city's racial dilemma failed to testify.

> The Grand Jury purposely excluded individuals directly involved in the racial disturbances in an effort to obtain . . . the true feeling of this cross section of the citizens of the county.[20]

The findings of the Jury clearly reflected the absence of Hayling's group. The Jury noted the city's racial progress; praised law enforcement officials; and blamed extremists like the Klan and Hayling for the city's problems.[21] But the most important finding the Jury made concerned a breakdown of communications between the races.

> The Grand Jury feels that there are many sincere and dedicated individuals, representing both races living in St. Johns County, and when given the chance to sit down and discuss these differences that they will be able to resolve the same, in so far as is humanly possible.[22]

McRae's criticism of Hayling and the Grand Jury Report caused the growing rift in the local NAACP to finally rupture. Hayling went too far for many local Negroes, and pressure from local leaders and Roy Wilkins forced Hayling out of the local organization. According to Hayling:

> Roy Wilkins' threat to me was that he would withdraw the local charter if I didn't step down. I told him (Wilkins), I'll send you your charter if you'll be in your office.[23]

Hayling and Eubanks resigned three days after the Grand Jury findings. They issued a statement in which they criticized federal Judge William McRae and local officials for inaction, and they explained that "new and less militant leaders could make more progress in breaking down the city's racial barriers."

The two men expressed hope that "divine wisdom would guide future efforts to heal the breach in human understanding in our nation's oldest city. If new leaders make sufficient progress in race relations, we feel that permanent retirement from the civil rights movement would be in order."[24]

The local NAACP, minus Hayling and Eubanks, sought immediate reconciliation with the city.

> In light of the recent findings and recommendations of the St. Johns County Grand Jury; the St. Augustine Branch of the NAACP would like to request a meeting with the City Commissioners at the earliest possible date. The implication of their findings was that when given a chance, well-meaning persons of both races would be able to sit down and discuss ways and means of establishing better racial relations and communications.[25]

Local officials never replied to the above letter. Perhaps they thought Hayling's withdrawal marked the end of racial tensions in the city. Perhaps they never had any intention of negotiating with local Negroes. Whatever the reason, St. Augustine missed another golden opportunity to solve its racial dilemma. The Negro grievances in St. Augustine were much more profound and ran much deeper than one individual or one group. As long as the city commission refused to negotiate, and Klan elements went uncontrolled, the entire community suffered the consequences.

Hayling remained on the sidelines only long enough to watch the local NAACP become stalemated. He then contacted Dr. Martin Luther King in Atlanta and joined the Southern Christian Leadership Conference (SCLC). Hayling met several times with King and his advisors, and he attended an SCLC meeting in Orlando, Florida on March 6, 1964. Hayling and King made plans at the Orlando meeting for a massive Easter desegregation campaign in St. Augustine.

Dr. Hayling's temporary retirement from local activity failed to ease the tense racial climate in the city. City officials allowed segregationist elements to continue their activities without any apparent harassment. On January 22, Mr. Charles Brunson and his wife attended a P.T.A. meeting. Brunson, a Negro deaf mute employed by the Florida School for the Deaf and Blind, enrolled three of his five children in a previously all-white elementary school. As the meeting progressed, several fire bombs destroyed Brunson's car. Later in the month, rifle shots hit Hayling's home, killing his pet dog. On February 11, the home of another Negro, whose children went to a former all-white school, mysteriously burned down. No vandals were ever caught or prosecuted in any of these cases.

Hayling and SCLC officials began preparations for a massive Easter drive to desegregate public accommodations in St. Augustine. The most pressing problem confronting SCLC concerned recruits for the coming drive. Hayling's small Youth Council lacked sufficient manpower to mount such a drive, and Hayling had little support among the local Negro adult population. Faced with this situation, SCLC advertised across New England for college recruits. Folders, pamphlets, and campus newspaper advertisements urged volunteers to spend their Easter in St. Augustine.

> This is not a vacation, these are serious demonstrations. Arrests are not planned at this time, but students must be willing to accept it . . . Students should previously secure a source of bail (up to $500) if at all possible.[26]

A St. Augustine student attending college in New England notified Mayor Shelley of the spring offensive. Shelley also received copies of several of the SCLC pamphlets and folders. On March 22, Mayor Shelley issued a statement in which he attempted to refute the contents of several of the SCLC folders. He made no mention of Negroes' attempts to negotiate with the city, and he blamed the city's racial problems on Hayling and the local NAACP. Mayor Shelley proudly pointed to Judge McRae's November ruling in favor of the city.

> At the conclusion of this trial held before a Federal Judge (McRae) in Jacksonville Florida, the Court gave the city officials a 100 per cent clean slate. The Court further severely criticized and reprimanded the leadership of the local NAACP. [27]

Undaunted by Shelley's remarks, a contingent of twenty white Northern college students arrived in St. Augustine a week before Easter. The students lived with Negro families and immediately organized for the coming struggle. On the night of March 25, SCLC held a mass rally at one of the local Negro churches. The next day students held a noisy demonstration at Murray High School, the local all-black high school. Caught up in the spirit of the demonstration the night before, many students shouted and pounded their feet. Still others refused to attend classes and demonstrated in the halls. Sheriff's deputies arrived at the school and arrested two white college students for organizing the disturbance.[28]

The Easter desegregation drive began in earnest on Saturday, March 28. Police arrested twenty-six persons at two segregated drug stores and a restaurant, while local officials placed their bonds at one hundred dollars each. As the demonstrations grew in size and intensity during Easter week and the following summer, bonds increased to seven hundred fifty dollars.[29] Police arrested ten more persons on Easter weekend, and several churches turned Negroes away from segregated services. Mrs. Peabody also arrived in St. Augustine on Sunday night.

> We went to St. Augustine, because although it is the oldest city in our country, it is totally segregated. One of Dr. King's followers telephoned me to say that many college students were going to St. Augustine to demonstrate during their Easter vacations, but that they needed older people too. He asked whether I knew of any people he might call. I said to him, 'Would I be of any use?'[30]

Attention now focused on Mrs. Peabody and several of her more famous companions, including Mrs. Donald J. Campbell, wife of the Dean of Episcopal Theological Seminary; Mrs. John Burgess, wife of the first Negro Episcopal Bishop in the United States; Professor Lawrence Burholder of the Harvard Divinity School; and William Sloane Coffin, Jr., the Chaplin of Yale University. Mrs. Peabody and her friends began their participation in the desegregation drive on Monday morning with a visit to the segregated Trinity Episcopal Church. The church hastily cancelled a scheduled 10:00 A. M. service, and Mrs. Peabody confronted several vestrymen and Rector Charles Seymour inside the church.

"Why don't you Northerners stay up North? You've got plenty of problems up there," said one vestryman.

"We have problems, and we are trying to solve them. You're not trying to solve your problems. We look upon ourselves as Americans, not as Northerners. Integration and civil rights are American problems," replied Mrs. Peabody.

"You have set us back five years down here," another vestryman told her.

"The Negroes have waited one hundred years," said Mrs. Peabody.[31]

Mrs. Peabody and her friends left the church and walked across the street to McCartney's Drug Store. The store's manager refused to serve the group, when Mrs. Peabody explained to him that the light skinned Mrs. Burgess was in fact a Negro. The flustered manager offered to pick up the check if the group left.[32] Mrs. Peabody led her group out of the store, and they spent the afternoon testing other restaurants and drug stores.

Despite the presence of Mrs. Peabody and a rapidly filling jail, local officials refused to change their positions on Negro demands or negotiations. They remained courteous to newsmen and firm in their belief that St. Augustine's racial problems were the product of outside agitators. They reasoned that as soon as Hayling and his New England friends grew tired and went home, the city's racial problems would go with them.

SCLC and Mrs. Peabody now resorted to a favorite tactic. They decided to have Mrs. Peabody and her friends arrested and jailed. Dr. King resorted to this tactic several times with a degree of success in such places as Birmingham, Alabama. Mrs. Peabody's arrest was designed to focus national attention on St. Augustine, but the resulting avalanche of bad publicity failed to budge the local power structure.

Mrs. Peabody, two white companions, and five local Negroes went to lunch on Tuesday, March 31, at the Ponce de Leon Motor Lodge. The restaurant, part of a country club complex north of the city, refused the group service. The manager summoned Sheriff Davis, who patiently read the state's anti-trespass law to the group. Mrs. Peabody remained firm in her refusal to leave, and Davis arrested the entire party. He charged the group with trespassing, conspiracy, and being undesirable guests.

While Mrs. Peabody and her friends attacked segregation at the Ponce de Leon Motor Lodge, SCLC moved on another front. A massive contingent of three hundred marchers moved down King Street toward the heart of town. The group moved peaceably, but a white man suffered injuries from a flying pop bottle, as he shouted obscenities at the group. The marchers moved into the downtown area, and about one hundred fifty of them converged on the Ponce de Leon Hotel's exclusive dining room. The marchers, most of whom skipped school, sat down in the hotel's dining room. City police arrived with dogs and cattle prods, and one hundred seventeen demonstrators found their way to the county jail.

Attention now turned to the county jail with its most famous inmate, Mrs. Peabody. Sheriff Davis, basking in national publicity, allowed Mrs. Peabody to hold a news conference shortly after she arrived.

> It's a very pleasant jail, and I have very pleasant company . . . I want to share the experience with my fellow demonstrators. If I got out immediately, there would be no point to it.[33]

Local Negroes and SCLC officials held a mass meeting the night of Mrs. Peabody's arrest. The results of the mass meeting indicated a shift in SCLC tactics. Integrationist forces faced a severe manpower shortage with nearly two hundred demonstrators in the county jail. Mrs. Peabody's arrest and the resulting publicity made further sit-ins unnecessary. (The purpose of the massive arrests was to focus national attention on St. Augustine.) Mrs. Peabody's arrest and a growing manpower shortage prompted SCLC to offer the city an opportunity to negotiate. The mass meeting approved a new list of demands, which superceded Hayling's demands of June, 1963. While the demands went beyond earlier requests, they were still quite moderate.

1. The immediate release, with all charges dropped against all demonstrators jailed.
2. The desegregation of all hotels, motels, department stores, restaurants, bowling alleys, swimming and bathing facilities and all other similar public accommodations.
3. The establishment of a bi-racial committee. The local chapter of SCLC shall name their representatives.
4. The desegregation of all public facilities such as parks, playgrounds, jail-house, and all other tax-supported facilities.
5. The integration of all public schools following the military districting lines.
6. The elimination of police brutality, especially the use of dogs and electric cattle prods.
7. The hiring of at least five Negro policemen with full civil service pay and responsibility privileges.
8. The establishment of equal job and promotion activities in all city and county employment.
9. The addition of Negro representation to the committee planning the Quadricentennial Anniversary of St. Augustine.
10. The guarantee that no person shall lose his (or her) job because of participation in civil rights activities.
11. The guarantee that students not be suspended or expelled from school for civil rights participation or in any manner penalized.[34]

SCLC also moved on the legal front. Lawyer William Kunstler flew immediately to St. Augustine.[35] Kunstler and Miami attorney Tobias Simon filed suit to remove the cases of the jailed demonstrators to federal court. Despite moving testimony from Mrs. Peabody, Hayling, and several others, U. S. District Judge Bryan Simpson denied the motion for removal.

Mrs. Peabody's arrest served its purpose well. Television, newspapers, and magazines across the country focused on St. Augustine. By Wednesday, April

1, some two hundred eighty-five persons packed the St. Johns County jail. Reverend Bernard Lee, an SCLC official from Atlanta, threatened to march on St. Augustine with a non-violent army. "It may be necessary to bring in part of our non-violent army that we have recruited from all over the country."[36] R. W. Saunders, Florida field secretary of the NAACP, appealed to Governor Farris Bryant to intervene in St. Augustine to "save our state from shame."[37]

Despite this publicity assault on the power structure, St. Augustine officials remained intransigent and unavailable for comment. Mayor Shelley finally broke official silence on April 2, in a curious statement to the press. He cited the city's racial progress, and he further explained his own views.

> I am a segregationist for one reason . . . God segregated the races when he made their skins a different color. I am not a racist. I have the deepest compassion for Negroes . . . St. Augustine has no White Citizens Council; and no John Birch Society . . . and to my knowledge no Ku Klux Klan.[38]

Mrs. Peabody posted bond on April 1, and left jail on the arm of Sheriff Davis. She flew home on Friday, April 3, and her departure marked the end of the Easter desegregation drive. White college students returned North to classes and SCLC called off further demonstrations. A contingent of workers stayed behind to plan a summer tutoring program and further demonstrations, but SCLC official Bernard Lee admitted grimly, "We've got to do some organizing here."[39]

The Easter campaign had little effect on the attitudes of most local officials. They expected the city to return to normal with Mrs. Peabody's departure. They steadfastly refused to see the deeply-rooted hate and prejudice which gripped the city. They preferred to blame the city's racial problem on "outside agitators." The more adverse publicity the town received, the further city officials retreated behind their own psychological barriers. Mayor Shelley went on NBC's *Today Show* on May 20, to combat the bad publicity the town received. His remarks clearly illustrated the position of the power structure.

> Mrs. Peabody did a disservice not only to St. Augustine, but to the nation as a whole. She did irreparable harm to race relations in the city which has made steady progress in eliminating racial barriers. We were picked on because we were celebrating our four hundredth anniversary.[40]

The Easter demonstrations helped set the stage for the "long, hot summer." The actors and props were all in place. On one side the power structure expressed confidence and intransigence, and Police Chief Stuart publicly gloated after a Boston riot involving eight hundred youths. He offered Boston (Mrs. Peabody's home) the use of some of his "peace-loving" police dogs.[41] On the other side a determined group of SCLC officials, white college students, and a handful of local Negroes looked forward to helping the city with the coming summer's activities. The curtain was now ready to open on one of the longest and bloodiest civil rights campaigns of the early 1960's.

THREE

"There's No White Man Scared of a Nigger"

Holstead "Hoss" Manucy lived at the end of a dead end road five miles north of St. Augustine. Fourteen children and a yard full of dogs graced his old, rundown frame house. The forty-five year old Manucy looked fresh off a Hollywood set in his battered black cowboy hat and cowboy boots. He played football for Sheriff Davis at St. Joseph Academy, and he was convicted for running moonshine in 1956. Manucy also served as a special deputy for Davis, and he reportedly led some fifteen hundred whites known as "Manucy's Raiders " Manucy's colorful appearance and rhetoric made him the darling of the press corps covering St. Augustine.

> Actually, if it gets much worse, there's only one way to stop it. We'll ask white people to fire every nigger in the county . . . There's no white man scared of a nigger. That's a proven fact in St. Johns County.[1]

Manucy took advantage of a ready-made situation in St. Augustine. Local officials remained intransigent and reluctant to exercise leadership in dealing with SCLC or the Manucy element. Aided by a news-starved press, Manucy stepped into the leadership vacuum. He became the spokesman for the community; a position he carefully nurtured and cultivated.

SCLC organizers worked diligently in St. Augustine after the Easter demonstrations. They conducted workshops in non-violent demonstrations and organized a summer tutoring program for Negro youths. Dr. Martin Luther King, Jr., head of SCLC, officially opened the St Augustine drive on May 26.

> Segregation attempts in the nations's oldest city will be a prelude to a long hot summer of similar efforts throughout the nation . . . We're here to plan for a long, hot, non-violent summer.[2]

41

Despite King's promises and the extensive organizational efforts, SCLC faced formidable opposition in St Augustine. The local power structure steadfastly refused to negotiate. SCLC hoped to force the power structure's hand with demonstrations designed to cripple the town's tourist economy. SCLC expected local merchants, businessmen, and moderates to exert pressure on the power structure to negotiate. But King and his aides underestimated the influence of the Ku Klux Klan and Hoss Manucy on the business community.

Manucy was largely a creation of the press. He reputedly led over one thousand whites known as "Manucy's Raiders." He also allegedly presided over the Ancient City Gun (Hunting) Club; an organization portrayed by the news media as being a Klan "front." Manucy himself did little to play down his newly won fame, and his flamboyant style endeared him to the large press and television array that descended on St. Augustine. Both television and newspaper personnel paid Manucy for interviews, and Manucy never disappointed his benefactors

> On at least one occasion during the week of June twenty-first, J. B. Stoner, Conrad Lynch, and Halstead Manucy left the Slave Market after receiving a contribution of cash from a T. V. network representative and went with that representative to his motel where they participated in a filmed interview.[3]

The one thousand "Manucy's Raiders" existed in fact only in the newspapers. No eyewitnesses or reliable reports ever placed Manucy in control or command of more than a few dozen "Raiders." The Ancient City Gun (Hunting) Club consisted of more than a thousand members, but the vast majority of the membership limited their activities to hunting. Alan Nease, the Chairman of the local School Board and a timber grower, allowed Manucy to organize the club, and Mauncy issued hunting memberships for a nominal charge. Mauncy and his club in turn patrolled Nease's property and watched for fires and illegal hunting. Mauncy maintained throughout the summer that he was not a member of the Klan, but he agreed with much of what the Klan stood for.

> No I'm definitely not knocking the Klan. Its a wonderful organization. A lot of people have the wrong idea about the Klan . . . Actually we're not tied to the Klan in any way.[4]

Despite Manucy's assurances and lack of real muscle, he exerted a great deal of influence. He spent part of his busy days lounging around Sheriff Davis' office, and local merchants and many moderates felt both the real and implied threat of Mauncy. Two dozen "Raiders," who seemingly operated with the blessings of the power structure, struck fear into the hearts of many people. Manucy's television appearances also added to his stature, and he became in effect the spokesman for the town.

SCLC also faced strong opposition from the Ku Klux Klan. Connie Lynch, a professional agitator, moved in and out of St. Augustine throughout the summer. J. B. Stoner, a Klan lawyer from Atlanta also made St. Augustine his base of operations. Lynch and Stoner led most of the Klan rallies in the Slave Market, and they perpetrated much of the violence which gripped the nation's oldest city.

SCLC opened its St. Augustine campaign on Wednesday, May 27. Some two hundred demonstrators marched from the St. Paul A. M. E. Church. (See Appendices B and C.) The march apparently caught segregationist forces by surprise, as no hecklers or white toughs occupied the Slave Market. Future marches followed the same route around the Slave Market, but this first march was one of the few peaceful demonstrations of the entire summer.

Following the demonstration, two SCLC officials, Harry Boyte and Reverend Andrew Young, conferred on Thursday afternoon with Wolfe, the most powerful element in the power structure. The men tried to impress upon Wolfe the importance of negotiations and the consequences of further inaction. Wolfe, however, refused to move, and Senator Verle Pope gave one explanation for Wolfe's reluctance.

Mr. Wolfe was sympathetic, but found himself on the opposite side of many of his friends (Upchurch). He finally refused to take any part in it.[5]

Following the meeting with Wolfe, SCLC again resorted to direct non-violent action. Police arrested fifteen demonstrators, as they attempted to integrate several lunch counters. SCLC also made preparations for another march on the Slave Market. Reverend Young assembled his forces outside the St. Paul Church. Parade marshals scanned the lines for possible troublemakers, and they hauled several young people out of line who had not attended training classes. The marchers finally moved forward singing, "Which Side Are You On, Boy?" and "We Shall Overcome." As the marchers moved forward, Reverend Young spoke through a megaphone.

I don't care what happens, we want you all to remain non-violent. If we overcome, it will be overcoming though love. If anybody curses you, walk straight ahead and say a prayer for them.[6]

As the marchers reached King Street, Police Chief Virgil Stuart stopped them and issued an ominous warning.

"Don't come any further unless you're prepared to get in serious trouble. It's my strong advice to go on back."

"We kind of feel," said Young, that "the only way we'll ever have any respect or . . ."

"Now listen," interrupted Stuart. "I'm not gonna argue with you. If you don't go back, my firm conviction is that some of you are going to get hurt. We can't protect you any further."[7]

Stuart's assessment of the situation proved to be very accurate. His twenty-five man police force was too small and inexperienced to handle trouble involving several hundred demonstrators. Sheriff's deputies and special deputies (citizen volunteers) beefed up the force, but the tiny contingent lacked both experience and desire to maintain law and order. Many of the segregationists in the Slave Market were friends and relatives of the local law enforcement authorities, and local authorities usually refused to crack down on these white toughs.

As the demonstrators marched down King Street toward the Slave Market, action focused on the downtown area. Between sixty and seventy whites occupied the Slave Market with a small contingent of law enforcement officials. The whites carried axe handles, chains, clubs, and bricks. A large group of television and newspaper personnel vied with the segregationists and policemen for good vantage points.

Young led his forces silently past the Slave Market on the King Street side. The demonstrators stopped to pause for a prayer, and the television lights and cameras lighted up the downtown area. As the television and news personnel opened up with their cameras, white segregationists opened up on the demonstrators. But the segregationists saved their most savage attacks for the news media. They smashed cameras, and several newsmen suffered worse beatings than the demonstrators. Harry Boyte, one of King's aides, attempted to take a picture of the violence. A white youth jumped on him and a policeman with a dog moved in. They all rolled to the ground, and a television reporter covered Boyte to protect him.[8]

Young managed to lead his marchers back into the safety of the Negro district. Despite several injuries, his people remained intact and never lost their poise. Sheriff Davis also headed into the Negro district and warned Young that city officials had prohibited all further demonstrations. Davis explained that future demonstrations were illegal without a city parade permit.[9]

Sporadic acts of violence continued into the night. Harry Boyte left the Slave Market and returned to the Holiday Inn. His son got out of the car and started to his room. Boyte noticed headlights approaching from his rear-view mirror. He wisely threw himself on the front seat of his car, as several loads of buckshot shattered his car windows. A beach cottage, rented for King, also came under a rifle and shotgun attack. No one occupied the cottage, but King and his aides had used it on previous nights.

Friday, May 29, signaled a temporary pause in the violence. Both sides paused to accuse each other of perpetrating the violence. King issued a statement calling for federal marshals, and he said the city was "under a reign of terror."

> In the last forty-eight hours we have witnessed raw and rampant violence even beyond what we have experienced in Alabama and Mississippi. All semblance of law and order has broken down.[10]

Mayor Shelley also issued a statement calling for all citizens to cooperate with law enforcement officials.

> I wish to assure all citizens of St. Augustine that we will do everything in our power to maintain law and order in our town . . . We intend to give you (newsmen) all the protection we can while you are in St. Augustine . . . St. Augustine has been picked, not because it is the most segregated city in America, but because it is the oldest . . . They (Boyte and Young) made it obvious they were going to continue to harass the city.[11]

Shelley also announced an organizational change. Sheriff Davis now commanded all state, county, and local law enforcement personnel. The Thursday night demonstrations clearly indicated the need for a uniform system of command. The new uniform command received its first test on Friday night as about fifty Negroes marched again toward the Slave Market. The Slave Market now resembled an armed camp with white segregationists, newsmen (now armed or with bodyguards), and police officials. Davis headed off a confrontation, however, when he persuaded the marchers to obey the ban on demonstrations.

Davis wasted no time in cracking down on arrested demonstrators. Judge Mathis ably assisted Davis by raising bonds to five hundred dollars per count for first offenders and one thousand dollars for second offenders. When police arrested white segregationists, their bond seldom exceeded one hundred dollars. Manucy, J. B. Stoner, and Connie Lynch lounged around Davis' office. Davis also constructed a large pen behind the county jail. Demonstrators occupied the pen from 11:20 A.M. to 4:30 P.M. in ninety-five degree heat. The only toilet in the facility consisted of a shallow hole in the ground. Both sexes used it, and a plywood wall hid occupants from the outside but not the inside of the compound. Davis also placed a group of male demonstrators in sweat boxes for singing freedom songs. Each box only measured seven feet by seven feet, and concrete points extended from the walls. Ten people usually occupied each box, and a standing position was a necessity in the crowded boxes.

SCLC now summoned lawyers William Kunstler and Tobias Simon. Simon telephoned Judge Bryan Simpson early Friday and informed him of an SCLC desire to apply for an injunction against the stopping of night marches.[12] Simpson agreed to hold hearings on Monday, June 1, at 2:00 P.M.

Sit-ins continued throughout the weekend in the racially troubled city. Lunch counters and churches refused to serve Negroes, and police arrested five more demonstrators. Car loads of armed whites cruised through the Negro district as tensions mounted. Rumors flew wildly about town. A massive invasion of Negroes threatened the town. Three more bus loads of demonstrators arrived from Alabama. These and other rumors caused near panic among many citizens. Few people ventured downtown, and many citizens carried weapons for the first time in their lives.

SCLC officials also conducted a skillful propaganda campaign, designed primarily to win support among local Negroes. King's entrance into St. Augustine won some converts, but only a handful of the county's ten thousand Negroes participated in the desegregation drive. SCLC published a pamphlet, "400 Years of Bigotry and Hate Maintained by Northern Tourist Dollars." The pamphlet presented SCLC's side of the civil rights movement in St. Augustine. SCLC also published its own newspaper, *The St. Augustine Liberator. The Liberator* contained favorable press articles and local news. SCLC designed this newspaper to counter the conservative and anti-civil rights bias of *The St. Augustine Record*. Mass meetings also continued in an attempt to win both converts and money.

The city commission also moved into action on Monday, June 1. A few hours prior to the federal court hearings, the commission passed two emergency ordinances. The first ordinance prohibited minors under eighteen from being on public streets or in public places between 9:00 P.M. and 5:00 A.M. A second ordinance prohibited vehicles from parking on forty-two streets in and adjacent to the downtown areas between 9:00 P.M. and 5:00 A.M. Mayor Shelley recommended the ordinances in an attempt to keep young demonstrators and segregationists from the downtown area.[13]

On Monday afternoon, Judge Bryan Simpson began hearing testimony for an injunction against city officials. Kunstler and Simon called a number of witnesses who testified to the lack of police protection, conditions at the county jail, and the outdoor "exercise" pen. Georgia Mae Reed, arrested May 28, gave damaging testimony concerning the excessive bails.

> The Court: Did anybody take you before a judge at anytime that you were in jail?
> The Witness: On Friday, they carried us before Judge Mathis. He told us that if we pleaded guilty that we could get out on bond, but if we didn't, he would arraign us on Monday. But he told this lady who works in there to raise our bonds to $3,000.[14]

City officials also presented a host of witnesses on Tuesday and Wednesday in an attempt to show that a clear and present danger existed in St. Augustine. SCLC officials admitted the danger, but they charged that inadequate law enforcement perpetrated the danger. Sheriff L. O. Davis damaged the city's case as Simpson closely questioned him about his "special deputies."

> The Court: And what is the number of these special deputies?
> The Witness: Well, I had around forty for fifteen days in Easter.
> The Court: Don't you know how many you've got?
> The Witness: No, sir, I don't.
> The Court: I think as a law enforcement officer, Sheriff, you can appreciate the danger in a situation where you have the members of the Klan or allied organizations in your organization as deputies.[15]

Simpson directed Davis to bring a list of his special deputies to court on June 3. Davis complied with the request and read the list of one hundred sixty-nine names into the record. When he read the name, Halstead Manucy, Simpson sat bolt upright. "Why that man's a convicted felon in this court!" exclaimed Simpson.[16]

After hearing all of the testimony, Simpson asked Kunstler to halt further demonstrations, pending a ruling. In the corridor outside of the courtroom, Kunstler conferred with Hayling and Young. "This is a very important thing," said Kunstler. "It will show the nation that we are responsible."[17] The two Negro leaders agreed, and Simpson promised a ruling as soon as possible.

Dr. King, who had been out of the city for more than a week, returned on Thursday, June 4. He addressed a mass meeting at a Baptist church, and the halls rang with his resonant voice.

> I want to commend you for the beauty and the dignity and the courage with which you carried out the demonstrations. I know what you faced. And I understand that as you marched silently and with a deep commitment to non-violence, you confronted the brutality of the Klan. But amid all of this you stood up. Soon the Klan will see that all of their violence will not stop us, for we are on the way to freedom land and we don't mean to stop until we get there.[18]

King held a press conference the following day and threatened new marches by the following week. He said he had to go to New York, but "I will be here a long time when I get back Tuesday."[19] SCLC also offered the city an olive branch at the same press conference. Hayling read the prepared statement.

> Now, the Federal Courts have given us a moratorium. During this time it is possible that we might come to enough accord to make further street demonstrations unnecessary. May we submit to you the following suggestions for redress of the grievances of the Negro community. We do not consider these to be considered terms about which we must bargain, but merely suggestions to which men of good will might respond in good faith. In a non-violent struggle, there is no victor or vanquished party. Both parties must come together to deal with any evil of injustice which exists in their midst. It is in this spirit that we submit these suggestions.
>
> 1. That all hotel and restaurant facilities be desegregated within thirty days.
> 2. That efforts be made on the part of the City of St. Augustine to employ at least five Negro firemen, four additional Negro policemen and three Negro office workers, all with complete Civil Service status, within ninety days.
> 3. That a bi-racial committee be established to deal with continuing problems of desegregation and the grievances of the Negro

community, with the St. Augustine chapter of SCLC naming two-thirds of the Negro representations.

4. That as an indication of the new climate of racial cooperation, the plaintiffs drop charges against persons peacefully demonstrating in behalf of their civil rights.

5. That applications be accepted from Negro citizens for any jobs available in St. Augustine, and that they be judged on merit rather than race.[20]

SCLC's offer went unheeded, and city officials set up their own press headquarters to tell the city's version of events. The city commission also repealed its night ordinances, as the truce made them unnecessary. On Sunday, June 7, *The St. Augustine Record* ran a two-page reprint of the "Dan Smoot Report." The article, entitled "Communism In the Civil Rights Movement," was paid for by the St. Johns County Chapter—Florida Coalition of Patriotic Societies. The article was the latest in a long series of articles and speakers that infested St. Augustine during the early 1960's. These speakers and articles made the civil rights movement, King, and communism synonymous. The Mayor, Chief of Police and many citizens saw the town's racial problems in terms of a communist plot.[21]

Judge Bryan Simpson, creator of the shaky truce, ended it on June 9. He lifted the ban on night demonstrations He also ordered city officials to discontinue the use of (1) the compound or exercise yard adjacent to the County Jail premises, (2) the "sweatboxes" adjacent to the County Stockade and (3) the padded cell in the County Jail, as punishment for real or fancied misconduct. He also ordered bonds to be set in the usual amounts of one hundred dollars.[22]

A few hours after Simpson's ruling, demonstrators again marched toward the Slave Market. They marched two abreast down King Street and around the Slave Market. The plaza again teemed with armed whites and television cameras. The whites attacked in force as the Negroes completed their march around Constitution Plaza. About twenty young whites broke through police lines and attacked the line of marchers. The segregationists singled out white demonstrators, and one marcher was knocked down and kicked repeatedly. He groaned and covered his head with his hands. A Negro boy covered the white youth with his body as the attack subsided.[23] Some beleaguered demonstrators fought back while others ran for the safety of the Negro district.

The "long, hot summer" promised by Dr. King now gripped the nation's oldest city. Local officials failed to take advantage of SCLC's offer for discussions made on June 5, and negotiations seemed more remote than ever. Sheriff Davis called on civic clubs, businesses, and local citizens for volunteers between the ages of twenty-one and fifty-five to serve as special deputies. As the issues moved into the streets after Simpson's truce, a civil war atmosphere hung over the town. Families became divided, and fear paralyzed the city. Innocent people suffered the consequences of a nightmarish situation, but motel owner James Brock felt the full wrath of both whites and blacks.

FOUR

"Don't Let the Illegitimates Grind You Down"

James Edward Brock moved to St. Augustine after World War II. He purchased the old Monson Hotel, and had it razed in 1959. The newly remodeled Monson Motor Lodge, located just down the street from the Slave Market, became a focal point for civil rights demonstrations. Most of the newsmen and all of the television crews covering St. Augustine made the Monson their headquarters. Brock encouraged their business and gave them special rates. While most businesses lost money during the first weeks in June, Brock's motel remained packed with newsmen.

The forty-two year old Brock appeared a most unlikely target for a civil rights controversy. He considered himself a moderate, but he refused to integrate his motel and adjoining restaurant for fear of reprisals. Brock, a pillar in the community, served as a Rotarian, as president of the local Community Chest Fund, as president of the Florida Hotel and Motel Association, and as a deacon in the Ancient City Baptist Church. But Brock found it impossible to remain on the sidelines during the "long, hot summer." A motel full of television cameras and newsmen proved to be the most powerful magnet in the community. Both integrationists and segregationists used the Monson as a focal point in their respective campaigns.

Judge Simpson's lifting of the ban on night demonstrations and the resulting violence of June 9 prompted Dr. King to call a news conference on the afternoon of June 10. King promised new demonstrations, as several busloads of demonstrators arrived from Savannah, Birmingham, and Wilmington, North Carolina. He also blasted local officials for not protecting his demonstrators.

> We are appalled by the unnecessary breakdown of law and order. It is obvious that the city police force is doing nothing to protect non-violent demonstrators. But this will not prevent us from continuing our struggle.[1]

King also telegrammed President Lyndon Johnson and again asked for federal intervention. Faced with intransigence by city officials, businessman, and the power structure, SCLC depended on federal intervention to break the siege.

> St. Augustine, Florida police stood by and watched as Negroes marching peacefully were brutally assaulted by white hoodlums. This was the most complete breakdown of law and order since Oxford, Mississippi . . . We urge you Mr. President personally to intervene in this city to prevent possible loss of life and needless destruction of property.[2]

Sheriff Davis asked King to notify him in advance of demonstrations in the interest of law and order. King immediately informed the sheriff of his intention to march again that night. Re-enforced by several busloads of young demonstrators, SCLC officials led about three hundred marchers toward the Slave Market. The Slave Market again resembled an armed camp. Between fifty and sixty young segregationists waited eagerly for the marchers to appear. More state police were also on hand, as Governor Bryant bolstered police forces with fifty additional troopers.

As the marchers approached the square, a group of about thirty whites broke through police lines and smashed into the marchers. They again singled out white demonstrators, and the Reverend William England, a chaplin at Boston University, felt the full fury of their attack. England vividly described his own plight.

> I was about thirty people behind the leaders, but I could see the leaders get hit by a big man in a red shirt. I heard some of them say, 'There's England, let's get him . . .' They grabbed me and tried to pull me into the bushes, but I fell down and they stood and kicked me for a while.[3]

The attack on June 10 marked the first time that law enforcement officers cracked down on white segregationists. A state trooper ordered the whites to disperse. When they refused to move, police opened up with tear gas. The enraged whites now attacked policemen as well as demonstrators. More tear gas finally forced an end to the hostilities. Police arrested five segregationists for disorderly conduct, resisting arrest, and carrying concealed weapons.[4]

Governor Bryant, determined to maintain law and order without federal troops, sent in more state troopers He also issued a statement in which he called for law and order in St. Augustine.

> I will not condone violence on any scale, and appropriate action has been taken to prevent it. I would not hesitate to exercise every power available to me as governor to insure that law and order prevail.[5]

On Thursday, June 11, President Johnson's office replied to King's request for federal marshals. Johnson's office denied the request. "We have been advised [by Bryant] that sufficient state law enforcement officers are present in St. Augustine to preserve law and order."[6] Johnson's repeated refusals to send in federal marshals took away the only leverage King had against the city. Without help from Washington, King now decided to increase the pressure on St. Augustine. The day before the federal refusal to send marshals, King announced he might go to jail. On Thursday morning, SCLC notified newsmen at the Monson Motor Lodge of King's intention to have lunch there. By the time King arrived, television cameras, police, and manager Brock occupied the restaurant. King and four others walked to the front door of the restaurant where Brock waited patiently.

"We want to have lunch—a group of five of us," said King.

"We can't serve you here. We're not integrated," replied Brock.

"We'll just wait around," said King.

"My name is Brock. I'm the manager here. As you probably know, you're on private property. I ask you on behalf of myself, my wife, and my children to leave."

"Does your invitation to serve tourists include Negroes?" asked Ralph Abernathy, another of King's aides.

Brock replied that the only provisions were for the Negro servants of white guests, who could go to the service area, where upon King remarked, "Do you understand what this does to our dignity?"[7]

The "debate" lasted for about twenty minutes, and police finally arrested King and his group after they refused to leave the restaurant. The group was taken to the county jail and charged with trespassing and conspiracy. Local officials later transferred King to Jacksonville, as they received several threats on King's life. As A. H. Tebault, editor of the *St. Augustine Record*, put it, "Medgar Evers was just a two-bit local philanthropist, and now he is a martyr. We don't want that to happen here."[8]

King's arrest failed to have any effect on the nightly marches. About two hundred demonstrators marched around the Slave Market on Thursday night, but a large police contingent prevented violence. Some two hundred law enforcement officials, many of them state troopers, lined the sidewalks around the Slave Market. The bottled-up segregationists hurled curses and fire crackers at the marchers, but the violence of previous nights failed to materialize. Police also found a cache of weapons near the Slave Market, including sulfuric acid, chains, and clubs. As the marchers headed for the Negro district, whites started after them. But the heavy police contingent forced the segregationists to turn back.

The violence of earlier marches and the threat of future violence now prompted action at the state level. State circuit attorney Dan Warren called a local Grand Jury into session to study the city's racial dilemma. The State Attorney General's office also went into federal court on Saturday, June 13, and asked Judge Simpson to ban night demonstrations. The Attorney General based his case on the threat of a clear and present danger in St. Augustine. State Senator Verle Pope also became involved. He began cautiously approaching local businessmen and moderates. He wanted them to take a more active, moderate stand, and he urged them to issue a statement to this end.

White segregationists also moved on new fronts. On Friday night, June 12, about two hundred white marchers led by J. B. Stoner marched through the Negro district. Stoner, a Klan lawyer from Atlanta, received able assistance from about one hundred policemen and some fifty newsmen. Negroes lined their sidewalks and politely applauded the marchers. Stoner started the march from the Slave Market with a fiery speech. He accused King of being a known associate of the Reds, and he injected the usual white supremacist rhetoric.

We whites are due more rights, not less. When the constitution said all men are created equal, it wasn't talking about niggers.[9]

The nightly marches cost SCLC a few injuries, but the daily sit-ins and resulting arrests depleted the movement's ranks. King still failed to generate massive local support for his cause, and SCLC resorted to using demonstrators from across the South. The use of such demonstrators created further problems for SCLC. Many of the out-of towners were teenagers, and their arrests created apprehension in their respective families. King finally worked out a deal with Juvenile Counselor Fred Brinkoff. Brinkoff agreed to release the arrested children, if King promised to return the children to their families.[10]

By Saturday, June 13, events seemed to take a more optimistic turn. The Grand Jury met, and King left jail to testify for over three hours. The State Attorney General was in federal court, and Senator Pope continued to work behind the scenes. Unfortunately, Pope represented only part of the power structure. The Upchurch (hard-line) wing of the power structure made its position quite clear on June 13th. U.S. Senator George Smathers, a close friend of Wolfe's, wired King on Saturday morning. He offered to pay King's bail if King left the state.[11] Upchurch also made his first public assessment of the situation in a statement issued by the local Quadricentennial Commission.

Until a year ago when St. Augustine was selected as a target to promote the national civil rights drive, we enjoyed excellent race relations . . . All Americans and all the world surely knows that St. Augustine is unjustly being used as a battleground . . . It was chosen for its publicity value and because of its helplessly small size . . . But let no one misunderstand. St. Augustine does not plan on rolling over and playing dead.[12]

J. B. Stoner addressed a packed Slave Market on Saturday night. After his speech, whites again marched on the Negro district. Stoner's two hundred marchers and police escort arrived in the Negro district only to be greeted by some five hundred Negroes. Whites carried Ku Klux Klan and Confederate flags; and one segregationist carried a sign, "Don't Tread On Me." The Negroes, not to be outdone, also carried signs, "Welcome—Peace and Brotherhood To You" and "We Love Everybody." Negroes also applauded and sang songs to the sullen white marchers. As the demonstrations ended, one march leader shouted to his followers, "Let's give a hand to our law enforcement officers for protecting us from those black savages."[13]

King posted a nine hundred dollar bond on Saturday and left for Yale University to receive an honorary Doctor of Laws degree. Local SCLC officials redoubled their efforts the following Sunday, June 14, with sit-in demonstrations in local segregated churches. Police arrested thirty-seven demonstrators, bringing the number arrested since Thursday, June 11 to one hundred twenty-seven.[14] Thirty of the demonstrators were arrested at the Monson restaurant when they refused to leave.

Sunday marked the most uneventful day in racial activity since Judge Simpson's lifting of the ban on night demonstrations a week earlier. Stoner held a Sunday night rally in the Slave Market, but SCLC called off a scheduled march to the area. Stoner also called off further marches into the Negro district, as both sides seemed to have exhausted their energies for the moment. The presence of more state police also helped to curtail activities. About one hundred fifty state police now occupied St. Augustine, and troopers now arrived on a daily basis.

Sunday marked the lull before another frantic week of activity. On Monday, attention focused once again on federal court in Jacksonville. The State Attorney General argued for a ban on night demonstrations. He attempted to show the danger of such demonstrations, but Judge Simpson refused to change his order with the following comments:

> I suggest rigid and strict law enforcement and some arrests and some real charges to be placed against those hoodlums that everybody down there seems to be afraid to move against . . . If the local law enforcement people are willing to let them come in there and take over the downtown section of the city without taking steps against them, maybe it's time for the State to step in and take charge of it.[15]

Governor Bryant, apparently prodded by Simpson's criticism, issued Executive Order Number One a few hours later. Bryant placed all law enforcement personnel in St. Johns County under state control.[16] He also replaced Sheriff Davis and placed Major J. W. Jourdan in command of his Special Police Force. Despite Davis' assurances that Bryant was not displeased with him, the circumstantial evidence went overwhelmingly against the Sheriff. Davis never cracked down on the segregationists. Stoner, Lynch, and Manucy lounged around his office. When the state tried to prove a clear and present danger in court, confiscated weapons had disappeared from the Sheriff's office. Police returned these weapons to their owners in many instances, and arrested segregationists seldom paid more than twenty five dollar fines. Bryant also hinted at his displeasure with Davis in his Executive Order. He required the Sheriff and Chief of Police to submit daily reports to Major Jourdan of the Highway Patrol. He also ordered Davis and Stuart to report all arrests and the names of all defendants delivered into their custody. The Governor also set up a special division of the new force to investigate "any arrest or failure to arrest on the part of any state, county, or city officer."[17]

Bryant's re-organized police force produced more effective law enforcement, but it also produced several glaring weaknesses. The new force, like the old one, consisted of many different agencies. Sheriffs' deputies, special deputies, local police, state police, state conservation officers and state beverage agents all served on the force. None of the agencies involved had any riot training, and they made many mistakes in dealing with the situation. While the old force under Davis cracked down on almost nobody, the new force cracked down hard on the segregationists. Bitter feelings toward the state police force resulted, as most St. Augustinians openly sided with the segregationists.

While state and local officials attempted to straighten out the police force, SCLC officials again attempted to obtain federal aid. Dr. Hayling and two of his aides, Henry Twine and Roscoe Halyard, spent the weekend and Monday, June 15, in Washington, D. C. as guests of AFL-CIO Local sixty-five. They participated in an AFL-CIO sponsored march to the Washington Monument. The protesters demanded passage of the Civil Rights Act. The St. Augustine delegation also met with Burke Marshall, head of the Civil Rights Division of the Justice Department, and George Sinclair, a special advisor to President Johnson. Sinclair assured Hayling's group that President Johnson kept his mind on the St. Augustine situation. The outspoken Hayling said that if President Johnson wanted to keep his eyes on the leadership of this civil rights movement, he should look in the St. Johns County Jail.[18] On Monday night SCLC held another mass meeting. Jackie Robinson, the former baseball great, addressed the gathering. He criticized President Johnson for his unwillingness to get involved in St. Augustine. Following the speech, some three hundred demonstrators marched on the Slave Market, but only about fifty whites occupied the market area. The march took place without incident, as a heavy police contingent ringed the plaza.

King returned to the city on Tuesday, June 16. SCLC continued its sit-in campaign in an attempt to fill the county jail. Fifty-one people were arrested, and police made most of the arrests at the Monson restaurant. Demonstrators also marched into the downtown area late Tuesday night, but police again prevented any incidents. The Highway Patrol also continued its crackdown. Patrolmen stopped cars and confiscated weapons, and they also charged several persons with possession of deadly weapons.

By Wednesday, June 17, the moderate wing of the power structure realized some tangible results. Senator Pope and bank president, Frank

Harrold, with some assistance from H. E. Wolfe, finally convinced twenty-six businessmen to take a stand. The businessmen issued their statement on Wednesday morning, but the statement contained little in the way of substance. The businessmen blamed outside agitators and bad publicity for the town's racial problems. They also promised to obey present and future laws, including civil rights laws. The most important element in the statement contained another call for a bi-racial committee.

Be it further resolved by this committee that we favor a study of the legitimate problems of this community by responsible local, law abiding citizens.[19]

While the statement of the businessmen had little lasting effect, it touched off a wave of frantic civil rights activity. King recognized the progress being made, but he rejected the findings of the businessmen. One spokesman for King called it "a segregationist statement which doesn't show much evolution. We'll have to keep up our program."[20] Most whites, including the Upchurch wing of the power structure, simply ignored the statement.

On Wednesday afternoon civil rights demonstrators staged a swim-in at St. Augustine Beach for the first time. As about thirty Negroes entered the water, about a dozen startled whites walked off the beach.[21] The beach swim-in marked a change in tactics by SCLC. The sit-ins proved too costly for King's forces, as police arrested the demonstrators immediately. The county had already integrated the beaches (1963), and the swim-ins received protection from the law, not arrests.

The "Special Police Force" continued its crackdown on weapons violators. The Force arrested more than one hundred twenty-five people in two days. Roadblocks and checkpoints appeared throughout the day, as police searched cars and confiscated weapons. State police even arrested one local plain-clothed policeman, as he investigated a weapons cache near the Slave Market. They took him to the county jail and booked him, despite his vehement protests. This incident and the approaching night demonstration enraged local whites. From this point on the "Special Police Force" enjoyed little support from most whites in St. Augustine.

On Wednesday night SCLC staged the largest and longest march of the campaign. Three hundred demonstrators converged on the Slave Market and the Monson Motor Lodge. SCLC almost seemed to be baiting the segregationists into an attack. They marched for nearly six miles through unlighted residential areas. The dark, narrow streets offered segregationists ample opportunity to attack the demonstrators, but no attack came. The marchers finally reached the Slave Market. Few whites occupied the area this night, and the demonstrators headed for Jimmy Brock's Monson Motor Lodge.

The marchers reached the Monson and prayed and sang for about fifteen minutes. The pray-in also marked the beginnings of a change in Brock. "I am a deacon in the Ancient City Baptist Church. I think it's terrible to use religion for publicity purposes."[22] His seventy-five year old mother-in-law, who lived at the Monson, suffered a heart attack during the demonstration. These two events and a coming swim-in turned Brock into a rabid segregationist.

There seemed to be no respite for Brock. The next morning a group of sixteen Rabbis and a few Negroes sought service in the Monson's restaurant. Brock turned them away, but a car with four Negroes and two whites soon stopped in front of the Monson. The group walked to the pool's edge, and Brock told them to leave. Two white men, already swimming in the pool, claimed the Negroes were their guests. The Negroes dived into the pool, and their act finally pushed Brock past the point of tolerance.

The enraged Brock left the pool area and returned with two containers of muriatic acid.[23] Brock poured the acid into the pool, hoping to bluff the demonstrators out. But his ploy failed, and an off-duty policeman lent some assistance. Henry Billitz took off his shoes and jumped into the pool. He flailed away at the swimmers until they finally left the pool. Police arrested them, and the swimmers brought the number of arrests at the Monson alone to two hundred sixty-nine. As Brock later said, "I regret it happened, but there is a limit to what anyone can endure."[24] Brock's friends guarded his pool for the remainder of the summer, and a Confederate flag flew over the Monson. Brock also erected a sign over the entrance to his restaurant, "Illegemati Non Carborundum" (Don't Let The Illegitimates Grind You Down).[25]

The arrest of a city policeman by state police and the Monson incidents caused angry reactions from the white community. *The St. Augustine Record* ran an angry editorial by Tebault.

The state police force apparently has assumed powers here which border on making the city a "police state" . . . They have assumed the power to clear the Plaza, a public park, of citizens when the integrationists march and demonstrate at night and search automobiles and pedestrians without search warrants in order to protect the demonstrators.[26]

In the same issue of *The Record*, however, Tebault carefully distinguished between state and local law officers. He praised the efforts of local officers, and he suggested a bonus of between one hundred and two hundred dollars for each local officer.[27]

The Grand Jury issued its findings on Thursday, June 18. After nearly a week of testimony from SCLC officials, city officials, and law officers, the Grand Jury suggested a thirty day cooling-off period. The Jury also suggested that King, SCLC, and segregationists forces demonstrate their good faith by leaving town during this period.

> Upon the expiration of thirty days, following the above suggested demonstration of good faith, this Grand Jury will reconvene to name a recommended bi-racial committee, composed of ten members, five Negroes and five whites, whose members have tentatively agreed to serve.[28]

King immediately rejected the Grand Jury proposals as being too one-sided. He instead proposed his own plan for racial harmony in St. Augustine.

> We would, therefore, propose that the Grand Jury be reconvened in the next few days and that the bi-racial committee mentioned in the presentment be appointed immediately. At the appointment of the committee, we would be willing to halt demonstrations for a week . . . If, at the end of this period of good faith communication, a reasonable attempt is made to comply with our requests, we will gladly accept this as a settlement.[29]

The Grand Jury rejected King's counter-proposal, and Jury foreman Aubrey Davis angrily denounced King on Friday, June 19.

> The Grand Jury will not be intimidated. We will not alter our presentment . . . On the day when it appears a sweeping civil rights bill will pass the Senate, Dr. King stands accused of bad faith and insincerity. It would appear he has no desire to actually achieve the goals he espouses.[30]

While the charges and counter-charges flew between King and the Grand Jury, SCLC continued swim-ins at the beach and nightly marches. King's forces still seemed to invite attack, as they repeatedly deviated from the usual march route. Large groups of whites followed the demonstrators on Friday night, hurling rocks and curses at the marchers. These longer marches and roving bands of whites made constant police protection almost impossible. So long as segregationists and demonstrators confined their activities to the Slave Market area, police offered effective protection since June 15.

Senator Verle Pope, concerned with the growing danger of widespread violence, asked Governor Bryant to ban night demonstrations. Bryant's state police officers also urged such a move, and Bryant banned all night demonstrations on Saturday, June 20. He also banned the use of public parks or any public facilities for demonstrations between the hours of 8:30 P.M. and sunrise.[31] Bryant's ban temporarily halted the night demonstrations, but ominous clouds hung over the city. One such cloud, Reverend Connie Lynch, returned to St. Augustine the day before Bryant's order. His presence breathed new life into segregationists' ranks and created a multitude of problems for everyone in St. Augustine.

FIVE

"But You Can't Sit Down With a Negro"

The Reverend Charles Conley (Connie) Lynch grew up in Clarksville, Texas, the son of a poor cotton farmer. Lynch quit school in the ninth grade, and finally made his way to California in 1936. After an army hitch in World War Two, he joined the Church of Jesus Christ, Christian. He later took the title of "Reverend" and began preaching his white supremacist dogma. In 1957 he became a traveling parson, traveling between fifty and seventy-five thousand miles per year in his 1958 Cadillac. He also became a California organizer for the National States Rights Party and one of its best fund raisers.[1]

Lynch helped organize the Klan in the St. Augustine area during the fall of 1963, and he returned to St. Augustine for "the long, hot summer." He based his philosophy on the inferiority of the Negro, and many people dismissed him as a crank. But his often incoherent speech and inaccurate Biblical quotations appealed to those hundreds of poor whites in the Slave Market. Lynch provided them with a ready scapegoat for their frustrations.

> Martin Lucifer Coon. That nigger says it's gonna be a hot summer. If he thinks the niggers can make it a hot summer, I will tell him that one hundred forty million white people know how to make it a lot hotter . . . When the smoke clears, there ain't gonna be nothing left except white faces.[2]

The day after Governor Bryant's ban against night demonstrations, a group of Negroes attempted to enter the Trinity Episcopal Church. Vestrymen locked the doors of the church, but the Reverend Charles Seymour left his pulpit and walked toward the doors. He personally unlocked the doors and escorted the Negroes into the church. Seymour's action touched off a bitter dispute within the church, and it provided an interesting look at conservative, right-wing influence in St. Augustine. Senator Verle Pope gave a graphic description of this element.

> There was a very active group, who might be said to be of a John Birch variety, who were very prominent and very strong. They were the leaders in the Kiwanis Club and Rotary Club. They were on the vestries in the churches. Wherever you turned it was the same group of people who were in power in these various organizations.[3]

Seymour and his vestry fought a running battle over the incident, but the admittance of the Negroes only marked one of several disagreements between Seymour and his vestry. On April 30, 1964, the vestry passed a resolution censuring the National Council of the Episcopal Church on the civil rights issue. One month later, the same vestry passed another resolution concerning the National Council of Churches.

> As of the thirty-first day of May, 1964, funds pledged to the Diocese of Florida by Trinity Parish shall be held in escrow at Security Federal Savings and Loan Association . . . until such time as the Diocese withdraws complete financial support from the National Council of Churches.[4]

Seymour's opposition on the vestry came from several local businessmen and A. H. Tebault, editor of *The St. Augustine Record*. After Seymour admitted the Negroes, the vestry passed a resolution on June 23, asking the minister to resign. They put the resolution on Seymour's desk, and Seymour forwarded it to Bishop Hamilton West, head of the Florida Diocese. The embattled minister also read the letter of resignation to his congregation the following Sunday. Seymour also clashed with his vestry over the behavior of the vestrymen during church services. The minister found the side doors of the church locked on several occasions (to keep out possible demonstrators), and several vestrymen engaged Mrs. Peabody in debate. Several vestrymen also cursed Negroes on church property during the integration attempt.[5]

Bishop West sided with Seymour and pledged the full weight of the Church in Seymour's struggle. West also went to St. Augustine and admonished the vestry in person.

> . . . continued disregard for and violation of the rubrics, canons, traditions, customs and usages in the doctrine, discipline and worship of the Episcopal Church can possibly end for each such vestrymen in suspension or excommunication, or both.[6]

Three vestrymen, including Tebault, immediately resigned. Seymour left St. Augustine at the end of the summer, but his case was not entirely an isolated incident. Whenever Negro offers for negotiations came before businessmen's groups, the city commission, churches, and civic clubs, the right-wing element surfaced. This element presented a hard line, and most white St. Augustinians followed this hard line throughout the agonizing summer of 1964.

While Seymour battled his vestry, integrationists and segregationists moved ever closer to the bloodiest showdown of the summer. Connie Lynch, who moved in and out of St Augustine, returned to the city on June 21. The fiery "minister" immediately generated new interest in the Slave Market. Crowds increased nightly from fifty to one hundred to several hundred. Lynch was by far the most effective of the segregationist speakers, and crowds in the Slave Market rose and fell with his appearances.

Although segregationist forces had no formal women's auxiliary, the women lent their support on June 21. About seventy-five women held an informal meeting and agreed to fire any domestics who participated in demonstrations. They also agreed to write their congressmen, support local businesses hurt by demonstrations, and they criticized King and Hayling.[7]

Governor Bryant's ban on all demonstrations after 8:30 P.M. forced SCLC and segregationists to alter their tactics. Both groups continued their confrontations in the Slave Market area, but the demonstrations now concluded before 8:30 P.M. SCLC also stepped up its swim-ins at St. Augustine beach during the mornings and afternoons. Demonstrators marched into the water daily, and white toughs attacked them. Hard-pressed police tried in vain to separate the groups, but the integrationists frequently suffered severe beatings at the hands of the whites.

Tensions continued to mount in the St. Augustine pressure cooker. Between Sunday, June 21 and Wednesday, June 24, SCLC forces conducted swim-ins two or three times a day. Segregationist attacks on the swimmers increased in intensity, and Negroes and whites continued early evening marches in the downtown area. The speeches of Connie Lynch also increased tensions in the Slave Market, as more than five hundred whites heard Lynch speak on Wednesday, June 24. Segregationists also showed their displeasure with white moderates. Six concrete blocks were thrown through the windows of Verle Pope's real estate office on June 21. Pope also received threats on his life, and he nearly withdrew his moderate support from the entire situation. "It would have been mighty easy for me to go fishing, and I would have been less than honest if I didn't say I was tempted to do it."[8]

By Wednesday, June 24, the nation's oldest city was on the verge of a racial explosion. Negroes again attempted swim-ins at St. Augustine beach, but white segregationists blocked their path to the water. Police made no attempt to disperse the whites, and the Negroes left the beach. King held a news conference after the attempted swim-in and called for a federal mediator. He felt a mediator was the only solution, because "whites who favor a settlement are afraid of the Klan element."[9]

On Wednesday afternoon about one hundred Negroes marched into the downtown area. Only a few whites occupied the Slave Market, and the Negroes returned to their churches Integrationists staged another march early Wednesday night around the Slave Market, as Connie Lynch concluded one of his inflammatory speeches. Over five hundred whites listened to Lynch earlier that evening, and Lynch and Stoner then led a march into the Negro district. As the white marchers returned to the Plaza, they found the Negro demonstrators marching on the opposite side of the Slave Market. The whites rushed across the Plaza at the Negroes, but a heavy police contingent prevented any violence.

SCLC moved into federal court on Wednesday in an attempt to have Bryant's ban lifted. SCLC, aided by the NAACP Legal Defense Fund, contended that Bryant's order directly contradicted Judge Simpson's order of June 15. Simpson immediately opened hearings on the motions, but the tensions building in St. Augustine refused to wait for a federal judge.

Thursday, June 25, began like other days of the preceding week. Late in the morning, the familiar hushed cry moved through the town, "Niggers on the beach." Most people ignored it, but many young whites stopped their jobs, piled into cars, and headed for the beaches. The scene at the beaches resembled earlier swim-ins. About thirty whites stationed themselves in knee-deep water and awaited the Negroes. About seventy Negroes marched down one of the ramps and onto the beach. Two Confederate flags, planted at the base of the ramp, provided a colorful backdrop for the Negro marchers. About one hundred state troopers surrounded the Negroes and escorted them to the water's edge.

At this point events began taking a different turn from previous days. Instead of letting the demonstrators take their chances with the segregationists, the troopers moved in between the whites and Negroes. "Come on in, you black bastards!" yelled one of the whites in the water.[10]

But the state police refused to back down. The whites listened in disbelief and anger as a state police captain called through a bull horn, "Let them go swimming. Let them in the water and stand back! Anyone blocking them will be arrested!"[11]

The Negroes attempted to enter the water, but the whites charged into the police lines in an attempt to get at the blacks. This time, however, the troopers waded into the whites and arrested several of them. One white youth, who resisted arrest, had his head split open with a billy club. The shocked whites could not believe it happened.

"Those finks!" cried a woman in disgust. "They didn't even beat the niggers at all!"[12]

The rage of the white crowd at the beach soon spread into the town itself. White youths hid assorted weapons in the Slave Market area. State police also felt the change in atmosphere. They hustled the trooper who had hit the white youth on the beach out of town.[13] The state police also viewed the Slave Market with some apprehension. Whites began gathering about 6:30 P.M., and a crowd of more than eight hundred angry segregationists soon packed the Slave Market and adjoining Plaza.

The Slave Market area provided the most ironical setting imaginable for the worst night of violence of the entire summer. A wax figure of Gandhi smiled benevolently at the proceedings from Potter's Wax Museum across the street. (See Appendix C.) The adjacent Matanzas Bay was named for a bloody massacre, and the movie theatre across the street featured "Law of the Lawless." The Slave Market itself, located in Constitution Plaza, provided even more irony. White masters auctioned slaves in the market before the Civil War, and freedmen later used the market to sell their various crops and other items. One hundred years later white masters again took advantage of Negroes on the steps of the Slave Market.

About 7:30 P. M. Connie Lynch mounted the steps of the Slave Market. He slipped out of his jacket and into a vest made from a Confederate flag. He coolly surveyed the crowd and began his speech. With the aid of the beach incident, he soon whipped the crowd into a frenzy. He also set the tone for the violence which followed.

They ask me, do you believe in violence? If it takes violence to defend our Constitution, the answer is . . . YES! . . . I favor violence to preserve the white race . . . Now I grant you, some niggers are gonna get killed in the process, but when war's on, that's what happens.[14]

Lynch concluded his speech with, "a nigger baby is no better than a monkey, so just smash his brains out!" The crowd roared its approval, as the Negro marchers neared the Slave Market. The white mob surged forward and someone yelled, "Let's get those black sons-of-bitches!" Several hundred whites attacked the demonstrators with clubs, chains and bricks. Most of the stunned demonstrators simply fell to their knees and covered their heads.

The police contingent numbered nearly two hundred, and they made a futile effort to protect the marchers. Police arrested five whites, but the crowd would not allow state troopers to arrest any more whites. Several hundred whites chanted "Let them go! Let them go!" The police promptly released the five whites and surrendered their authority to the mob.

The Negroes re-grouped and continued their march around the Plaza. The white mob charged across the Plaza and hit the demonstrators on the other side. Rebel yells, curses and cries of agony filled the hot, sultry air. Some Negroes ran for their lives, but others bore the full fury of the attack. One magazine writer attempted to protect a thirteen year old Negro girl, who was trembling and seeking shelter in some bushes. Her dress had been ripped away, and blood poured from a shoulder wound.

"Let that gorilla go!" shouted three whites who tried to seize the girl.

"Run!" the newsman shouted at the girl. She darted away as he blocked the path of her pursuers. The whites paused to beat and kick the newsman, but the girl reached the safety of the Negro district.[15]

Nineteen demonstrators required hospitalization, and scores of Negroes suffered minor cuts and bruises. Manucy, Stoner and Lynch held a news conference following the melee and promised more violence. Manucy blamed the violence on the "brutality" of the state patrolmen on the beach. Manucy said, "Violence will continue as long as Negroes continue to invade the public beach, which has been used by whites for hundreds of years."[16]

Governor Bryant flew to St. Augustine the day after the bloody confrontation. He ordered eighty more state troopers into the city and promised a tighter ban on night demonstrations. He also met with Wolfe and other community leaders, and he hinted at a solution to the city's racial problems. "I can only say that I have taken steps to open communications between the two opposing sides."[17]

While Bryant worked to bring about some solution to the city's problems, SCLC demonstrations and swim-ins continued through Saturday, Sunday and Monday. White meetings in the Slave Market also continued, but the swim-ins and rallies appeared to have lost most of their steam. The Thursday night violence of June 25 marked the end of massive street violence, as both sides seemed worn out by the bitter confrontation.

Governor Bryant's efforts at opening negotiations produced results on Tuesday, June 30. He announced the formation of a four-man bi-racial committee. Bryant asked the committee to serve until the Grand Jury named a permanent committee mentioned in its presentment of June 18. The violence of June 25 apparently persuaded Bryant to act. The Civil Rights Act of 1964 passed the Senate on June 17, and President Johnson signed it into law on July 2. Further bloodshed over public accommodations seemed pointless, and Bryant pointed out the futility of violence in his statement.

> Whether we agree with the civil rights bill or not—and I do not—it is time to draw back from this problem and take a look down the long road, at the end of which somehow, we must find harmony . . . We cannot solve this problem through violence. Violence is anarchy, and anarchy is the enemy of freedom.[18]

King called a press conference and announced a twelve to fifteen day ban on demonstrations. Manucy also canceled segregationist meetings for two weeks, and eighty motel and restaurant owners agreed to comply with the Civil Rights Act. SCLC withdrew its contempt motion from federal court, and the worst of the city's racial dilemma appeared to be over.

Bryant's temporary truce contained several serious defects which surfaced soon after Bryant, King and local businessmen made their pronouncements. Manucy spoke only for his "Raiders," not for the Ku Klux Klan. Stoner and Lynch had no intention of curtailing their activities. Bryant's bi-racial committee apparently existed only in the newspapers.[19] Without communication between the two sides, any truce had to be very shaky.

Bryant's truce offered both sides a way out of their respective situations. Police crackdowns on whites (over three hundred arrests since June 15) hurt Manucy's forces. One segregationist leader said, "We couldn't stand those bonds when they got as high as fifteen hundred dollars."[20] The truce also appealed to businessmen who lost an estimated ten million dollars during the "long, hot summer." SCLC also benefited from a truce. The Civil Rights Act made demonstrations to desegregate public accommodations unnecessary, but King's forces also needed an excuse to call off the marches. The truce allowed SCLC to stop the demonstrations, without appearing to give in to segregationist forces.

Both sides complied with the truce. Negroes began testing motels and restaurants, and local businessmen reluctantly complied with the new Civil Rights Act. Signs over many cash registers read, "Any Money Spent Here

By Negroes Will Be Donated To Goldwater For President." The only element which failed to comply was the Klan. On July 4, over two hundred robed Klansmen marched through town to the Slave Market. Klan speakers urged resistance to the new Civil Rights Act during the brief rally. The Klan continued to hold meetings throughout July, and the Klan rallies reminded local businessmen of both real and implied dangers.

While local businessman continued to comply with the Civil Rights Act, SCLC encountered increasing opposition from the Klan element after the July 4 rally. White toughs harassed groups of SCLC workers, and several integrationists were beaten and chased from restaurants. On July 5, a carload of whites stopped on the Vilano Beach bridge and attacked five Negroes. The whites beat the Negroes, who were doing nothing more than fishing. One Negro required hospitalization after the whites severely beat him with a bicycle chain.[21]

Manucy ignored his promise of a two week truce, and his "Raiders" began open intimidation of local businessmen. On Thursday, July 9, Manucy's pickets appeared in front of the Monson Motor Lodge. The pickets carried signs stating, "Delicious Food. Eat With Niggers Here," and "Niggers Sleep Here, Will you?"[22] Brock gave into the pressure as did most other restaurants and motel owners. Within a week after the appearance of "Manucy's Raiders," St. Augustine's public accommodations again closed their doors to Negroes.

SCLC promptly went back into federal court on July 15. Armed with the new Civil Rights Act, SCLC attorney's filed three suits against local motel and restaurant owners. The suits also named Manucy and several others as Class II defendants. Brock and other restaurant and motel owners testified against Manucy and his followers. Their testimony clearly showed their fear of Manucy. At one point during Brock's testimony, Judge Simpson stopped questioning the terrified Brock. Simpson asked Brock to name the pickets, but Brock hesitated.

> You know you put me in a very unpleasant position when you ask me this up here . . . Because I recognize that you're not going to be too happy—too interested in my welfare, and I'm just a little bit frightened to be talking like this.[23]

Brock's fears turned out to be more than justified. The Klan held rallies on July 16, 17, 18, and 19 outside of the city. Vandals struck Brock's motel with fire bombs on the night of July 21. King also returned to the city on July 16 and threatened new demonstrations.

> We have gone too far to turn back. We seek to solve the problems by negotiations, but if necessary we will again put on our walking shoes to walk the streets of the city.[24]

Judge Bryan Simpson finally ended the fears and frustrations of "the long, hot summer." Simpson listened to testimony from Manucy, local officials, and local businessmen for nearly three weeks. On August 5, he destroyed the segregationists with a series of sweeping orders. He ordered restaurants and other public facilities desegregated. He ordered Manucy to stop "intimidating, threatening, or coercing anyone asserting rights under the Civil Rights Act."[25] Throughout the month of August, Simpson continued to strike at segregationist forces. He ordered the Flagler Hospital's snack bar desegregated on August 13. He also ordered Charles Lance, a special deputy, to resign his position on August 19.[26] Simpson found Lance guilty of harassing integrationists who engaged in testing motels and restaurants.

Isolated acts of vandalism, beatings, and threats continued throughout July and August, but Simpson's orders defused the situation. Manucy stayed in and out of federal court until October, and he ceased to be a threatening force after early August. Simpson's orders put teeth into the Civil Rights Act, and his forceful, controversial rulings finally brought an end to the violence and intimidation in St. Augustine.

Local officials and most white St. Augustinians viewed Simpson's orders as attacks on the city. On September 27, *The St. Augustine Record* carried a long, front page editorial entitled, "Law, Justice In County Feel Lash of Federal Court Power." The editorial contained quotes from most local authorities in the county, concerning the abuses of federal court power. Judge Charles Mathis expressed a typical opinion.

> The faith and confidence of the lawyers, laymen and law enforcement officers in the Federal Judiciary system has been shaken, if not destroyed, by the action of the Federal District Court in Jacksonville in cases entertained and considered as Civil Rights cases. The citizens of St. Johns County now see this court as a threat to their freedom rather than as a question of their rights.[27]

On August 5, the Grand Jury made a final attempt at appointing a permanent bi-racial committee After a thirty day waiting period, the Jury appointed five whites and five local blacks to the committee.[28] Three of the whites resigned within a week of their appointments, and the bi-racial committee never held a meeting.[29]

"The long, hot summer," like an old soldier, faded away during the last weeks of August. The long, bitter struggle over public accommodations in the nation's oldest city was finally at an end. Many factors influenced the city's refusal to negotiate Negro demands, but a native American racism also pervaded the city. The legal battle over public accommodations ended with the signing of the Civil Rights Act on July 2, 1964. But the social, economic, and moral battles over public accommodations remained to be fought. Reverend Charles Seymour humorously summarized St. Augustine's dilemma of racism.

> I've often thought that we could solve the problem of public accommodations by taking all the chairs out of restaurants and motels. You know you can stand up with a Negro and lay down with a Negro, but you can't sit down with a Negro.[30]

Epilogue

By the end of August the worst of the city's racial dilemma appeared to be over. The sounds of marching feet and fiery speeches gave way to car horns and milling tourists. The Highway Patrol returned to duty elsewhere, and Stoner and Lynch no longer plagued the city. "Hoss" Manucy was occupied in federal court, and Dr. King turned his energies and efforts to new endeavors. The "long, hot summer," finally ended, and a degree of normalcy returned to the city. Most citizens enjoyed the new found peace and tranquility, and August was a time for contemplation and reflection.

Most white St. Augustinians and local officials viewed the civil rights movement in their city as an invasion by "outside agitators." They believed that the city was chosen for its publicity value. Local officials never tired of pointing to Negro "progress" in the city, insisting that St. Augustine's racial problems were no better or worse than most other cities across the South. So long as Negroes "stayed in their places," the city enjoyed "excellent race relations."

St. Augustine was singled out in 1964 by SCLC for massive demonstrations. The city possessed obvious publicity value as the nation's oldest city. The city's request for nearly a half million dollars in federal funds created another issue and made federal intervention and support a possibility. Hayling had an organization ready to affiliate with SCLC, and the Negro dentist had already brought some national publicity to bear on St. Augustine. Hayling enjoyed little support from most local blacks, but the divisions in the black community were not confined to St. Augustine. Civil rights groups faced the same apathy and fear by local Negroes across the South. Besides, the presence of King usually calmed the fears of local blacks. When King and his lieutenants decided to move into St. Augustine in March, 1964, the city must have looked like an easy target. The tourist economy was very vulnerable to demonstrations, and moderate businessmen would surely negotiate. The police force numbered only about twenty-five men, and the only jail in the county could be easily filled with demonstrators if necessary. SCLC seemed to hold all the cards in March.

But King's forces clearly underestimated the situation in St. Augustine. The demonstrations severely damaged the town's economy, and many businessmen like James Brock favored negotiations. But the issues in St. Augustine never reached the conference table. "Manucy's Raiders" and the Klan effectively silenced the business community. When the business community became paralyzed, the power structure could have led them to the negotiating table. But the power structure split. Wolfe vacillated between negotiation and inaction. Senator Pope and Frank Harrold, a local banker, finally got involved. But Frank Upchurch, an influential local attorney, and the rest of the power structure followed a hard line Without help from the power structure, the businessmen were at the mercy of Manucy.

The division of the power structure and news coverage gave Manucy far more power than he deserved. In the absence of a unified power structure that spoke forcefully for the city, Manucy became the unofficial spokesman for St. Augustine The colorful "special deputy" frequently appeared on television news programs. He provided newsmen with far more colorful comments on the situation than did any member of the power structure. It was no accident that Manucy's stature declined appreciably shortly after the television crews left town.

Another factor integrationist forces failed to consider was the right-wing element. This group was hard to define or identify, but everyone from Senator Pope to Dr. Hayling acknowledged its existence. Businessmen, National Guard officers, and a few doctors and lawyers made up the bulk of this group. Some right-wingers belonged to formal organizations—Dr. Hardgrove Norris headed the St. Johns County Coalition of Patriotic Societies, and others were prominent in the local White Citizens Council. Many belonged to no organization, but all were united by their determination to resist a communist-infested civil rights movement. Prominent in civic clubs, businessmen's organizations, and churches, the right-wing managed to intimidate other moderate elements like the clergy.

The clergy maintained an ostrich-like posture throughout the summer. Most Protestant ministers refused to incur the wrath of their congregations, and most churches conducted segregated services. Reverend Seymour took a stand, but most Protestant ministers faced powerful, conservative opposition to integration. Monsignor John P. Burns of the local Cathedral, the city's largest church, issued just one statement—on June 21, 1964. He urged Catholics to refrain from violence (Manucy was Catholic), and he asked his congregation to work for peace.

It is a precept of our Catholic faith that we love all men as our brothers in Christ and that we treat them with fraternal charity.[1]

Faced with frightened and silent moderate elements, King's forces turned to Washington. SCLC repeatedly asked for federal intervention and the severance of federal funds for St. Augustine's Quadricentennial celebration. SCLC failed to achieve either objective. The federal funds were in the able hands of Senator George Smathers, a close friend of both H. E. Wolfe and President Johnson. Johnson's advisors and the Justice Department consistently refused to send marshals or mediators into St. Augustine. One plausible reason for federal inaction was Barry Goldwater. Johnson, a Southerner, simply did not want to send troops or marshals into the South during an election year.

St. Augustine's bitter racial confrontations left indelible impressions on the town and its citizens. Integrationist forces achieved their primary goal of desegregating public accommodations, including the county's public beaches. But SCLC failed in its other demands, including the formation of a bi-racial committee. The most lasting effect of the "long, hot summer," however, was a marked change in attitudes. The summer of 1964 destroyed the city's ancient racial divisions and preconceptions. Whites viewed these old "understandings" as "excellent race relations." Many Negroes like Hayling, however, viewed the situation "as a master-slave relationship."

The attitudes of the white community underwent a subtle but distinct change. The racism remained intact, but St. Augustine's white population underwent a sophistication of prejudice following "the long, hot summer." Throughout the summer of 1964, the hottest racial issue was public accommodations. Heated discussions broke out among whites over the dangers of eating or drinking after Negroes. "I won't drink after no Nigger or eat off the same dishes!" After 1964, whites turned their attentions to a bitter fight over court-ordered school desegregation and busing.

Regardless of the interpretation or the subtlety of the change, virtually everyone noticed a difference in the Negro community. The "yasuh, Mr. Charlie" attitude of many blacks died in the streets of St. Augustine. While many Negroes did not actively support the movement, scores of Negro homes contained pictures and momentos of Dr. King. Although Negroes failed to improve their economic, political, and social positions in St. Augustine, they had experienced a conversion of spirit. They still held the poorest jobs, attended run-down schools, and most lived in sub-standard housing. But the beatings, the curses, the bricks and the broken promises of the "long, hot summer" forged a new Negro. He was at long last free. "Free at last! Free at last. Thank God Almighty, we are free at last!"[2]

APPENDIX A

ST. AUGUSTINE, FLORIDA

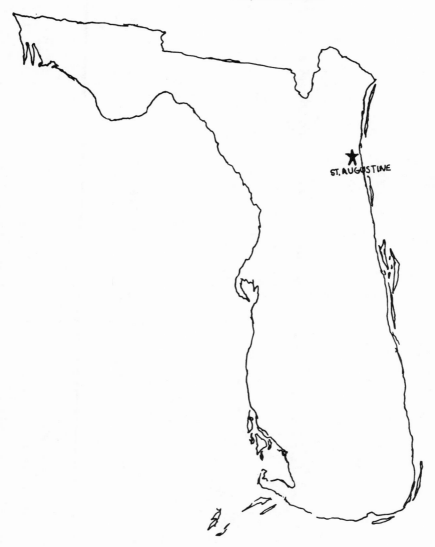

ST. AUGUSTINE

APPENDIX B

DOWNTOWN AREA OF ST. AUGUSTINE

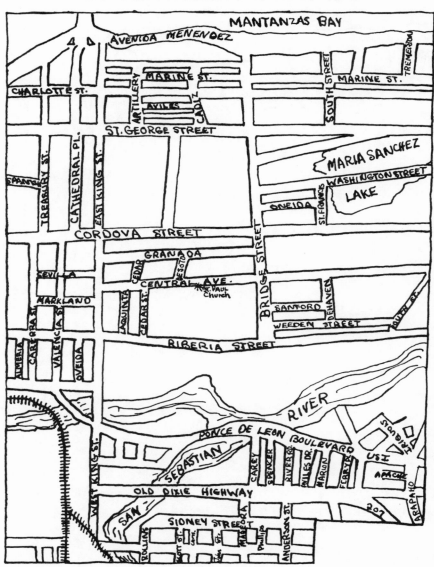

APPENDIX C

SLAVE MARKET AREA OF ST. AUGUSTINE

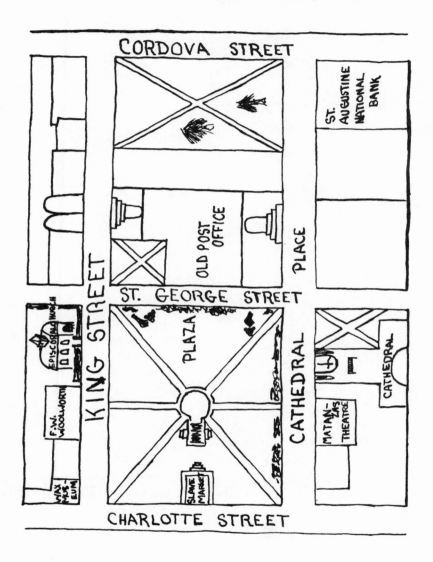

Notes

INTRODUCTION

1. *U. S. Bureau of Census—County and City Data Book—1962*. (A Statistical Abstract Supplement.) U. S. Government Printing Office, Washington, D. C., p. 62.
2. *Florida Statistical Abstract—1967*. Bureau of Economic and Business Research. University of Florida, 1967, p. 102.
3. Martin Waldron, "After Dark in St. Augustine," *Nation*, 198 (June 26, 1964), 648.
4. Larry Goodwyn "Anarchy in St. Augustine," *Harper's* 230 (January, 1965), 76.
5. I have only sketched the major figures of the power structure who played a part in the city's racial drama. I purposely left out many minor figures who did not figure in the 1964 disorders.
6. *U. S. Bureau of Census—County and City Data Book—1962*, p. 63.
7. Letter, Mayor Shelley to Florida Advisory Committee On Civil Rights, August, 1963.
8. Verle Pope, private interview, St. Augustine, Florida, March, 1971.
9. "Violence Erupts Here as Negroes Continue Sit-Down Demonstrations," *The St. Augustine Record*, March 17, 1960, p. 1.

CHAPTER ONE

1. Part of Hayling's dental school financial aid carried the stipulation that he must practice in a "deprived" area for five years. St. Augustine qualified as such an area.
2. Dr. Robert B. Hayling, private interview, Cocoa Beach, Florida, March, 1971. (Hayling made this statement to me, not to Johnson.)
3. Letter, Vice-President Johnson to NAACP, March 7, 1963.
4. Dr. Robert B. Hayling, private interview, Cocoa Beach, Florida, March, 1971.
5. *Ibid.*
6. *Ibid.*
7. *Ibid.*
8. Letter, NAACP to City Manager Charles Barrier, June 24, 1963.
9. Larry Goodwyn, "Anarchy In St. Augustine," *Harper's* 230 (January, 1965), p. 77.
10. Dr. Robert B. Hayling, private interview, Cocoa Beach, Florida, March, 1971.
11. "St. Johns Trio Denies Race Incident Charges," *The Florida Times Union*, July 4, 1963, p. 29.
12. Dr. Robert B. Hayling, private interview, Cocoa Beach, Florida, March, 1971.
13. *Ibid.*

14. Senator Verle Pope, private interview, St. Augustine, Florida, March, 1971.

15. "Time For Adult Action and Common Sense," *The St. Augustine Record*, July 6, 1963, p. 1.

16. "Mayor Shelley Makes Statement to Citizens on Racial Tensions," *The St. Augustine Record*, July 7, 1963, p. 1.

17. Telegram, SCLC to Johnson, July 8, 1963.

18. "Demonstrations by Juveniles Prohibited Here," *The St. Augustine Record*, July 23, 1963, p. 1.

19. Fred Brinkoff, private interview, St. Augustine, Florida, March, 1971.

20. "Bail Asked For Four Negro Teenagers in St. Johns," *The Florida Times Union*, September 12, 1963, p. 18.

21. "Four Convicted at St. Augustine," *The Florida Times Union*, July 30, 1963, p. 20.

22. Mable N. Chesley, "Nine Fined in St. Augustine Sit-In Charge," *Daytona Beach Morning Journal*, August 2, 1963, p. 3.

23. *Ibid.*, p. 3.

24. Letter, Hayling to Johnson, August 3, 1963.

25. "Report On the Open Meeting In St. Augustine, Florida." Unpublished report by the Florida Advisory Committee to the U. S. Commission on Civil Rights, August 16, 1963, p. 2.

26. "Ancient City Teems with Unrest," *Daytona Beach Morning Journal*, August 17, 1963, p. 1.

CHAPTER TWO

1. The biographical sketch of Mrs. Peabody is based upon Robert K. Massie, "Don't Tread on Grandmother Peabody," *Saturday Evening Post*, 237 (May 16, 1964), p. 76.

2. David M. Chalmers, *Hooded Americanism*, (Chicago: Quadrangle Paperbacks, 1965), p. 366.

3. Mr. Ron Messina, private interview, St. Augustine, Florida, March, 1971. (This is Messina's account of the first Klan meeting held in St. Augustine.)

4. "Twelve Seized in St. Augustine," *The New York Times*, September 1, 1963, p. 41.

5. The Slave Market is a partially enclosed platform located in the center of town in a public park. The market, used generations ago during slave trading days, became a focal point for both white and Negro demonstrations.

6. "Jury Deadlocks On Arrest Charge in St. Augustine," *The Florida Times Union*, October 2, 1963, p. 26.

7. Police arrested four Negroes in August, 1963 for littering when they attempted to give out handbills, but they took no action against the same activity by the Klan.

8. The account of the Klan meeting is based upon several eyewitness accounts, the most valuable being, Reverend Irvin Cheney, *St. Augustine Ku Klux Klan*

Meeting, Unpublished Report—Florida Council on Human Relations, September, 1963, p. 1.
9. Ron Messina, private interview, St. Augustine, Florida, March, 1971.
10. Reverend Irvin Cheney, *St. Augustine Ku Klux Klan Meeting,* Unpublished Report—Florida Council on Human Relations, September, 1963, p. 5.
11. Hayling, private interview, Cocoa Beach, Florida, March, 1971.
12. Reverend Irvin Cheney, *St. Augustine Ku Klux Klan Meeting,* p. 7.
13. *Ibid.* p. 8.
14. Hayling, private interview, Cocoa Beach, Florida, March, 1971.
15. "Court Asked to Prevent St. Augustine Interference in Racial Demonstrations," *The Florida Times Union,* September 27, 1963, p. 26.
16. Florida Advisory Committee to the U. S. Commission on Civil Rights, Press Release, October 20, 1963.
17. "St. Johns Gets Aid in Probe of Slaying," *The Florida Times Union,* October 26, 1963, p. 26.
18. "St. Augustine Negro Area Strafed by Whites in Cars," *The New York Times,* October 30, 1963, p. 24.
19. "Ancient City NAACP Loses Court Fight to Demonstrate," *The Florida Times Union,* November 16, 1963, p. 26.
20. *Presentment of St. Johns County Grand Jury,* December 16, 1963, p. 1.
21. *Ibid.,* p. 2.
22. *Ibid.,* p. 3.
23. Hayling, private interview, Cocoa Beach, Florida, March, 1971.
24. "Two NAACP Officials Quit Posts in Ancient City," *The Florida Times Union,* December 20, 1963, p. 27.
25. Letter, Local NAACP to City Manager Barrier, January 9, 1964.
26. "Florida Spring Project SCM—SCLC," Pamphlet distributed by SCLC throughout New England, March, 1964. (Mimeographed.)
27. Mayor Shelley, Public Statement, St. Augustine, Florida, March 22, 1964.
28. "Two Whites Held After School Row," *The Florida Times Union,* March 27, 1964, p. 30.
29. "Twenty-Six Seized in St. Augustine," *The New York Times* March 29, 1964, p. 33. (By the middle of the "long hot summer" some individual bonds reached three thousand dollars or more.)
30. Robert K. Massie, "Don't Tread on Grandmother Peabody," *Saturday Evening Post,* 237 (May 16, 1964) , 76.
31. *Ibid.,* p 76 (Reverend Seymour corroborated this conversation in an interview in December, 1970 in New Orleans, Louisiana.)
32. Reverend Charles Seymour, private interview, New Orleans, Louisiana, December, 1970.
33. "Mrs. Peabody Is Jailed Overnight In Sit-Ins," *The Daytona Beach Morning Journal,* April 1, 1964, p. 1.
34. "List of Demands," SCLC Mass Meeting, March 31, 1964. (Mimeographed.)
35. William Kunstler, *Deep In My Heart,* (New York: William Morrow and Company, 1966) , p. 272.

36. "More Demonstrators May Be Called Upon," *The Daytona Beach Morning Journal*, April 1, 1964, p. 1.
37. Telegram, Saunders to Bryant, April 1, 1964.
38. "St. Augustine Mayor Sees Negro Demands For First Time," *The Florida Times Union*, April 2, 1964, p. 24.
39. "Negro Student Tutoring Seen For St. Augustine," *The Daytona Beach Morning Journal*, April 4, 1964, p. 1.
40. "Mrs. Peabody's Act Seen Harmful to All," *The Florida Times Union*, May 21, 1964, p. 11.
41. "St. Augustine Offers to Help Boston Combat Rioting," *The Florida Times Union*, April 15, 1964, p. 18.

CHAPTER THREE

1. "Manucy's Raiders—A White Force In St. Augustine," *The Miami Herald*, June 14, 1964, p. 14.
2. "Race Protest Start Vowed in St. Johns," *The Florida Times Union*, May 27, 1964, p. 29.
3. *Racial and Civil Disorders In St. Augustine*, Report of the Legislative Investigation Committee of the Florida Legislature, February, 1965, p. 141. (The payoffs to Manucy were common knowledge, and several reliable sources close to Manucy corroborated these payments.)
4. "Manucy's Raider's—A White Force in St. Augustine," *The Miami Herald*, June 14, 1964, p. 14.
5. Senator Verle Pope, private interview, St. Augustine, Florida, March, 1971.
6. "Moment of Truth in America's Oldest City," An unpublished account of the first night's march by an unknown author, June, 1964, p. 4. (Mimeographed.)
7. *Ibid*. p. 11.
8. Pat Watters, "The American Middle Ground," *New South*, September, 1964, p. 8.
9. Claude Sitton, "Two Hurt In Clash In St. Augustine," *The New York Times*, May 29, 1964, p. 10.
10. "Night Riders Fire on Dr King's Aide," *The New York Times*, May 30, 1964, p. 14.
11. "St. Augustine Tense as Marchers Halted," *The Florida Times Union*, May 30, 1964, p. 23.
12. William M. Kunstler, *Deep In My Heart*, (New York: William Morrow and Company, 1966), p. 289.
13. "St. Augustine Extends Curfew, Curtails Parking In Peace Bid," *The Florida Times Union*, June 2, 1964, p. 20.
14. *Johnson vs. Davis*, No 64-141-Civ.-J (M.D. Fla. 1964), Transcript of Proceedings, June 3, 1964.
15. *Young vs. Davis*, No. 64-133-Civ.-J.(M.D. Fla. 1964), Transcript of Proceedings, June 2, 1964.

16. *Ibid.*, June 3, 1964.
17. William Kunstler, *Deep In My Heart*, p. 294.
18. *Ibid.*, p. 295.
19. "More Ancient City Marches Threatened, *The Florida Times Union*, June 6, 1964, p. 22.
20. St. Augustine Chapter SCLC, press release, June 5, 1964.
21. Pat Watters, "The American Middle Ground," *New South* September, 1964. (Mayor Shelley considers the most accurate account of the St. Augustine disorders to be, A. G. Heinsohn, "St. Augustine: Rape of the Ancient City," *American Opinion*, ed. by Robert Welch, October, 1964.)
22. *Johnson vs. Davis*, No. 64-141-Civ.-J. (M. D. Fla. 1964) Preliminary Injunction, filed June 9, 1964.
23. "Violence Breaks Out During Night March," *The Florida Times Union*, June 10, 1964, p. 29.

CHAPTER FOUR

1. "Whites Routed by Tear Gas in St. Johns Row," *The Florida Times Union*, June 11, 1964, p. 20.
2. Telegram, King to Johnson, June 10, 1964.
3. "Police Rout Mob At St. Augustine," *The New York Times*, June 11, 1964, p. 1.
4. *Ibid.*
5. "Bryant Adds Patrolmen at Ancient City," *The Florida Times Union*, June 11, 1964, p. 20.
6. Letter, Lee C. White, Counsel to the President to King, June 11, 1964.
7. William Robert Miller, *Martin Luther King, Jr.*, (New York: Avon Books, 1968), p. 201.
8. Pat Watters, "The American Middle Ground," *New South*, September, 1964, p. 4.
9. William Robert Miller, *Martin Luther King, Jr.*, p. 202.
10. Fred Brinkoff private interview, St. Augustine, Florida, March, 1971.
11. Telegram, Smathers to King June 13, 1964.
12. "Quadricentennial Leaders Hit at Irresponsible Criticism," *The Florida Times Union*, June 14, 1964. (Upchurch explained his position to me in an interview in March, 1971. He refused to let me tape his remarks, but he felt King had no chance to win in St. Augustine. He also favored letting King "hang himself" right in St. Augustine.
13. Pat Watters, *New South*, p. 4.
14. "St. Augustine Racial Activity Slows Down," *The Florida Times Union*, June 15, 1964, p. 24.
15. *Young vs. Davis*, supra Transcript of Proceedings, June 15, 1964.
16. Governor Farris Bryant, "Executive Order Number One," reprinted in *Report of the Legislative Investigation Committee*, February, 1965. p. 89.

17. *Ibid.*, p. 4.
18. The account of the Washington trip is based upon, "Local Leaders Take Part In Washington Maneuvers." *St. Augustine Liberator*, June 30, 1964, p. 4. (Hayling and Twine both verified the Washington trip in March, 1971 interviews.)
19. "Local Business Leaders Adopt Resolution on Racial Situation Here," *The St. Augustine Record*, June 17, 1964, p. 1. (*The Record* published the complete text of the statement.)
20. "Dr. King's Plea Moves Seventeen Rabbis To Join St. Augustine Protest," *The New York Times*, June 18, 1964, p. 5.
21. *Ibid.*
22. "Genial Ancient City Businessman Caught In Middle of Race Issue," *The Florida Times Union*, June 21, 1964, p. 22.
23. "Acid Test," *Newsweek*, 63 (June 29, 1964), p. 27. (Muriatic acid is actually a weak acid used for cleaning pools. It is not harmful, especially diluted in water.)
24. "Genial Ancient City Businessman Caught In Middle of Race Issue," *The Florida Times Union*, June 21, 1964, p. 22.
25. *Ibid.*
26. A. H. Tebault "Two Sides To The Coin," *The St. Augustine Record*, June 18, 1964, p. 1.
27. A. H. Tebault, "City Police and Sheriff's Deputies Rate A Bonus," *The St. Augustine Record*, June 18, 1964, p. 4.
28. *Presentment of St Johns County Grand Jury*, June 18, 1964, p. 4.
29. Martin Luther King, Jr. "Answer to Presentment of Grand Jury," press release, June. 19, 1964, p. 2 (Mimeographed.)
30. "Efforts For Racial Peace Bog As Jury Rejects Negro Demands," *The Florida Times Union*, June 29, 1964, p. 22.
31. Governor Farris Bryant, "Executive Order Number Two," reprinted in *Report of The Legislative Investigation Committee*, February, 1965, p. 101.

CHAPTER FIVE

1. J.B. Stoner, the Klan attorney, became a close friend of Lynch. Stoner ran for Vice-President of the U.S. in 1964 under the banner of the National States Rights Party. Although rumors persisted that certain right-wingers in St. Augustine paid Lynch to come there, no concrete evidence verified this rumor.
2. Trevor Armbrister, "Portrait of an Extremist," *Saturday Evening Post*, 237 (August 22, 1964), p. 80. (The biographical sketch also came from this article.)
3. Senator Verle Pope, private interview, St. Augustine, Florida, March, 1971.
4. "Resolution Concerning the National Council of Churches," adopted by the Vestry of Trinity Episcopal Church, May 31, 1964. (Mimeographed.)
5. Reverend Charles Seymour, private interview, New Orleans, Louisiana, December, 1970.

6. "Rector of St. Augustine Backed By Bishop West of Florida," *The Witness*, 49 (July 23, 1964) , p. 3.

7. "Women Join Efforts To Combat Race Agitators," *The St. Augustine Record*, June 22, 1964, p. 1. (The practice of firing local Negroes who participated in demonstrations was widespread and quite effective.)

8. Senator Verle Pope, private interview, St. Augustine, Florida, March, 1971.

9. "Whites Negroes Cross Paths; St. Johns Police Avert Fight," *The Florida Times Union*, June 25, 1964, p. 26.

10. "St. Augustine Mob Attacks Negroes," *The New York Times*, June 26, 1964, p. 1.

11. *Ibid.*

12. *Ibid.*

13. The day after the incident *The St. Augustine Record*, whose editor never tired of criticizing biased news coverage, printed the name and badge number of the trooper.

14. Trevor Armbrister, "Portrait of an Extremist," *Saturday Evening Post*, 237 (August 22, 1964), p. 80. (The account of the events of June 25 is a combination of newspaper and magazine articles and several eyewitnesses, including the author.)

15. The account of the girl and the newsman is found in, "St. Augustine Mob Attacks Negroes," *The New York Times*, June 26, 1964, p. 14.

16. *Ibid.*

17. "Bryant Boosts Trooper Force In St. Augustine," *The Florida Times Union*, June 27, 1964, p. 1.

18. "Truce Flags Up In Ancient City As Bryant Appoints Study Unit," *The Florida Times Union*, July 1, 1964, p. 32.

19. No city official or Frank Upchurch, Sr., knew of any such committee or who its members might have been. No Negro official or Hayling knew anything about the committee, and no evidence exists that the committee ever held a meeting.

20. "Businessmen Vote In St. Augustine to Obey Civil Rights Law," *The Florida Times Union*, July 2, 1964, p. 18.

21. "Negroes Beaten At St. Augustine," *The New York Times*, July 6, 1964, p. 19.

22. The quotations on the picket signs are based upon first hand observations by the author.

23. *Plummer vs. Brock*, No 64-187-Civ. J. (M. D. Fla. 1964), Transcript of Proceedings, July 28, 1964.

24. "New Marches Seen In St. Augustine As Negroes Vow To Oppose Klan," *The Florida Times Union*, July 17, 1964, p. 25.

25. Plummer vs Brock, No. 64-,187-Civ.-J. (M. D. Fla. 1964), Order for Interlocutory Injunction, filed August 5, 1964.

26. *Plummer vs Brock* supra, Transcript of Findings, August 19, 1964.

27. "Law, Justice In County Feel Lash of Federal Court Powers," *The St. Augustine Record*, September 27, 1964, p. 1.

28. *Further Presentment of St. Johns County Grand Jury*, August 5, 1964, p. 2.

29. Otis Mason (a black member of the committee), private interview, St. Augustine, Florida, March 1971.
30. Reverend Charles Seymour, private interview, New Orleans, Louisiana, December, 1970.

EPILOGUE

1. "Cathedral Cautions Catholics," *The Florida Times Union*, June 21, 1964, p. 22. (Burns' references to brotherhood and love apparently applied only to whites. The Catholic schools in St. Augustine refused to admit Negroes until August, 1964.)
2. Martin Luther King, Jr., Speech given during the 1963 March on Washington at the Washington Monument, August, 1963, p. 3. (Mimeographed.)

Bibliography

INTERVIEWS

Arnade, Charles W. University of Florida. March, 1971.
Brinkoff, Fred. St. Augustine, Florida. March, 1971.
Chalmers David M. Gainesville, Florida. February, 1971.
Hayling, Robert B. Cocoa Beach, Florida. March, 1971.
Mason, Otis. St. Augustine, Florida. March, 1971.
Messina, Ronald. St. Augustine, Florida. March, 1971.
Pope, Senator Verle. St. Augustine, Florida. March, 1971.
Seymour, Reverend Charles. New Orleans, Louisiana. December, 1970.
Upchurch, Frank, Sr. St. Augustine, Florida. March, 1971.

BOOKS

Chalmers, David M. *Hooded Americanism*. Chicago: Quadrangle Paperbacks, 1965.
Florida Statistical Abstract—1967. Bureau of Economic and Business Research. University of Florida, 1967.
Kunstler William M. *Deep In My Heart*. New York. William Morrow and Company, 1966.
Miller, William Robert. *Martin Luther King, Jr.* New York: Avon Books, 1968.
U. S. Bureau of Census—County and City Data Book—1962. A Statistical Abstract Supplement. (Washington: U. S. Government Printing Office, 1962.)

REPORTS

Cheney, Irvin. *St. Augustine Ku Klux Klan Meeting*. Unpublished Report—Florida Council on Human Relations, September, 1963.
Further Presentment of St. Johns County Grand Jury. August 5, 1964.

"Moment of Truth In America's Oldest City." An unpublished account of the first night's march by an unknown author. June, 1964. (Mimeographed.)

Presentment of St. Johns County Grand Jury. December 16, 1963.

Presentment of St. Johns County Grand Jury. June 18, 1964.

Racial and Civil Disorders In St. Augustine. Reports of the Legislative Investigation Committee of the Florida Legislature. February, 1965.

Report On The Open Meeting In St. Augustine, Florida. Unpublished Report—Florida Advisory Committee to the U. S. Commission On Civil Rights. August 16, 1963.

COURT CASES

Johnson vs. Davis. No. 64-141-Civ.-J. (M. D. Fla. 1964). Transcript of Proceedings. June 3, 1964.

Johnson vs. Davis. No. 64-141-Civ.-J. (M. D. Fla. 1964). Preliminary Injunction. Filed June 9, 1964.

Plummer vs. Brock. No. 64-187-Civ.-J. (M. D. Fla. 1964). Transcript of Proceedings. July 28, 1964.

Plummer vs. Brock. No. 64-187-Civ.-J. (M. D. Fla. 1964). Order for Interlocutory Injunction. Filed August 5, 1964.

Plummer vs. Brock. No. 64-187-Civ.-J. (M. D. Fla. 1964). Transcript of Findings. August 19, 1964.

Young vs. Davis. No. 64-133-Civ.-J. (M. D. Fla. 1964). Transcript of Proceedings. June 2, 1964.

PERIODICALS

"Acid Test." *Newsweek.* June 29, 1964, p. 27.

Goodwyn, Larry. "Anarchy In St. Augustine." *Harper's.* January, 1965, pp. 74-81.

Heinsohn, A.G. "St. Augustine: Rape of the Ancient City." *American Opinion*, ed. by Robert Welch. October, 1964.

Massie, Robert K. "Don't Tread on Grandmother Peabody." *The Saturday Evening Post.* May 16, 1964, pp. 76-78.

"Rector of St. Augustine Backed by Bishop West of Florida." *The Witness*. July 23, 1964, p. 3.

Watters, Pat. "The American Middle Ground." *New South*. September, 1964, pp. 4-20.

NEWSPAPERS

Daytona Beach Morning Journal. January 1, 1963 to August 31, 1964.
Florida Times Union. January 1, 1960 to August 31, 1964.
Miami Herald. June 1, 1963 to August 31, 1964.
New York Times. June 1, 1963 to October 23, 1964.
St. Augustine Liberator. June 30, 1964.
St. Augustine Record. January 1, 1960 to August 31, 1964.

MISCELLANEOUS PRIMARY SOURCES

Bryant, Governor Farris. "Executive Order Number One." Reprinted in *Report of the Legislative Investigation Committee*. February, 1965.

_____."Executive Order Number Two." Reprinted in *Report of the Legislative Investigation Committee*. February, 1965.

Florida Advisory Committee to the U.S. Commission on Civil Rights. Press Release. October 20, 1963.

Florida Spring Project SCM—SCLC Pamphlet. March, 1964. (Mimeographed.)

Hayling, Robert B. to Vice-President Johnson. Letter. August 3, 1963.

Johnson, Lyndon [as Vice-President] to NAACP. Letter. March 7, 1963.

King, Martin L. "Answer to Presentment of Grand Jury." Press Release. June 19, 1964. (Mimeographed.)

King, Martin L. to Vice-President Johnson. Telegram. June 10, 1964.

"List of Demands." SCLC Mass Meeting. March 31, 1964. (Mimeographed.)

NAACP to City Manager Charles Barrier. Letter. June 24, 1964.

NAACP to City Manager Charles Barrier. Letter, January 9, 1964.

"Resolution Concerning the National Council of Churches." Adopted by the Vestry of Trinity Episcopal Church. May 31, 1964. (Mimeographed.)

St. Augustine Chapter SCLC. Press Release. June 5, 1964.

Saunders, R. W. to Governor Bryant. Telegram. April 1, 1964.

Shelley, Joseph. Public Statement. March 22, 1964.

Smathers, Senator George to Martin L. King. Telegram. June 13, 1964.

Southern Christian Leadership Conference to Vice-President Johnson. Telegram. July 8, 1963.

White, L. C. to Martin L. King. Letter. June 11, 1964.

St. Augustine and the Ku Klux Klan:

1963 and 1964

EDWARD W. KALLAL, JR.

Contents

ONE

Introduction
and
Chronology

On June 25, 1964, the day St. Augustine's militant segregationists made their most physical effort to purge the community of integrationists, mob action occurred both during the day at St. Augustine Beach, and during the evening when integrationist marchers had the temerity to interrupt J. B. Stoner's oration before 900 persons.[1] Since the 300 persons who attacked the marchers peeled off from Stoner's audience, one can reasonably infer that Stoner, national chairman of the National States Rights Party, hidden member of the United Florida Ku Klux Klan, and possessor of a special passport that allows him admittance to any United Florida Klavern,[2] had a hand in provoking the violence. The violence at the beach was different. What Aryan's heart would not pound with pride on seeing a tall blond woman in a white bathing suit lead the attackers against the integrationist foe?[3] And what Aryan would not be righteously incensed on seeing a state trooper fracture the skull of a participant of that attack, Richard Cubbage, age nineteen?[4]

The violence at the beach and at the rally, which was held in the Old Slave Market, points out that Klansmen were not the only militant segregationists. Whether or not Cubbage was a Klansman, the blond certainly came from outside the Klan's ranks. On the other hand, Cubbage's age symbolizes the leading role youths took in the violence. Further, since the Klan is a small organization, the 900 at the rally and the 300 attackers were not all Klansmen. One suspects Halstead "Hoss" Manucy, leader of the Ancient City Gun Club, correctly analyzed the crowd: "Just ordinary people go out to these speakings and things and just listen."[5]

The Klan, then, did not stand alone in the physical fight against integration. To borrow a phrase that D. R. "Billy" Mathews used to describe the integrationists in the Congressional Record, the militant segregationists were ". . . undisciplined cadres of juveniles, thrill seekers, and agitators."[6] Klansmen, as well as their brothers of the quasi-Klan Ancient City Hunting Club, were agitators. The juveniles and the thrill-seekers came not just from the Klan and the Ancient City Hunting Club, but also from the community at large. The actions of the agitators cannot be understood outside of the context of the three. In its relationship to allied groups and to the community, then, is the Klan to be understood.

As a backlash organization, the Klan had a narrow base of popular support. Many persons condemned the Klan's disposition to violence in the defense of the white race; many persons found the Klan repulsive. The Citizen's Band Radio Club felt impelled to write to the *St. Augustine Record* to disavow any connection with the racial disturbances: "Every time we ride down the street with our antennas waving in the breeze, people turn and look at us like we're criminals."[7] The Klan and the Hunting Club used C.B.'s to coordinate their activities.[8]

Yet the Klan is, however repulsive, a genetically American group. Professor Chalmers, after all, named his study of the Klan *Hooded Americanism*. The Klan claims to represent one hundred per cent Americanism. The unfortunate truth is that the Klan is not un-American: Klansmen reflect and magnify attitudes and dispositions found throughout American society. To understand the relationship of the Klan to other parts of society is to understand (1) why unaffiliated members of the society—"white citizens determined . . . to prevent integration"[9]—joined the Klan as militant segregationists, (2) how militant backlash groups could, when needed, spring from the community as home-grown, quasi-Klans, and (3) why the community, in its crisis of trembling institutions, would allow the Klan to exercise its militant backlash tactics and, indeed, turn the defense of the community's cherished institutions and ideas over to the Klan.

Further, an appreciation of the Klan's Americanism guards against stereotypical thinking and scapegoatism. If the Klan was essentially an alien organization, one could—and some do—focus all violence and misdeeds committed against integrationists on the Klan itself or portray the violence as wholly Klan-inspired and thus purge the society of guilt. This conception of the Klan, the society, and the violence is nonsensical: it distorts the empirical facts and attempts to cover up society's dirty linen. Paradoxically, some of that dirty linen is the counter-vein of violence committed by Negroes against the segregationists. The Americanism of the Klan prompts me to concur with the *St. Augustine Record:* "The Responsibility For Any Further Racial Violence Rests With Us All."[10]

The second chapter, then, argues that the Ku Klux Klan is an organization drawing its membership from the lower and lower-middle classes[11] and exhibiting a disposition to violence, fraternalism, nativism, anti-communism, and racism. That none of these traits are unique to the Klan but rather that many other groups and people also exhibit these traits—albeit in varying combinations—demonstrates the Americanism of the Klan.

In addition to examining the interrelationships between the Klan and its society, one should look at both the crisis that brought Klansmen out into the streets and what Klansmen did to fight integration in that crisis. The crisis, indeed, was genuine and punctuated with violence. It ranged from the shootout at National Association for the Advancement of Colored People (NAACP) turned Southern Christian Leadership Conference (SCLC) leader Dr. R. Hayling's house and the antics of his "army"[12] to a swan-song beating of Al Lingo in October, 1964.[13] One may very easily criticize militant segregationists for their actions in the crisis; but righteousness does not necessarily make good history. "It is a mistake to dismiss the reaction as calculated or cynical, for it was often deeply felt and deadly serious."[14] This reaction must be considered in the context of Negro violence towards the white race and in the context of the threat posed to long-standing and cherished institutions.

The foremost threat, of course, was to the segregated way of life. But the events in St. Augustine were only part of the evidence of the attempt to destroy segregation, or perhaps one should say the attempt to destroy the rights of association and property as guaranteed by the First Amendment. Rioters took to the street only thirty-eight miles to the north of St. Augustine in Jacksonville; New York and Chicago witnessed riots. When the integrationists came to town, St. Augustinians were worried and stunned. So traumatic an experience was the integration drive that the *St. Augustine Record* ruefully commented: "It's a wonderful city, at least what's left of it after the twin disasters of Martin Luther King and Hurricane Dora."[15]

But the marching legions of King, whom St. Augustinians widely regarded as a Communist, joined in constituting the crisis a smaller and more traditional element of crises: the strike. As president of the St. Johns County Chapter of the Florida Coalition of Patriotic Societies, Dr. Hardgrove Norris busied himself by warning the populace that "under revolutionary guidance the Negro moves in mass and in so doing, spills over the rights of others."[16]

Norris and his family were also concerned by the infringement of property rights. Thus, his son worked as a strike breaker for the Florida East Coast Railway and, as a consequence, suffered a wound.[17] The strike, which the FEC won, began in January of 1963 and lasted through the civil rights crisis. Hence, the latter crisis built upon the festering of the older problem—a problem that also occasionally burst into violence. The stability and good order of the community faced a perplexing variety of threats.

The Klan and the community it was attached to moved to stave off these threats. The resulting events—the admixture of threats to or crises of the stability of the St. Augustinian way of life and the community efforts to stave off the pending changes for the worse—are subject to various interpretations. These interpretations present differing views that emphasize this aspect or that in the endeavor to present a reasonable explanation of the events. The interpretations range from Robert Hartley's[18] golden-opportunities-slipping-through-the-fingers of the establishment thesis to Pat Watter's[19] Negroes standing for all Americans' rights in the face of anarchy to Stoner's and Manucy's[20] thesis that argues that the militant segregationists really won the Battle of St. Augustine. A brief survey of these theses will put my argument in perspective.

Klansmen were the agitators in Matthews's trilogy, but their activities can be further categorized. Klansmen from Jacksonville rallied their support for their St. Augustine brethren; Klansmen tried to bolster their thin ranks by recruiting when the persons in the community at large were feeling a certain solidarity with the hooded order. Klansmen articulated the views and frustrations of all participants in backlash. Klansmen organized and led the counter marches that "white citizens determined to resist integration" staged, although the Ancient City Hunting Club gave a helping hand. Klansmen organized the picketing of integration restaurants and motels; the Klan orators had an unsalutory effect on the disposition of crowds. Occasionally, Klansmen resorted to violent intimidation.

Klansmen and members of allied organizations were joined in the struggle against integration and in their methods of struggle by many segments of the community. Accordingly, one must be careful and ascribe to the Klan only the deeds and misdeeds that can be documented as the Klan's. One may suspect that Klansmen were driving the two cars that followed the Jacksonian's car out of St. Augustine and showered it with small caliber gunfire and rocks. But one cannot prove that Klansmen were behind the wheel.[21] To assume that a Klansman pulled the trigger is to ignore the attitude of the larger community and to fall into the same kind of stereotypical thinking that characterized both sides. Hence:

As an abhorred, but integral, member of society and especially as a member of those desiring to prevent integration and the concomitant destruction of social institutions, the Ku Klux Klan played a leading, but stereotyped, role in the militant backlash movement.

Chronology

In order to understand the Klan's role in the crisis, the scaffolding of the crisis is needed. The tide of integration broke over the community of St. Augustine in two waves. The first occurred in 1963 and was largely a local affair with local participants. The dominant integrationist organization was the NAACP. Dr. Robert Hayling, dentist and Korean War veteran, was the catalyst that generated the disturbances. The St. Augustine branch of the NAACP wrote to Vice-President Johnson requesting he not come to help dedicate the Arrivas House. The NAACP requested that President Kennedy block federal funds for the city's Quadricentennial celebration.[1] June saw the beginning of picketing, various meetings between the city and the NAACP, and the end of discrimination at public buildings. On July 1, militant segregationists shot it out with Hayling's followers in front of Hayling's house.[2]

In July, picketing continued; sit-ins began; Juvenile Court Judge Mathias prohibited juveniles from picketing or demonstrating. The police made sit-in arrests, which integrationists protested with a demonstration in front of the county jail. In September, the school system peacefully, tokenly, integrated. Police thoroughly broke up an integrationist Labor Day meeting in the Plaza; the Klan held several rallies outside of town. Klansmen severely beat Hayling and three friends for spying on their meeting. Hayling petitioned Federal District Court to enjoin city officials from interfering with demonstrations. Following the Labor Day arrests, City Manager Barrier prohibited all parades, demonstrations, and large open air and public meetings.[3] On October 25, Ancient City Hunting Club member William Kinard and three compatriots drove by NAACP leader Goldie Eubanks', home to "cuss" him. Kinard paid for it with his life when a "lucky" shot from a .38 caliber pistol fired one block away from Kinard's moving auto hit him in the head.[4] Militant segregationists retaliated several nights later by

101

peppering several "juke joints," homes and businesses with shotgun and .22 caliber rifle fire. One militant segregationist also heaved a live grenade that did not explode at one of the nightclubs, Harlem Gardens.[5]

Police arrested several NAACP members in connection with the slaying, but a key prosecution witness mysteriously disappeared. Tensions eased in November and December as the Federal District Court dismissed the NAACP petition (". . . the plaintiff did not come into court with clean hands.") The city lifted the ban on marches and demonstrations; a Grand Jury blamed extremists in the integration forces and the Ku Klux Klan, "which does not represent the majority view of the white citizens of St. Augustine," for the unrest. Hayling and Eubanks resigned from the NAACP to make way for less militant leaders.

The last two months of 1963 and the first two months of 1964 saw the recession of the first wave of integration and the rise of the second wave—the national phase, which featured national leaders for the integrationists and a mixed bag, national and local, for the militant segregationists. During 1964, the dominant integrationist group was King's SCLC. January and February were punctuated with violent vandalism. Fires ravaged the car of a man whose children were attending a previously lily-white school and the home of another man whose children were integrating a school.[6] Various car and home windows were broken with gunfire and rocks; an FEC train was blown up. Snipers shot up Hayling's home in an act that Mayor Shelley called dastardly.[7] Hayling joined the SCLC, requested aid from King, and planned the "Spring Project" with King in Orlando. Between March 28 and April 3, the well-publicized Spring Project, featuring college students and Mrs. Peabody, mother of the Governor of Massachusetts, picketed, sat-in, and attempted to break down segregation in churches and in restaurants. Police arrested around 125 persons during the project, which ended when classes started and when Mrs. Peabody left. The SCLC planned for June; police occasionally arrested demonstrators during April and May.

The integrationists began their all-out effort to integrate the private sector of St. Augustine with marches in late May.[8] Integrationists began their flood-the-jail tactics. Militant segregationists attacked newsmen. Following the violence of May 28, the city banned nighttime marches to the Plaza. Police turned back a night march May 31; sit-ins continued. Federal District Judge Bryan Simpson, in Jacksonville, finally ruled June 9 to remove the ban on night marching. An undercurrent of violence, involving beatings and vandalism, marked the lull in demonstrations from June 3 to June 9. Throughout the rest of June, the integrationists marched. Catching on, the militant segregationists started marching on June 11; they continued to plague integrationist marchers, newsmen, and police. Violence continued and reached a crescendo on June 25, four days after the integrationists began wade-ins. Nightly militant backlash rallies, frequent marches, the integrationist's various tactics, and the numerous acts of violence and vandalism contributed to the civil war atmosphere. Governor Bryant turned the command of law enforcement agencies over to a state officer and on June 20 banned night marches. The violence continued after June 25, but police provided adequate protection to wade-in demonstrators on June 29. With the passage of the Civil Rights Law of 1964, Governor Bryant arranged a halt to the demonstrations in early July. However, Klansmen, ever patriotic, marched on July 4.

Violence occasionally burst forth during July, as integrationists tested the newly integrated restaurants. Klansmen picketed for resegregation and conducted rallies. On July 24, two Molotov cocktails cracked through the plate glass window of Monson Motor Inn, scene of integrationist efforts prior to the Civil Rights Act and of backlash efforts after the law.[9] In August, Judge Simpson ordered the restaurants to re-integrate and enjoined the Ancient City Hunting Club from interfering. As the tension died, the Klan and the Hunting Club passed the leadership of backlash over to a newly forming White Citizens Council.

TWO

The Klan and Society

The Ku Klux Klan, as an organization drawing its membership from the lower and lower-middle classes of society and exhibiting a disposition to violence, nativism, fraternalism, anti-communism, and racism, was not a foreign or alien body in St. Augustine society. Rather, the Klan was an integral member of the society. Although many persons voiced disapproval of the Klan—Sheriff Davis calls J. B. Stoner a "rabble rouser"[1]— the Klan was a member of society because features of the Klan, except the membership base, were also exhibited by various other groups in society. Thus, the Klan was, in a sense, 100% American.

Membership Base

The sixth factor, the membership base of lower and lower-middle classes, does set the Klan off from some other segments of society. That the Ancient City Hunting Club shares this factor and that it shares with the Klan methods of opposing integration are the reasons for my labeling the Club a quasi-Klan.[2] Dr. Norris's Chapter of the Florida Coalition of Patriotic Societies and the women who resolved to fight integration by firing any domestics engaged in "racial demonstrations"[3] represent different social strata and different approaches to the crises at hand. The social position of members in the Ancient City Hunting Club and in the Klan helps explain why they became leaders in militant backlash. My argument on the composition of membership rests on three types of sources: on information from the House Committee on Un-American Activities; on the information from and results of James W. Vander Zanden;[4] and on assorted other analyses of the Klan. Since I am not familiar with the selection procedure of the Committee's investigation, I justify my use of its material by associating myself with Vander Zanden's statement on the problem:

This sample is of unknown representativeness and it is undoubtedly biased, yet it probably reflects the occupational breadth of the Klan's membership.

Accordingly, caution should be taken into account in evaluating the following interpretations.[5]

Vander Zanden's 153 Klansmen fall into four categories: (1) skilled workers; (2) marginal, small businessmen; (3) marginal white-collar workers; and (4) unskilled and semi-skilled workers in transportation and larger industries. Fifty-one, or 33%, belong in category (1). Eleven, or 7%, are in category (2). Thirty-six, or 24% belong in category (3). Fifty-five, or 36%, are in category (4). In the first three categories, which constitute ninety-eight, or 64%, Vander Zanden argues, Klansmen are in the upper rungs of the lower class and the lower rungs of the middle class. the Klansmen in these categories are in an intermediate position between clear-cut lower class and clear-cut middle class jobs; "their status is insecure and they are anxious."[6] This group of Klansmen have the example of and aspire to be middle class, but hitherto do not quite cut the mustard. On the threshold of the middle class and wanting desperately to get in, these Klansmen "internalize the success goals"[7] of the middle class, but still have to face the anomaly of their non-achievement. Two concerns thus arise. On the one hand, the Klansman searches for reasons to explain his failure to achieve full middle class status.[8] On the other hand, the Klansman endeavors to maintain his grip, however precarious, on the middle class.

Vander Zanden's fourth category, with fifty-five, or 36%, of the Klansmen, ranks solidly in the blue collar working class; the group does not have the middle class "teasingly" in front of it. Nonetheless, he argues, they are still frustrated and insecure. They live in an economy that considers some unemployment normal. Cutbacks in production now and again mean cutbacks in jobs now and again. Klansmen in this class are never sure the job will be there tomorrow. Further, many of these workers left the strong ties of family and friends to work in the new large industries that came to Southern cities after World War II. The Klansmen were participants in C. Vann Woodward's bulldozer revolution. If one remembers the two-tier society of the South in the 1960's, and if one remembers that destruction of the two-tier system would mean spiraling competition for these jobs—not to mention the distasteful prospect of brushing elbows with Negroes at lunch counters—then one can understand these working men's commitment to segregation and their determination to fight integration.

Of the 172 Klansmen who testified before the House Committee on Un-American Activities in 1965 and 1966, occupational material was available for 122, or 71%. Although some overlap between these Klansmen and those in Vander Zanden's sample surely occurred, I was forced to create two additional categories: (5) jobs with higher prestige or better pay than categories (1) through (4); and (6) jobs with lower prestige or poorer pay than categories (1) through (4). Eleven, or 9%, of the Klansmen had jobs in category (1). Twenty-five, or 20%, had jobs in category (2). Nineteen, or 16%, had jobs in category (3). Twenty-eight, or 33%, had jobs in category (4). Twenty-three, or 19%, had jobs in category (5). Sixteen, or 13%, had jobs in category (6). Hence, eighty-three, or 68%, of the Klansmen interviewed by the Committee had jobs that fell into the categories that Vander Zanden established. However, thirty-nine, or 32%, of the Klansmen fell into categories (5) and (6) and thus merit some attention.

Category (6) comprises those workers whom I could not, in good conscience, include in category (4) (See explanation of Table 1). Included in this category were, among others, loggers, criminals, Klansmen who worked full time for the hooded order, and employees of minor industries. Nonetheless, the explanatory model for category (4) applies also to this category. Certainly, the argument that the Klan has a lower and lower-middle class base is not endangered, and the 13% of this category could be added to the 68% of categories (1) through (4). Thus, 81% of those Klansmen interviewed are in the categories of the lower and lower-middle classes.

The 19% of the Klan in category (5) represent an exception. Is the exception overwhelming?[9] I think not. The category, literally, is all occupations with status above the lower-middle class. So defined, compared to the Klan's 19%, a disproportionate amount of Americans' jobs would fall into it. That 81% of the Klansmen tested do not join Americans in the "great middle class" indicates, I believe, a significant definition of Klansmen. Category (5) ranged from foremen to a vice-president of a school board to attorneys to a self-employed farmer and cattle rancher who had interests in oil and timber and was owner of a four-seat airplane.[10]

That these exceptions are not overwhelming can be seen even more clearly on combining Vander Zanden's and my results. Out of 275 Klansmen, sixty-two, or 23%, are in category (1). Fifty-five, or 20%, are in category (3). Thirty-six, or 13%, are in category (2). Eighty-three, or 30%, are in category (4). Twenty-three, or 8%, are in category (5). Sixteen, or 6%, are in category (6). Combining the lower and lower-middle class categories of (1) through (4) and (6) produces an impressive 252 Klansmen, or 92%. Having

8% of the Klansmen in higher categories does not skew the Klan's base of support from the lower and lower-middle classes.

The sample for education may be too small—both numerically and percentage of Klansmen interviewed—to give an accurate impression of the educational status of the Klansmen. Nonetheless, of the Klansmen interviewed, most terminated their education at some stage of high school. Nineteen, or 27%, of the Klansmen dropped out of high school; twenty-three, or 33%, graduated but did not attend any college. Categories (2) and (5) sandwich these two groups, which comprise 60% of the Klansmen in the education group. Category (2), which was eight years of schooling or less, had twelve, or 17% of the Klansmen, whereas category (5), which was formal schooling beyond high school but with no degrees, had nine, or 13%. Only insignificant numbers of Klansmen received no education, a bachelor's degree, or post-bachelor work. Most of the Klansmen interviewed, then, thought that a high school diploma represented enough, or more than enough, formal schooling.

The distribution of age among these Klansmen is important when one remembers the major role played by community youths in St. Augustine's militant backlash. The youths probably were not Klansmen.[11] Out of the 124 Klansmen in the age group, which made up 72% of the total Klansmen interviewed, fifty-three, or a full 43%, were between the ages thirty-one and forty inclusive. This 43% is equal to the combined totals of the categories that sandwich the thirty-one to forty group. Twenty-six, or 21% were between the ages of twenty-one and thirty inclusive; an equal number were between forty-one and fifty inclusive. Most of the Klansmen interviewed were either in their thirties, headed for their thirties, or coming from their thirties. Only one Klansman interviewed was a teenager.

Other observers corroborate Vander Zanden's and the House Un-American Activities Committee's placing the Klan in the lower and lower-middle classes. Even the Klan of the 1920's is moving from John Mecken's "good solid middle class" to Kenneth Jackson's description: "Having fought his way above the lowest rungs of the financial ladder, the potential Klansman remained something less than a success."[12] Chalmers offers a similar description of the Klan of the 1960's. "He stood at the juncture of the middle and working classes, with middle class identifications but without its prestige occupations and status." The Klan's anti-semitism, Chalmers explains, stems in part from "his financial and social insecurity."[13] The marchers in the Klan-organized counter-march of June 14, 1964 were, although not all

Klansmen, farmers, mechanics, carpenters, and few, if any, white collar workers.[14] A few days earlier, the marchers in the Klan's march, again although not all Klansmen, included barbers, gas station attendants, cab drivers, postmen, and workmen from Fairchild-Stratos, a company that repairs airplanes.[15]

"Hoss" Manucy, who has a high school education, agrees with the more learned observers. The trouble with the Civil Rights Bill of 1964—the Constitution of 1964, as Manucy puts it—is that it is only for black people. "Lower class white people can't get the breaks they [the blacks] can get." After all, the Ancient City Hunting Club also hunted deer. The Club was organized in part: "so the little man could have a place to hunt."[16]

The Ku Klux Klan and quasi-Klans, then, are organizations of the lower and lower-middle classes. Their precarious position in society makes them sensitive to demands from those outside of society for a fundamental restructuring of the society, a restructuring that would allow those outsiders into the society. Not wanting to share what little of the pie they had with their neighbors and realizing that their neighbor's share would come from their part and not from the part of those above the lower and lower-middle class socially, the Klansmen vehemently turned to militant backlash.[17]

Violence

In addition to its lower and lower-middle class base, the Klan exhibits a disposition to violence, just as the society that spawned it exhibits a disposition to violence. The disposition, then, defines the Klan and puts it in a wider social context.

American society in the 1960's was a violent society; the Klan reflected and magnified the violence. Americans in 1963 witnessed the assassination of the President of the United States. That John Kennedy was the fourth man to be murdered out of thirty men who had occupied the office demonstrates that although violence is the exception in American politics, violence falls within, not without, the political sphere. Race relations have always been tinged with violence. The relations were heated by the attempts at "forced integration." If the Klan was violent, it had pleanty of company.

And the Klan was violent. Imperial Wizard Robert Shelton noted: "We're not in favor of violence, but the law of survival is the first one."[1] *The Klan Ledger*, official organ of the White Knights of the Ku Klux Klan of

Mississippi, which was the most violent of the collage of 1960 Klans—during the summer of 1964, federal authorities arrested thirty-six White Knights and charged them with seven murders and related felonies[2]— was as indiscreet as Shelton.

> We are deadly serious about this business. We have taken no action as yet against the enemies of our State, our Nation, and our Civilization, but we are not going to sit back and permit our rights . . . to be negotiated away by a group composed of atheistic priests, brainwashed black savages, and mongrelized money-worshippers, meeting with some stupid or cowardly politician. Take heed, atheists and mongrels, we will not travel your path to a Leninist hell, but we will buy *YOU* a ticket to the Eternal if you insist.[3]

Klansmen came out feet first against, in Wilhoit's phrase, the "egalitarian revolutionaries."[4] On May 12, 1963, after a cross-burning meeting of the Georgia and Alabama Klans, bombs blew up in a Birmingham motel and the Birmingham home of A. D. King, presaging the attacks on his brother, Martin's cottage in St. Augustine. The three hour riot that followed the blasts led Mayor Hanes to observe that "Martin Luther King is a revolutionary."[5] The Klan was implicated, as it was in two blasts in September of 1963. With J. B. Stoner, hero of St. Augustine militant segregationists, on hand, a bomb exploded in a Birmingham church. The bomb killed four black children.[6] A few nights later, Connie Lynch, the other Klan hero of St. Augustine, succinctly analyzed the situation for a sympathetic St. Augustine audience at a Klan rally:

> In the first place, they ain't little. They're fourteen or fifteen years old—old enough to have venereal diseases . . . In the second place, they weren't children. Children are little *people*, little *human beings*, and that means white people. There's little monkeys . . . there's little dogs and cats and apes and baboons and skunks and there's also little Niggers. But they ain't children . . . . And in the third place, it wasn't no shame they was killed.[7]

So inspired by Reverend Lynch, who "knew his business real well,"[8] and others, such as Weldon Don Cothran, Florida Grand Dragon of Shelton's Klan,[9] Florida Klansmen demonstrated their disposition to violence. After all, Robert Pitman Gentry, kligrapp (secretary) of the Robert E. Lee Klavern number 508, Jacksonville, testified that Klansmen were not interested in "getting troublemakers out" of the Klan.[10] Instead, they made trouble. At the above meeting, on September 18, four local members of the NAACP, including Dr. Hayling, had the temerity to spy on the meeting and suffered grievously for their mistake. Summoned by Reverend Cheney, Sheriff Davis may well have saved their lives. One Klanswoman whispered to her husband: "Go get the head chopper . . . and get the rope, and for God's sake, take off your robe and leave it in the car."[11] When Sheriff Davis arrived, most Klansmen had departed, leaving the four integrationists, beaten with fists and motorcycle chains, lying on the ground. Noting that he could lay two fingers in the head wound of Hayling, Sheriff Davis rather politely summed up the situation: the Klansmen "beat the tar out of 'em."[12]

Jacksonville, a short thirty-eight miles north of St. Augustine, was the heart of Florida Klandom. Boasting of six Klaverns, Robert E. Lee's numbers 506, 508, 513, 514, 518, and 520, Jacksonville witnessed Klan violence. Klansmen N. L. Wood, G. Knouse, V. Glen, and J. E. Higginbottom pummeled sixty-two year old J. E. Land on suspicion of having an affair that would lead to mongrelization.[13] In early February, 1964, Jacksonville Police uncovered a cache of 800 sticks of dynamite with fuses and caps.[14] A few days later, Klansman William Rosecrans, thirty years old and from Indiana, demonstrated the excellence of the dynamite and his backlash elan by exploding some dynamite under the home of G. Gillian, whose six year old grandson, Donald Godfrey, had recently deflowered lily-white Lackawana School.[15] With local police and the FBI in hot pursuit, Rosecrans abandoned his car—leaving in it three sticks of dynamite—and fled to St. Augustine with the alleged aid of Buddy Cooper, Exalted Cyclops (leader) of the St. Augustine Klavern number 519. Cooper reportedly got Rosecrans a job at Nick's Boat Yard under the name James Lewis, but Manucy betrayed him in early March when Manucy suspected Rosecrans had bombed a Florida East Coast train and when Sheriff Davis offered Manucy part of the FEC reward money.[16] Rosecrans received seven years in jail for his crime but four indicted Jacksonville Exalted Cyclopses were eventually vindicated. Stoner conducted the defense, pleading with the jury to remember white supremacy and the rights of white people. He was impressed when a Catholic on the jury was not biased against the Klansmen.[17]

During the civil rights demonstrations in St. Augustine, Klansmen, quasi-Klansmen, and "white citizens determined to fight integration," attempted to physically expel the "egalitarian revolutionaries," who were understandably intimidated. A spokesman for King demonstrated either personal paranoia or the gravity of the expulsion attempt. "We've got to go through with them [marches] even if we're mowed down with machine guns."[18] One suspects a good deal of paranoia or consciousness of the news media was involved in that statement, but one can not deny the Klan's hand in St. Augustine violence.

But in what direction did that hand attempt to direct the violence? Some observers suggest the Klan and quasi-Klan had a restraining influence on the young "white citizens determined to prevent integration." The *New York Times* reported that Cochran engaged in the following dialogue at a Slave Market (the focal point of the civil rights demonstrations) rally on June 19, 1964:

> Cochran. "The Klan has been accused of violence—they say seventy-six years ago we used to lynch niggers."
>
> A few men in the crowd. "Let's lynch some tonight."
>
> Cochran. "Now wait a minute, we can't do that, because there would be hundreds of federal officers in here if we did."[19]

Sheriff Davis reports his "liaison officer" Manucy restrained overzealous militant segregationists: "If whites got too rowdy, Hoss would get 'em in line."[20] Stoner qualifies the irenic purpose of the Klan and quasi-Klan along lines similar to Cochran's. The Klan did not really restrain the "white citizens determined to prevent integration," but the Klan did prevent some attacks on the police because the Klan did not want the national guard to move in.[21]

Other observers see the Klan following the path marked out by the September 18 meeting. While Sherrif Davis saw most violence coming from white juveniles in the Plaza, national news services saw it coming from Klansmen.[22] The *New York Times* considered that most violent opposition to integration came from Klansmen and "other whites from surrounding towns and rural areas." The *Times* also reported that Stoner was riding in a car with a two-way radio and a passenger whose revolver rested on his lap.[23] *Life* saw the Klan as the fountainhead of the violence, analyzed the Slave Market mobs to be "Klan-infested," and argued that Klansmen were night-riding to terrorize the Negro section of town. To prove the last point, *Life* offered several instances of terrorism, the perpetrators of which managed to elude police.[24] Police Chief Virgil Stuart analyzed the militant backlash mobs to consist of boys and men. The latter were (of course) out-of-towners, some of whom were Klansmen.[25] On July 5, 1964, a group of militant segregationists, undoubtedly Klansmen or quasi-Klansmen, assailed Richard

Eubanks, accused slayer of Kinard, member of the Ancient City Hunting Club and brother of Manucy's son-in-law. Although arrested, Exalted Cyclops Buddy Cooper saw the charges against him dismissed.[26] Hartley, historian of St. Augustine, looks upon Klansmen Stoner and Lynch as perpetrating "much of the violence which gripped the nation's oldest city."[27]

Klansmen were not alone in violence. Aside from the integrationists' violence, which is discussed below, other participants in backlash were violent. One should be careful, however, not to overemphasize violence—Sheriff Davis and Stoner both thought it was built up in the press—[28] but violence was none the less evident.

Sporting blue jeans, tee shirts and ducktail haircuts, and in the spirit of the South Carolina youths who chanted "5, 6, 7, 8, we don't want to integrate, 7, 8, 9, 10, we don't want the monkeys in," St. Augustine's young men in their late teens and early twenties played the juvenile thrill seeker to the Klan's agitation. At both the beaches and the rallies, a young St. Augustinian, more often than not, would be the one to attack the integrationist. As Stoner reflected: "The youth were more interested in taking direct action." Young men held the attention of police and "burly young whites" discussed strategy at motel dining rooms.[29] The beaches were almost the exclusive front for the young, although, we will recall, not the exclusive front for males. Having "found something they could have a lot of fun at,"[30] the youths would line up in the water, throw sandballs, and taunt the integrationists. (It is interesting to note that Manucy may well have exercised a great influence over these youths—see below on the Club.) Several times the integrationists chose not to go into the water and several times the youths attacked the integrationists. Presumably, their youthful enthusiasm boiled over.

Similarly, those who attacked the integrationists as they marched were also young. Sheriff Davis describes the youths' favorite tactic: "There would be ten to twelve guys in the park who would rush one part of the line—maybe one cop in that part—would force five or six blacks out the other side of the line, bop 'em two or three times and keep on going."[31] The Klan, according to Stoner, had "'bout all the young white boys there cooperating with us."[32] A sample of the newspaper reports of the violence bears that assertion out. The *St. Augustine Record* reported mostly teenagers participating in the violence against integrationists on May 19, 1964. City Manager Charles Barrier noted that the large number of minors were creating a dangerous situation. "A near riot" occurred June 9 when men joined the youths in attacking marchers. The *St. Petersburg Times* reported youths throwing sulfuric acid at marchers, though Sheriff Davis says it was oil of mustard. The *Tampa Tribune* argued that when dusk fell, gangs of young white youths "take over" the town. In short, St. Augustine's youths did not flinch from violence in militant backlash. "You'd be surprised how much trouble a bunch of teen-aged young kids can give you."[33]

The Klan's disposition to violence further recedes into the landscape of St. Augustine's violence when the Klan's betters and the youth's elders occasionally dabbled in violence. On June 18, 1964, as the Florida Legislative Investigation Committee tersely put it: "Two whites and four Negroes invaded Monson Motor Lodge private pool for guests creating famous TV show . . . Tension again mounted higher."[34] What could stir (and frighten) the respectable more than an invasion of private property? Only seeing the police not defend private property is worse. When the six jumped into the pool, State Troopers on hand declined to aid the local policemen, one of whom jumped into the pool after the demonstrators and the rest of whom flailed at the demonstrators with clubs. Incensed at this improper display of police behavior, thirty or so angry businessmen surrounded the State Troopers and berated them for nonfeasance. When integrationists marched on Monson around midnight, many businessmen were waiting, baseball bats in hand, to defend the sanctity of private property. Sheriff Davis persuaded the integrationists not to attempt to hold a rally on private property because, not only would that rally be morally and legally wrong, but also that "these people would hurt them."[35]

Compared to the alleged violence of the St. Augustine Police Department and the St. Johns County Sheriff Department, the verifiable Klan violence pales by comparison. Critics level charges against the local law enforcement agencies, especially the Sheriffs' Department: of using electric cattle prods and dogs to rout demonstrators, of personally pummeling integrationists, of maintaining inhuman jail conditions, and of standing around passively while militant segregationists beat up integrationists. Very little evidence exists to indicate police or Sheriff's deputies personally pummeled the integrationists. Richard Eubanks, accused slayer of Kinard, filed suit against Sheriff Davis and two deputies for allegedly beating him with a blackjack in 1962; the SCLC decried police brutality as unbelievable.[36] Conclusive proof is lacking in both cases.

What of the electric cattle prods and of the dogs, which were bought and trained by funds donated by the public-minded citizens in 1963? In what manner and for what purpose were these law enforcement tools used? In July, 1963, police used cattle prods on sit-in demonstrators who refused to move. Bertell Duncan accused Sheriff Davis of poking her in the arm as she walked down the street the last day of August, 1963. On Labor Day, police broke up a rally in the Slave Market for lacking a permit. In the process, Goldie Eubanks, local NAACP leader, received two blows from a cattle prod as the police "herded" the demonstrators to police cars. Eubanks deflected the first blow with his hand; the second thrust struck him in the cheek.[37] Sheriff Davis conceded the use of cattle prods in breaking up demonstrations, especially sit-ins. The Sheriff Department's standing rule was not to pick up prisoners. Davis points out that Judge Simpson never ruled against the use of the cattle prod.[38] Although inspiring fear, police dogs, despite charges to the contrary, found their main duty in protecting integrationists.

On June 10, 1964, Simpson ordered Davis to refrain from putting prisoners into sweat boxes, closet-like cells with rough plaster, and padded cells, and thus foreclosed a peculiar form of violence that integrationists experienced. The punishment is peculiar because I know it was used, but beyond that, what happened is hazy. Sources disagree on the duration of the stay, the reasons for the punishment, and even if the punishment was originally intended for integrationists. The *Alligator* maintains that Davis, infuriated by some local prisoners joining the demonstrators in singing freedom songs, "took all the white demonstrators into the sweatbox."[39] Davis, on the other hand, maintains that since the local prisoners were cussing the Negro demonstrators, who were cussing back, he started to take the local boys to the sweatbox. The demonstrators jailed with the local prisoners insisted on going to the sweatbox also.[40] The facts, in short, are murky, as they are concerning the exercise pen outside the jail. Assertations of a concentration camp jail would certainly aid my thesis of militant backlash and community involvement, but such an assertation lacks solid ground.

Aside from the use of cattle prods, the most violent act of the police was really no act at all. The police were indecisive: they wavered between, on the one hand, their sympathy for backlash and personal friendship for many militant segregationists—Davis and Manucy are friends—and, on the other hand, their devotion to their duty to uphold the law. Hence, the police had a spotty record on protection. Sheriff Davis's initial policy toward wade-ins allowed his deputies to go into the water only if attackers were drowning someone. A prudent policy, perhaps, and convenient for the officers who were thus spared from having to clean their tools; a policy, however, not designed to minimize violence.

This policy contrasts with the police action June 10, 1964, when 150 policemen (100 local, 50 state) routed 300 jeering militant segregationists with tear gas when the militant segregationists attacked the marching integrationists.[41] Although on June 25, after Cubbage's head split on the beach, the police lines folded under the onslaught of 300, on June 24, the police protected the marchers from 1,000 militant segregationists, who occasionally tossed cherry bombs.[42] The local policeman's devotion to duty kept his sympathy for backlash checked most of the time; occasionally, the sympathy overruled the duty and the policeman turned his back.

Although one expects misdeeds from the Klan and its disposition to violence, one is surprised by the ugly teeth St. Augustinians showed—the youth, the businessmen, the police. This acceptance of violent backlash to expel unwanted integrationists and to stave off attacks on the social system demonstrates the oneness of the Klan and society. In a very real sense, the Klan was serving the town's wishes—wishes so greatly desired that the Klan did not have to do all the dirty work itself. The Klan whispered in St. Augustine's ear and St. Augustine responded. The Klan and the Ancient City Hunting Club, Stoner remarked, encouraged violence against integrationists; "the local citizens certainly helped out with the enthusiasm and all."[43]

Nativism

Nativism, the favoring of native-born persons over immigrants, just as violence does, identifies the Klan and links the Klan to society. Although minor when compared to the more pressing problems of the day—fighting Communists and keeping Negroes in their place—nativism is not only exhibited by both Klansmen and other St. Augustinians, but it also helps explain a major component of St. Augustinian stereotypical thinking: the blame for the civil unrest lies with outsiders.

To a nativist, the antithesis of himself would be an internationalist. Only for sinister reasons would someone trade away his native heritage of Americanism. Dr. Hardgrove Norris explained to the St. Augustine Lions Club: "the Negro is the vehicle by which this revolution is carried, being chosen by an international communist meeting."[1] In June of 1963, the St.

Augustine chapter of the Daughters of the American Revolution felt impelled to set some facts straight. In May, a misguided soul wrote the *Record* and argued that UNESCO was a means of stopping, not fostering, communism.[2] In a lengthy reply, the DAR asserted that UNESCO was indeed communist and had the sinister goal of fostering one world government. One of the purposes of the Florida Coalition for Patriotic Societies was to fight this threatening internationalism. "And of course the local propagandists for the United Nations are much disturbed by any outfit that spreads the truth."[3]

Klansmen are also concerned by internationalism. Prospective Klansmen had a myriad of Klans to choose from. Consequently, the various Klans published "reasons why *YOU* should join the____Ku Klux Klan." One reason for joining the Original Ku Klux Klan was that only "native-born, white, Gentile Americans make up the membership." The White Knights of the KKK of Mississippi was made up of "native-born, white, Gentile, and protestant American citizens who are sound of mind and of good moral character."[4] Some are more discriminating than others. The Original KKK believes in getting America out of the United Nations; the White Knights were concerned with alien forces entering America bent on its destruction. The Original KKK believes in disenfranchisement of all foreigners who have not been in America for twenty-one years. The Original KKK was concerned that the UN charter had usurped the U.S. Constitution; the Klan stood firmly opposed to UNESCO and the World Health Organization. Klansmen were aware of the international threat.

On a local rather than a national level, nativism works into the stereotype of outside agitators. That is, once in the habit of distrusting outsiders, one finds it easy to blame outsiders for misfortune. One social scientist noted that in adverse times, persons tend to focus the blame for their troubles on outsiders—the scapegoats.[5] Conclusion number seven of the Florida Legislative Investigation states, in part: "Such racial problems as faced the city very probably could have been amicably solved by the Negro and white citizens of St. Augustine had they been free from outside agitators."[6] Many St. Augutinians hold this view and, in doing so, forget that St. Augustine had such a chance in 1963, when virtually all participants in civil rights disturbances were from the community.

Manucy, leader of the indigenous quasi-Klan, the Ancient City Hunting Club, witnessed outsiders—integrationists—invade his beloved St. Augustine. Manucys have been in St. Augustine for over 200 years, having landed in

New Smyrna and walked to the Ancient City. Manucy, like other Minoricans, has deep roots in St. Augustine. "That's why we like to fight for it."[7]

As a vestige from the highly-nativistic 1920's, the Klan of the 1960's still believed they represented 100% Americanism. This nativism can be expressed negatively—anti-foreigners or anti-outsiders. But many other St. Augustinians shared this nativism—demonstrating it through a distrust of outsiders, outside America or outside St. Augustine, and through a pride in heritage. According to the historian Charles Arnade, St. Augustine's leaders, like Manucy, had a mania for genealogy.[8]

Fraternalism

Like other nativists, Klansmen thought it important to associate with 100% Americans. The Klan of the 1960's did not, in its salespitch, key upon its fraternalism; but the Klan was nonetheless a society wherein like-minded persons could gather under a common identity. What Frank Tannenbaum said of the 1920's Klan holds true today and explains the third major identifying Klan trait that also unifies it with its society. The Klan, he tells us, appeals to the same set of interests that fills small towns with secret and fraternal orders.[1]

St. Augustine, a small town in the early 1960's, was a city of joiners. A myriad of clubs, societies, and fraternities offered themselves to the public, appealing to differing interests, desires, and backgrounds. For horticulturists, St. Augustine boasted of the Altrusa Club, the Iris Garden Club, the Gallandia Garden Club, the Cherokee Garden Club, the Camelia Garden Club, the Azalia Garden Club, the Poinsettia Garden Club, the Corissa Garden Club, and the Arnaryllis Garden Club. The ladies could choose from the Theta Alpha chapter of Beta Sigma Phi, from Epsilon Sigma Alpha, or, if the blood was bluer, from the Maria Jefferson chapter of the Daughters of the American Revolution. The men became Moose; the ladies became Women of the Moose. The civic-minded joined the Rotarians, the Kiwanians, the Lyons Club, or the Jaycee Wives Club. Veterans had the Veterans of Foreign Wars, the American Legion, and the American Legion Auxiliary Club. More exotic were the Ancient City Cootiette Club, the Pilot Club, and the Don Pedro Menendez Society. The Ashlar Lodge called St. Augustine home, as did Elks, Shriners, the Knights of Columbus and the Scottish Rite bodies. Whatever the taste, St. Augustine had the organization.

On September 27, 1963, a little more than ten days after the Klan meeting that ended with four beaten people, the *Record* printed the following article on page five: "Kiwanis Club's Kids' Day Set For Tomorrow." In the same spirit of friendly cooperation with and service to the community, the *Record* printed, directly underneath the above article: "KKK Holds Rally Tonight and Sat." In the integration crisis, when people turned to the Klan and the Hunting Club for backlash leadership, the *Record* hauled them out of disrepute and placed them on an equal par with their brethren: the Elks and the Moose. Thus, the *Record* would provide pertinent information to its readers. Dates, times, and locations of Klan meetings, an organization the *Record* called the "South's oldest secret society,"[2] were often posted so that those desiring to attend, could attend.

Internally, as well as in the eyes of the local press, the Klan and the Ancient City Hunting Club were groups that, like other groups in St. Augustine society, united persons with common interests, desires, and background. Imperial Wizard Shelton defines the Klan as a fraternal order for Caucasian Christians.[3] The common purposefulness can be seen in the Hunting Club. Manucy called it simply a club that people could join to be able to go hunting. Theoretically, anyone could join—"even had nine local niggers hunt out there one time." But in reality no "local niggers"[4] or for that matter few middle and upper class men joined. The problem was that the "big man'" had all the pastures; so the club, membership cards and all, provided the "little man" who wanted to a place to hunt. These men, united in their love of the pursuit and their common social status, found a means of identity and of pursuing their love in the Hunting Club.

These men were also united in their repugnance of integration and their determination to prevent integration. The Klansmen, although lacking grounds to hunt on, were united also in their economic background and in their desire to prevent integration. Hence, in terms of uniting persons of common background and interests, the Klan is indistinguishable from the Kiwanis.

Anti-Communism

To many St. Augustinians, twin threats were ready in 1963 and 1964 to tear the society asunder. Not only were integrationists trying to topple the pillar of segregation but communists were trying to play Sampson to all the pillars. Indeed, a sinister blending occurred between the two groups. As Hartley and Chalmers point out,[1] many St. Augustinians and their leaders worried about communism and the threats it posed to their society. The Klan also was concerned about the evils of communism. The fourth identifying, yet unifying, trait of the Klan was anti-communism.

With occasional assists from the John Birch Society, the St. John County Chapter of the Florida Coalition of Patriotic Societies made herculean efforts to stave off the communist threat by saturating St. Augustine with information. By sponsoring speakers, by writing letters to the editor, and by purchasing advertisements, these patriots sounded the alarm. Karl Boorslay discussed "Why we are losing the cold war" with St. Augustine's Rotarians.[2] Karl Prussian articulated on the subject "Inside a Communist Cell."[3] Both Major Bundy and the popular William Strube considered the topic of the Communist Threat to American Internal Security.[4] The Birch orator Lt. Colonel Thieme took to the airwaves to lecture on ". . . a subject which should be of vital interest to everyone at this time: Are you a Christian or A Socialist?"[5] Loy Lee Capo was the Patriotic Societies' hardworking essayist who often fired off letters that were spiced with "facts" such as Lee Harvey Oswald being an avowed Marxist and a Jack Ruby being the son of a Russian soldier.[6] On Kennedy's assassination, the John Birch Society bought a one page I-told-you-so-ad entitled "The Time Has Come."[7] On the other hand, the Patriotic Societies were bothered enough by the Munich test ban treaty that the Coalition took out a full page ad imploring St. Augustinians to stop the "Treaty of Moscow."

St. Augustinians not only responded whole-heartedly to the patriot's message, but demonstrated a keen awareness of their own. A dedicated fighter against communism, Dr. Norris found himself "a speaker in much demand." The Kiwanians invited him to speak on that "lulling hypodermic needle," the test ban treaty; the St. Augustine Independent Luncheon Club listened to him explain communist gains and tactics around the world and in the United States.[8] Three hundred people turned out to listen to Reverend Hargis. William Strube attracted a large audience.[9] Citizen Leary took out an ad to warn against co-existence. The communists scored a stunning victory, a letter tells us, when the Supreme Court banned mandatory prayer in the schools.[10] And the Elks held an annual essay contest on the communist danger.[11]

St. Augustine's leaders were also dedicated to the principle of anti-communism. While discussing the defeat of the Saskatchewan Socialist Party,

Mayor Shelley dared America's liberals to throw off their cloaks and confess what they really are: socialist.[12] Senator Strom Thurmond advised the local chapter of Young Americans for Freedom to fight communists with the fear of God in their hearts.[13]

The House Committee on Un-American Activities doubts the authenticity of the Klan's anti-communism. "It is obvious that Klans are cynically exploiting public antipathy to communism in order to advance their white supremacist objectives."[14] No enterprising Klan orator would turn down a chance to appeal to a crowd's particular antipathy. Speakers found that an exposition on the Jewish conspiracy warmed up audiences nicely.[15] Even though communism was a secondary threat to Klansmen, it was nonetheless a threat. Since the 1930's, the Klan had been fighting Communism. The Klan was so anti-communist that it went into a "prolonged flirtation" with various American fascist organizations.[16]

Indeed, Klansmen were concerned over the pernicious influence of the disciples of Marx. The White Knights' satanic enemies were domestic communists; bi-racial committees were Soviet organizations. Joining the Birchers, Klansmen saw through the communist hoax of Kennedy's assassination. Right-minded Americans should join the White Knights because they stand for total segregation and total destruction of Communism in all forms and because, if Communism will be stopped, it will be stopped in the South.[17] With its effective program against Socialism, Communism, and ultra left-wing Liberalism, the Original Ku Klux Klan opposed free communist literature flowing through the U.S. mail system and stood against any government professing friendliness to America and, at the same time, trading with communist countries. As was Mayor Shelley, the Klan was aware.

One peculiar aspect of communism haunted St. Augustinians because it seemed to materialize in the Ancient City itself— communism's tie to the integration movement. Many persons from a wide range of backgrounds believed in this connection. Given the perfidy of communists and their long record of attempted subversion, the nexus between communism and integration answered a lot of questions of those bewildered by the integrationists' sudden militancy. Why *was* the Negro suddenly unhappy with his place? The nexus was sinister and doubly-dangerous. The combination of cunning, coolly conspiring communists with the ferociousness of persons "barely removed from the jungle" was nightmarish. While the theory appears a shallow one, there is no functional difference between a communist-integrationist conspiracy and a Klansman-backlash conspiracy

121

wherein Klansmen conceive, plot, and carry out every violent act of militant backlash. Conspiracy theories, wherever they appear, explain complex problems with an excess of elegance and simplicity.

Ever in the forefront of the foes of communism, the Florida Coalition of Patriotic Societies published a two-page ad on the Dan Smoot Report during the height of the civil rights crisis. The ad painstakingly traced the sinister forces behind the NAACP and civil rights.[18] The area presses were aware of the nexus: editorials noted that the Civil Rights Bill went beyond the wildest hopes of Socialist-Liberals,[19] and that, with Harlem in flames, even national networks began looking for communists.[20] St. Augustine's (white) citizenry was critically aware of the nexus. Citizen Calhoun lambasted the "Evil" Rights bill and called President Johnson a socialist.[21] A cab driver analyzed the integration drive: "You know this is communist-inspired and the niggers are being used."[22] Infuriated on being driven from the Slave Plaza, one militant segregationist issued that vilest of epithets: "Communist Niggers."[23] Law enforcement officers also knew a Red when they smelled one. Harry Boyte, King's aide, requested that a policeman return his confiscated camera. The policeman shot back the logical reply. "Let Khrushchev buy you a new one." [24] Another policeman warned an impressionable young University of Florida student: "These marches are communist inspired."[25] To the right-wing organizations, to the local presses, and to the beleaguered people, the nexus was obvious.

Many of St. Augustine's leaders, on the state level and on the local level, agreed with Judge Clayton Jones of Albany, Georgia. "The Machiavellian hand of Khrushchev is behind this agitation."[26] From just north of the border the Georgia Commission on Education issued an informative pamphlet entitled "Communism and the NAACP" which found its way to St. Augustine.[27] Among other points, the pamphlet notes that Adam Clayton Powell was a communist, that Martin Luther King was leaning towards communism, if not already there, and that the NAACP and communism had 2,200 affiliations of public record.[28] A Florida Legislative Investigation Committee considered the nexus so obvious that it tried to compel the Miami branch of the NAACP to disclose its membership list.[29] Another Legislative Investigation Committee, the one assigned to St. Augustine, felt compelled to provide information on Martin Luther King . . . "not generally known to the public." As the Committee ironically notes: "Yet curiously enough the communist press has never attacked . . . King for any of his activities."[30] Mayor Shelley had fifteen documents irrefutably proving how deeply the civil rights movement was mired in communism.[31] Frank Upchurch, Jr., a local power broker,[32] introduced Dr. Norris to the Rotarians. The doctor spoke on the subject of communism in the civil rights movement.[33] Both the chief of police and the sheriff thought that communism festered in the civil rights movement. On being asked if he wanted to make any final comments on the integration crisis of St. Augustine, Sheriff Davis noted that King never rejected the idea of his going to that communist school.[34]

Just as St. Augustine's state and local leaders, police forces, press, right wing organizations, and citizens perceived the nexus between integration and communism, so too did St. Augustine's Klansmen and quasi-Klansmen perceive the nexus. John Herbers observed that the nexus was ". . . readily accepted by the poor whites who are the activists in the racial struggle."[35] Imperial Wizard Shelton denounced the communist conspiracy behind the civil rights movement.[36] Joining the cab driver and the Georgia Commission of Education, J. B. Stoner angrily lambasted the integrationists as the "willing tools of the Communist Jews."[37] Connie Lynch addressed a rally at the Slave Market and informed his audience that Martin Luther King associated with communists and that, in fact, integration was communism.[38] And Holstead "Hoss" Manucy came out and said what every segregationist believed: King was a communist.[39]

Klansmen demonstrated their Americanism by firmly opposing communism. Many persons concerned with the crumbling of segregation found the reason why it was crumbling in communism. Klansmen subscribed to the nexus theory. But Klansmen, unlike Mayor Shelley, did not see communism as the major threat to the stability of St. Augustine society. In other words, one could oppose integration from more than one position. Some people really feared communist gain in integration success; some people were incensed merely by the "uppity niggers" and the prospect of blacks eating in the same restaurants as white folks eat in. Klansmen worried about communism, but not as much as they worried about race. In retrospect, Stoner labels communism "a factor, but not the factor" in the formation of the Civil Rights crisis.[40] Manucy, also in retrospect, pointed up the major weakness (other than the lack of evidence) in the nexus theory: "What good would it be to the Communists?"[41]

Racism

In the 1960's, the Ku Klux Klan dedicated itself to concerns of race. To preserve the separation of the races, to keep America a white man's country, to maintain the integrity of white womanhood, Klansmen viciously fought integration. But these concerns extended beyond Klansmen. Barzum argues that racism was not a function of social class or of education;[1] Vander Zanden observes that the "great mass" of Southern whites believed in Negro racial inferiority.[2] Although many were racists, which means one who believes in races and usually believes in the inferiority of one of the races, St. Augustinians differed in emotional attachment to racism from time to time and from person to person.[3] Some St. Augustinians tried to set themselves off from the Klan by drawing a subtle distinction between being a segregationist and being a racist. Racism is a salient feature of the Klan. Racism also created a substantial bond between the Klan and its community.

Integrationists recognized rampant racism, and at times deliberately evoked the worst of racist nightmares. Raising the specter of miscegenation, integrationists would hold hands during marches.[4] According to one observer, the integrationists occasionally stopped in the business section to kiss and to fondle each other ". . . for the sole purpose of getting these old redneck crackers riled up."[5] Grown men sat down on the curb and cried. St. Augustinians ". . . couldn't believe any white person could be that crummy."[6] Integrationists may have been singing about the brotherhood of man when they sang "We love everybody," but all racists could hear was sordid designs on their loved ones. Integrationists deliberately brought forth the racism that was common to Klansmen and other members of the community. Provoked by the tactics of the integrationists and by, more fundamentally, the simple presence of the integrationists, many St. Augustine citizens, with increasing vehemence, aired their racial views. Citizen Lindsley was sickened and saddened to see a "hysteria-ridden Negro group" request that the federal government deny funds for St. Augustine's Quadricentennial.[7] Lindsley felt betrayed because St. Augustine was one of the "most racially liberal-minded cities of Florida." In nearby Clay County, Kennedy's popularity dropped to twenty-three per cent because he was "jamming too many civil rights down people's throats."[8] Since, according to Counselor Upchurch, ninety-nine percent of St. Augustine whites stood opposed to the Civil Rights Act,[9] then one is not surprised at the reaction of local prostitutes to the prospect of sharing their cell with Mrs. Peabody, mother of the governor of Massachusetts, and her integrated entourage: "We don't want no niggers in here with us."[10] According to Hartley, after the passage of the Civil Rights bill, the community's racism remained, but became subtle racism.[11] Subtle as a brickbat: on July 21, 1964, two local men threw a brick through the plate glass window of Kling Tile Co. A note accompanied the brick and warned "Fire niggers or go out of business."[12] Waitresses preferred to quit than to serve in integrated restaurants.[13] The local police wavered between duty and prejudice. At one moment, a Deputy sheriff shouts "There's a nigger lover." At another moment, an officer warns a beach heckler, "You shut your mouth . . . This beach is integrated."[14]

The Civil Rights Act of 1964 forced the Ancient City's restaurants to integrate. Pressured by militant segregationists and by other businessmen to re-segregate[15] the restaurants needed little persuasion. Indeed, they showed remarkable ingenuity in avoiding the law. The Palms Congress Inn announced it would serve parties of all Negroes but not integrated parties.[16] Lunch counters closed in variety stores; restaurants "closed for alterations." Some establishments gave notice that all money from black patrons would go to Goldwater's campaign fund. Other establishments displayed signs proclaiming that no out-of-state persons (and hence no out-of-state commerce) would be served. One restaurant using strictly Florida food did a good business. The Restaurant Association announced that . . . "integration of places of accommodation is obnoxious to us."[17] Restaurants often provided militant segregationist J. B. Stoner with free meals.[18] Restaurant owners mirrored the populace's attitude on "the racial question."

The city's leaders showed the same stereotyped face as the citizens' and the restaurant owners'. As was Sheriff Davis, Mayor Shelley was a segregationist because "God made us different."[19] As he admonished citizens to beware the radical fringe of both races, Shelley explained that there was no such thing as equal people.[20] Since he approved seven of nine applications to send children to previously segregated schools, the school superintendent argued that the school system had integrated.[21] The city government was not strictly racist. City Manager Barrier reported that twenty-seven out of 150 city employees were Negro. Out of the twenty-seven, the highest-ranked one was a waterworks crew foreman. The City did remove segregation from public places when requested to do so, but adamantly refused to interfere with private segregation, which was not in the City's jurisdiction.

Dr. Hayling and his NAACP youths began picketing segregated drug stores' lunch counters in June of 1963. At the City Commission meeting of

June 28, the Mayor reiterated the city's position on integration: that the city had no authority over private segregation, that the public facilities were not segregated (as of June 16), that a bi-racial committee would be powerless and hence useless, and that anybody could take civil service exams. The Mayor went on to ask that any pickets refrain from obstructing sidewalks. One commissioner asked that persons picketing be of good moral character. Later in the meeting, doubting the efficacy of persuasion, the Commission passed an emergency picket law. Henceforth it was unlawful to picket by creating fear and violence, by preventing ingress and egress to businesses, and by walking back and forth, loitering or remaining on street or sidewalk in front of businesses for the purpose of persuading persons from entering the place of business, excluding persuading persons not to work. The city may have lacked the power to force the integration of private concerns but the city found the power to obstruct private attempts to force the integration of private concerns.[22]

As were other persons in St. Augustine society, Klansmen were, to a man, racist. The Reverend Connie Lynch found parallels between murdering four black girls and killing rattlesnakes.[23] An orator with a portable microphone explained the dynamics of integration to an approving crowd of 600 to 700 persons. "When people go to church together, that is social equality, which eventually leads to intermarriage. And that is the purpose of race relations—to bring about interbreeding between the whites and the niggers."[24] With the battlecry of "Niggers ain't got no God," Klansmen fought for the government that Lynch described: of the white man, by the white man, and for the white man.[25] Consciously imitating an American war hero, Stoner explained ". . . the only good nigger is a dead nigger."[26] When talking about men being created equal, Stoner pointed out . . . "the constitution wasn't talking about niggers."[27] Klansmen's stereotype of race extended to Jews and anti-semitism raised its head now and again. The House Committee on Un-American Activities was correct in emphasis, if not in exclusiveness, when it concluded that white supremacy was the only objective the Klan seriously advanced.[28]

To be sure, to travel from Mayor Shelley's polite pronouncements on race to the Klansmen's vulgar pronouncements on race is a long way to go. The path, however, is straight and logical. Although Klansmen are identified by their extreme racism, Klansmen are genetically linked to and come out of the context of a race-thinking society.

Brothers in Arms

As an organization attracting lower and lower-middle class persons to the cause of militant backlash, the Ku Klux Klan had a disposition to violence, nativism, fraternalism, anti-communism, and racism. I will discuss the Klan's role in militant backlash in St. Augustine in Chapter III. None of the characteristics of the Klan are unique to the Klan: other groups and other persons possessed the characteristics, although one may argue not in the same combination or with the same conviction. That is, different organizations may possess this trait or that, or different persons may decline to put into practice what their thought dictates. In explaining the Klan's role in backlash, the social class membership, the racism, and, to a lesser extent, anti-communism seem to be the more important traits. These traits provide Plato's "cause of a thing" as opposed to "the condition without which it could not be a cause."[1] Attempting to preserve what was rightfully theirs—jobs and race—forms the sufficient cause of Klansmen's actions.

Aside from the above ways of thinking and ways of life, the Klan had more physical ties to two groups in St. Augustine society: the Sheriff's Department and the Ancient City Hunting Club. The Club is an enigma. Despite similar goals and a great interaction between its personnel and the Klan's personnel, the Club refused to yield its identity to the larger group. The Ancient City Hunting Club was, in effect, a home-grown Klan. What were the Klan's ties to the Club?

Ancient City Hunting Club

A short, muscular, pot-bellied man, Holstead "Hoss" Manucy organized the Hunting Club in 1961 or 1962. Manucy is a quick witted man: he can avoid answering questions with the best of politicians. In September of 1964, Federal Judge Bryan Simpson ordered Manucy to produce a membership list of the Club on peril of contempt of court. "Hoss changed his mind after an hour's meditation in jail and supplied a list of the members . . ."[2] Manucy derived that list by random selection from the St. Augustine telephone directory.[3] Despite the misinformation, Simpson aptly described the Club as a hydra-headed organization.[4] The larger head pertained to the 1,000 or so "little men" who hunted deer and patrolled on the land of Alan Nease.[5] The Sheriff described this head as "just a bunch of old crackers [who] go out here in the woods." One joined by hunting, although one was expected to

127

contribute to the Club to get a membership card. Davis says two dollars; Manucy says three dollars or more.[6]

The other hydra's head was the militant backlash quasi-Klan. (Manucy confirmed Hartley's supposition that a group called "Manucy's Raiders" with 1,000 nightriders existed only in fiction.) Estimates of the size of the militant backlash group range from a few dozen to 150 or so.[7] This Ancient City Hunting Club was probably around fifty men. During an interview, Manucy noted that the Club had a membership of about 1,100, that all the members of the Club possessed citizen band radios, and that the Club had thirty-two CBs in St. Augustine. There is no reason for all the members of a "little man's" hunting club to possess radios; I doubt that 1,100 men did actually have them. On the other hand, using CBs in militant backlash seems reasonable and was reported. Thus, given that the Club was probably a county-wide organization, one hundred fifty—all of whom were Catholics—seems a reasonable number.

This part of the Club acted unusually for a hunting club. Manucy went around to different parts of the state to organize more hunting clubs to "let them know what was going on here."[8] Simpson suspects that Manucy's check stubs (on the club's account) marked "eats for the boys" and bail bond "for the boys" were for this part of the club.[9] An interesting aspect of the Club was the involvement of Manucy's children. As did many other of St. Augustine's youths, Hoss's older sons played an active role in militant backlash. Hoss had a powerful influence on other youth indirectly through his sons.

> His kids were the ones he worked through. Hoss had a lot of relatives and he worked through their kids . . . they looked up to Hoss; whatever he said was gospel to them . . . [Manucy's sons] went out and got these kids fifteen, sixteen, seventeen, eighteen years old and they'd go right along with 'em.[10]

Although denying that the Club was involved in violence on the beach, Manucy concedes that the attackers of the integrationists were "kids and individuals." The *New York Times* noted that, on June 20, Manucy waited on the beach until the wade-in demonstrators arrived. Manucy then radioed compatriots. Shortly thereafter, four cars of militant segregationists arrived to cleanse the beach.[11] Manucy's backlash influence spread out over the community's youths.

The Club and the Klan worked intimately together. Klansmen and Huntsmen mourned together. After a .38 slug killed Huntsman William

Kinard, causing him to discharge the number 7 1/2 birdshot in his shotgun through the floor of the car, the Klan and the Club gathered for the funeral. The Reverend Connie Lynch assisted in the ceremonies; Buddy Cooper, Exalted Cyclops of the local Klavern number 519, was an active pallbearer. The honorary pallbearers included Holstead Manucy, Bart Griffen, the Exalted Cyclops of Klavern number 513, Jacy Harden, Jacksonville Klansmen, Eugene Spegal, former Exalted Cyclops of number 513, and W. Eugene Wilson, Jacksonville Klansmen and National State Rights Party organizer.[12] Both the Klan and the Club held meetings in the basement of the Surf Side Casino.[13] When the Klan threw rallies, Huntsmen showed up.[14] Klansmen and Huntsmen worked closely on militant backlash projects. Huntsmen helped arrange a hiding place for Rosecrans, Klan bomber of the home of a six-year old integrationist.[15] Manucy helped the Klan secure a site for their rallies.[16] The Klan and Club worked together in preparing militant segregationist marches.[17] Manucy visited Lynch and Stoner at their motels; they returned the courtesy.[18] To Manucy, Stoner was a "helluva nice guy" with whom he worked closely; Manucy knew Lynch "real well" and worked closely with him. Stoner concedes he worked closely with Manucy.[19] Indeed, Stoner observes on the membership rolls of the Klan and the Club; "there was some overlap."[20]

Yet the Club remained a home-grown quasi-Klan and was not a bona fide Klavern. Stoner denied that the Club was a Klavern.[21] Manucy lauded the Klan, evaded the question of his own membership in the Klan, but definitely denied that the Club was a Klavern.[22] After all, Manucy asks rhetorically, who ever heard of a Catholic Klansman? Stoner had: he argued that most of the St. Augustine Klansmen were Catholic.[23] The adamant avowals of organizational difference, the slight differences in policy—the club agreed to Judge Simpson's truce of July 1, 1964; the Klan declined to agree[24]—and the appeal of the Club to youth, an appeal entirely lacking in the Klan, all argue for the existence of a quasi-Klan.

Deputies

Most observers agree on the intimate relation between the Klan and the Ancient City Hunting Club. In addition, many assert that the KKK had a strong influence in the St. Johns County Sheriff's Department. Integrationists vehemently charged that the Department was Klan infested. State Attorney Dan Warren ordered an investigation of Klan infiltration of the Sheriff's office.[25] Judge Simpson accused Davis of being a Klansman. Manucy claimed that he regularly exchanged information with the Sheriff's Department and the Police Department. *Life* charged that several hundred of Davis's Special Deputies were Klansmen.[26] The Sheriff admitted that several members of the Club and perhaps one Klansman were deputies.[27] Further, Chalmers claims that Stoner and his Klansmen lounged on the front steps of the jail; the House Committee on Un-American Activities adds that Davis allowed the Klan to use the jail for meetings and to borrow Sheriffs Department cars.[28] And Manucy claimed that Davis, Stoner, and Lynch were good friends.

On the other hand, Davis states that the Klan stayed strictly away from him.[29] Calling Stoner a rabble rouser, Davis claims that Stoner and Lynch visited his office only twice—and then just to secure permits to parade. Although several Huntsmen (including Manucy) and perhaps some Klansmen were Special Deputies, the 200 figure is surely too large. Many of the deputies were businessmen. At any rate, the Sheriff was not a Klansman. The Klan asked him to sign up, but after Hayling was beaten September 18th, Davis declined: ". . . the initiation is so horrible that I don't believe I could stand it."[30] Thus, it seems that the Ancient City Hunting Club, if not the Klan, did succeed in penetrating the Sheriffs Department. Even if integrationists' fears of a dark conspiracy seem far fetched, the fears do seem to have some basis in fact. Anyway, to the integrationists, the penetration gave a sinister complexion to the forces that resisted them by militant backlash.

THREE

The Klan's Role
in the Crisis

Despite the multifarious connections between it and St. Augustine society, the Ku Klux Klan played a definite role during the crisis of 1963 and 1964. The Klan was the agitator in Matthew's trilogy. The community responded to that agitation and that leadership. To understand the segregated community's reaction to the revolutionary prospect of integration, one must attempt to understand the crisis atmosphere. This attempt constitutes the first section of this chapter. Various scholars have understood the crisis of integration and reaction in various ways. The second section attempts to briefly present the interpretations. The final section concerns the various agitational activities of the Klan: the support of the Jacksonville Klans, the recruitment activities of the Klan, the articulation of racist views and frustrations through the leading of rallies, the effort to beat the integrationists at their own game by counter-marching, the organization of pickets, and the intimidation of those who differ with the Klan.

Crisis

"This City Shall Survive!" St. Augustine, the *Record* editorialized on April 5, 1964, survived attacks by the French, the Indians, the British, and the pirates. Surely the city will survive a civil rights invasion. That the newspaper felt impelled to issue such a stirring manifesto indicates, however, that some question existed in people's minds whether the city would survive. The whirlwinds of crisis beleaguered St. Augustinians. They feared for the basic social structure of their community. St. Augustine was, according to J. B. Stoner, "a town stirred in a crisis."[1] As the SCLC correctly stated: "In times of desperation, desperate men do desperate things."[2] What were the elements of this crisis, which would drive men to desperate things?

Troubles Abroad

The first element of the crisis was non-St. Augustinian: 1963 and 1964 were turbulent years for America. Some feared that violence would rip the country apart. St. Augustinians had the backdrop of turbulence to compare the events in their community to. Many cities felt the unwelcome vibration of marching—and charging—through its streets. Birmingham was a veritable battleground. Klansman gunned down suspected integrationists in Georgia.[3] New York tasted racial violence in 1963 and 1964. Chief of Police Stuart offered to assist Boston in maintaining the peace after Boston had sent St. Augustine Mrs. Peabody and then found itself in the embarrassing position of having its own civil rights disturbances.[4] "Hoss" Manucy indicated that he received favorable mail from the North because ". . . they were raising hell up there."[5] And so they were: riots broke out in Rochester, South Chicago, Philadelphia, Elizabeth, Paterson, Jersey City, Washington, DC and Phoenix.[6]

St. Augustine was not the only city in the Sunshine State in which integrationists threatened the right of association. In June of 1963, a man was foolish enough to purchase a ticket for a segregated movie theater in Gainesville. In the ensuing battle, integrationists beat a militant segregationist, threw bottles, and destroyed a militant segregationist's automobile. Militant segregationists returned the volley of bottles and shot an integrationist for good measure. As they tried to integrate two theaters the next day, integrationists showered cars with stones and bricks.[7] While Gainesville's City Commission set up a bi-racial committee, pickets were out in Daytona Beach, Tallahassee, and Miami.[8] In Deland, the Sheriff routinely suspended a Deputy Sheriff who accidentally and fatally shot a Negro in the face after the Negro hit him in the County Courthouse.[9] In 1964, Lakeland, Tallahassee, Ocala, and Pahokee had civil rights pains. Klansmen marched in Lake City.[10]

Just forty miles to the North, in Jacksonville, the civil rights struggle was intense. Both the NAACP and the Klan were active in Jacksonville: the former picketed, the latter rallied. In early March, 1964, the NAACP, 300 strong, marched downtown to protest the city's failure to name a bi-racial committee.[11] Later, police dispersed a NAACP-organized protest rally in front of the Municipal Courthouse.[12] Fearing the worst, Mayor Haydon Burns swore in the city's 496 firemen as special police on March 21. His nightmare came true: gangs of integrationist youth roamed the streets breaking windshields; molotov cocktails seared Governor Burn's campaign headquarters. Persons threw rocks, bottles, and firebombs at stores in Negro areas. Integrationists damaged transit buses, brutally beat up pedestrians and persons pulled from cars. Taunting youths chased newsmen from the streets. From a passing car, three militant segregationists shot and killed the mother of six. Police arrested over 300 integrationists.[13]

Violence occasionally erupted in Jacksonville throughout 1964. The experiences of that city and numerous other American cities served ominous warning to St. Augustinians. They realized that the Ancient City was not immune from racial disturbances and, considering the violence in other cities, feared that violence would develop from integrationist efforts. People were apprehensive.

Labor Unrest

The second component of the crisis situation was the longest strike in the labor history of the United States. The non-operating unions of the Florida East Coast Railway walked off the job on January 23, 1963. At first, the strike caused great consternation among segments of the county population, since the FEC was important in shipping the large potato and cabbage crops. The County Commission requested a federal takeover of the FEC.[14] However, management proved quite capable of striking-breaking; the Area Two Strike Committee of St. Augustine settled in for the long siege. Just as police arrested juvenile integrationist pickets, so too did police arrest juvenile FEC pickets.[15] Using scabs and management personnel, the FEC thanked people in potato country " . . . for their patience during the current work shortage."[16] Although avowing non-involvement, the strikers began to give the railroad's insurance company headaches. On February 26, 1964, in the 201st intentional lawless act against the FEC during the strike, two dynamite bombs derailed two freight trains and destroyed or damaged six engines and thirty-three freight cars in St. Johns County.[17] Governor Bryant created a twenty-one man investigation team; Mayor Shelley requested that the National Guard protect the FEC's track. Manucy tried to collect the $100,000 reward by turning in Klansman Rosecrans.

The strike lingered on in 1964. Police occasionally arrested vandalizing strikers. The strike added a degree of violent uncertainty to a St. Augustinian's world. Would a loved one lose his life? Would one's crops rot in the fields? Would the strike depress the economy further? St. Augustinians had one more thing to worry about.[18]

Integration

The third and most important ingredient of the crisis was the local integration effort. Hayling's sit-ins and King's marching legions wanted to destroy St. Augustine's time-honored way of life. In a sense, this threat is a major theme throughout this paper. Thus, the topic needs but brief consideration here. The point is that only those who think they have nothing to lose are willing to see a drastic re-organization of society. Integrationists, Wilhoits's egalitarian revolutionaries, directly threatened St. Augustine's "peculiar institution;" an institution, of course, shared with most local societies in America. Many St. Augustinians resented the assault on their social system—an assault made worse because it was "outside agitators" carrying it out. The threat of crumbling institutions distressed St. Augustinians.

Economics

The fourth component of the crisis came in part from integrationist tactics and in part from people's inclination to avoid violence. In 1963 and 1964, tourism and agriculture were the two mainstays of St. Johns County economy.[19] In an effort to force integration on the community, integrationists tried to bring pressure on the community by disrupting the tourist trade. They were successful. Sheriff Davis ruefully commented that the integrationists ". . . did one thing they said they were going to do—they made us crawl."[20] Integrationist pickets appeared at Jacksonville airport to ask people to avoid St. Augustine.[21] A former vice-president of the Chamber of Commerce estimated revenue losses in tourism (1964) to be five to eight million dollars out of a maximum of fifteen million tourist dollars annually.[22] Tourists, 26,174 strong visited the Castillo de San Marcos in April, 1964; that number represents a forty percent drop from the 44,115 that visited the fort in April, 1963. The 33,838 that visited the fort in June, 1964 compares with the 63,689 visitors in June, 1963 for a forty-seven percent decline. The fort saw forty-eight percent fewer persons in July, 1964 compared to July, 1963 when 43,908 visitors passed through the turnstiles instead of 84,174. The fort had 44,065 tourists in August of 1964 compared to 78,449 in August of 1963 for a decline of forty-four percent.[23]

In addition, the sightseeing vessel Victory II was fifty percent behind 1963; the City Museum was thirty percent behind.[24] The tourist trade was in shambles. Remembering the threat posed to agriculture by the FEC strike, St. Augustinians, when thinking about tourism, had good cause to worry.

Vandalism

A fifth component of the social crisis, one that heightened tensions, that put people on edge, and that gave the crisis an ugly countenance, was the undercurrent of vandalism. As was the crunch on the tourist trade, most of the vandalism stemmed from the effort to integrate St. Augustine. Some of the vandalism cannot be attributed to either side: on October 30, 1963, gunfire raked the home of a "white male in a predominately Negro area." Police recovered five .22 caliber bullets and a .30-.30 caliber bullet.[25] During the "Spring Project," vandals broke all the windows of Chimes Restaurant.[26] State Senator Verle Pope thought that "either extreme" might have thrown the six concrete blocks through his insurance company's windows.[27] Chief of Police Virgil Stuart pointed out that race issues were deeply involved in the vandalism; it involved whites against colored and colored against whites.[28] Disrespect for private property from both integrationists and militant segregationists deepened St. Augustine's crisis.

William Gore, grocery store owner, found himself on the wrong side of integration. Three nights in the first week of June, 1964, persons who were "apparently Negro boys" heaved rocks through the windows of his grocery store. A couple of days later, four rifle shots slammed into his car, which was parked in front of his store.[29] Back in 1963, a young man in a "black mob" of twenty-five to thirty men fired his pistol at a passing car, which had a six-year old girl and a seven-year old boy as passengers. Bullets went through the trunk and grazed the bumper.[30] Ten nights later, three or four integrationist youths threw bottles at a woman's car.[31] In 1964, Negroes, in a passing car, threw bricks through a Southern Bell supply truck. Others shot at the car of militant segregationists.[32]

But militant segregationists matched the integrationists brick for brick and shot for shot. After the *Record*, in a fit of civic patriotism, printed its address and owner, Martin Luther King's cottage on the beach became a favorite target for militant segregationists. On May 28, buckshot and rifle fire smacked into the cottage. On May 30, persons unknown turned on the cottage's electric stove and placed a blanket on it. Volunteer firemen doused the smoldering blanket. On June 8, militant segregationists sacked the cottage: they broke windows, smashed furniture, pulled cabinets off the kitchen walls, and attempted to burn the cottage with rags soaked in an inflammable liquid. Again volunteer firemen showed up for duty.[33]

Although shotgun pellets broke the front window of the band director of the local Negro high school and riddled his neighbor's car, a brick broke B. James's window.[34] A hail of .30-.30 bullets slammed into a Jacksonville integrationist's car and a young militant segregationist's rifle fire shattered Ivy Wood's windshield and grazed his shoulder.[35] Such vandalism on both sides, attacking property and verging on criminal assault, lay in the background of the headline-grabbing marches and sent an ominous message to St. Augustinians on the possible course of the integration-militant backlash struggle.

Integrationists' Violence

As if the above components were not enough for the crisis, hard-pressing integrationists seemed willing to resort to force in knocking down the pillars of segregation. Combined with the other factors, this willingness drove embattled and apprehensive St. Augustinians into the arms of the militant backlash Ku Klux Klan and the quasi-Klan Ancient City Hunting Club.[37] Even if one accepts Klineberg's idea that the relative frequency of Negro aggressive violence and occasional group violence must be considered in the context of societal rejection of the Negro, one also should appreciate Sheriff Davis's position regarding the aggressive intent of the integrationists. One integrationist official habitually singled out Davis and said: "When we bury this man six feet deep in the streets of St. Augustine, we'll get what we want."[38] Dr. Hayling provoked the most concern. In June of 1963, after the brutal murder of civil rights activist Medgar Evers, Hayling warned that he and others were arming themselves and would shoot first, ask questions later. A couple of weeks later, four teenage militant segregationists followed two of Hayling's friends back to Hayling's home. The teenagers threw a brick and received a blast from a shotgun in return. They left, but returned with their own shotguns to shoot at members of "Hayling's police force." [39] Judge Mathias dismissed charges against both integrationists and militant segregationists.[40] Hours later, Willie Holt, seventeen, one of the recently acquitted members of "Hayling's police," was arrested in possession of a .30 caliber repeating rifle equipped with deadly soft-nosed, hollow pointed cartridges. The gun, reported the *Record*, belonged to Hayling.[41]

In October of 1963, a twenty-one year old member of the NAACP and messenger for Hayling sauntered into court with a loaded .32 caliber pistol in his pocket. Hayling owned the gun.[42] Given that police arrested members of the NAACP for the slaying of Ancient City Hunting Club member Kinard, it appeared that the egalitarian revolutionaries were willing to resort to violence to achieve their revolutionary goal: the destruction of segregation. As the moderate State Senator Verle Pope commented of Hayling: "I would never negotiate with a man who would have given out guns to children."[43]

Occasionally, mobs sympathizing with integration attacked persons not sympathizing with integration. At least twice, integrationist mobs heaved bricks, rocks, bottles, and sticks at police officers.[44] In July, 1963, a group of 300 marched on the county jail to chant their protest over the jailing of several juvenile integrationists. When Mrs. Cook, wife of the jailer, "foolishly walked out the front door," the protesters knocked her down, kicked her, and scratched her.[45] Two dozen brave lads dragged seventy-two year old Oscar Thompson, vendor of vegetables, and pummeled him in late June, 1964. In August, 1963, eight "Youthful Negro hoodlums" beat up two thirteen-year-olds.[46] Militant segregationists, in their hit and run attacks on marching integrationists, occasionally provoked the integrationists into fighting back and "a lot of times the blacks would come out on top."[47]

However, to local law enforcement officials, the most nefarious aspect of integrationist violence was not violence committed by their own hands, but rather violence deliberately provoked to cast themselves as pious sufferers. In June, 1964, the marching integrationists repeatedly changed their routes. This policy minimized police protection and invited attack.[48] On the Plaza, if the marchers saw a group of disgruntled citizens milling about, the integrationists would march towards them forcing the police to clear a path. Thus, on June 25, the day of the largest militant backlash attacks, an exasperated Sheriff Davis, with blood splattered on his shirt, could declare that King finally had what he desired: violence in the streets.[49]

Acceptance of Militant Backlash

St. Augustine's crisis, which included outside examples of integration turbulence, violence, tension, and economic dislocation from the FEC strike, the social threat in integration's drive to destroy a way of life, economic depression, vandalism, and indications that integrationists, despite claims to non-violence, intended to use violent means to gain their ends, was very real.

As Chalmers would say, the heat was on. And who would not be edgy? Even if one dislikes St. Augustine's decision to accept, with an upturned nose, the Klan's proffered assistance, one should not scorn St. Augustine for that decision. After all, other cities, such as Birmingham, made similar decisions. In St. Augustine, beset with an exigent situation, Klansmen found a willing audience.

When faced with the crisis that stemmed in the main from the desires of integrationists, the elements of the community ideologically committed to segregation and angered that outsiders came in trying to force St. Augustine to change its way of life backed towards militant backlash and its organization which was genetically American, the Ku Klux Klan. St. Augustine never gave the Klan a unanimous welcome. Corresponding to the intensity of the threat to the community was the community's propensity to accept the Klan's militant backlash.[50] The community accepted the Klan and its goals at times more, at other times less. There were two peaks in the integration crisis of 1963 and 1964: fall of 1963 and summer of 1964.

Prior to the high tensions of September and October, 1963, the Mayor and the local press firmly extolled moderation. The *Record*, in its July 2 editorial "Time for Adult Action and Common Sense," decried the inflammatory actions of Hot-Heads and called for parents to take action to prevent further violence stimulated by Racial Agitators. In his statement to citizens on race relations, Mayor Shelley admonished citizens to beware the radical fringe of both races and urged respect for law and order.[51] The editorial "The Middle Ground" argued the necessity of moderates working out the problems of the community.[52] After Kinard's slaying, the Mayor appealed that both sides refrain from retaliating and to leave justice "in the hands of those authorized to dispense it."[53] The grand jury of St. John's County concluded that the unrest was due to militant Negro leaders and the Ku Klux Klan and that the Klan did not represent the majority view of white citizens.[54]

Perhaps the Klan did not represent a majority of the white citizens, perhaps it did. 1963 was a tremor compared to 1964's earthquake, but militant segregationists embarked on a series of retaliations. When these retaliations culminated in the shooting at Hayling's house, the *Record* considered it high time that elected public officials demanded and enforced the laws to the maximum of their abilities.[55] After all ". . . nothing happens in . . . [St. Johns] County that the power structure does not sanction.[56] As

Mrs. R. N. Gordon noted: " A hostile element was brought out that we didn't realize existed."[57]

As the tension grew in June, 1964, many, though not all, St. Augustinians inched toward an acceptance of militant backlash. Militant segregationist leaders detected wide community support. Manucy asserted that all whites thought alike. Stoner asserted that the "whole community was practically solid in support of our activities."[58] Local officials contemplated calling in George Wallace to lend the benefit of his experience in dealing with King.[59] In the vernacular of the *Record*, militant segregationists changed from "young white toughs" to "white citizens opposing Martin Luther King's integration drive." The *Record* would print the time, place, and directions to Klan meetings. Although a group of businessmen headed by Pope promised to obey all laws (including the imminent Civil Rights Act), many observers thought that the business community tolerated the militant backlash acts of violence. *The St. Petersburg Times* reported businessmen allowing young militant segregationists to set the mood of the town; Hartley argues that Manucy's shooting star of influence included his being the spokesman for the town.[60] Indeed, according to Hartley, most St. Augustinians openly sided with the segregationists.[61]

The stars and bars of the Confederacy were the symbols of militant backlash. From flags waving defiantly at the beach, on car antennas, at rallies, and on marches, one could suppose a militant segregationist was close at hand. In their hour of crisis, St. Augustinians recognized the symbol of backlash and responded to it. Stoner tells us: "I'd walk around some times with my eighteen-inch confederate flags on a stick and everybody was always agreeing with me and cheering me even when we weren't having a meeting."[62] Although the demonstrations adversely affected most businesses, the demonstrations greatly stimulated a variety store's business. The store, which usually sold about a dozen confederate flags a year, sold thirty-six dozen confederate flags in ten days of June, 1964.[63]

Interpretations

St. Augustine, when faced with the crisis of integration, turned toward militant backlash and the preponderant militant backlash organization, the Ku Klux Klan. The Klan's actual role in militant backlash will be discussed below. Various scholars and others have interpreted the integration crisis of

St. Augustine. The purpose of this section is to present some of those interpretations for the sake of comparison.

Hartley's MA thesis, "A Long Hot Summer: the St. Augustine Disorders of 1964" is the most comprehensive of the works on St. Augustine's integration crisis. In strict, though sometimes mistaken,[1] chronological order, the thesis considers several aspects of the crisis: the involvement of the judiciary, the indecisiveness of community leaders and clergy, the brutality of the militant segregationists—in sum, the thesis covers most of the ground. The order that he sees in the crisis is: (1) integrationists initiate non-violent demonstrations; (2) "white toughs" react with violent reprisals; (3) the power structure ignores Negro demands; (4) negotiations fail; (5) pressures build and explode in the streets.[2] Hartley emphasizes (3)—he repeatedly refers to the golden opportunity to solve the unrest that the power structure let slip through its fingers.[3] The key influential persons vacillated, thus allowing the less influential business community to be intimidated by the Klan and Manucy, who nevertheless became spokesman for the town. Because of the vacillation, the native American racism, the right-wing element, and the ostrich-like clergy, Manucy and the Klan were able to frighten and silence moderates.

Chalmer's *Hooded Americanism* makes him dean of the Community Acceptance school of interpretation. His pithy examination fits necessarily into his overall consideration of the Klan. The popular and police sentiment gave the Klan "a high degree of local immunity" that enabled the Klan to successfully turn to violence.[4] The demeanor of resistance to integration of local officials and open racism and collaboration with the Klan displayed by local law enforcement officials encouraged a united front of Protestant Klansmen and Catholic Huntsmen. This front attacked, at the beaches and at the Plaza, the beleaguered integrationists and newsmen. Only the Governor's intervention, the Congress's intervention with the Civil Rights Act of 1964, and the federal judiciary's intervention could bring a semblance of peace to the community.[5]

Another Community Acceptance interpretation is Goodwyn's "Anarchy in St. Augustine."[6] A bi-level power structure, with a solid segregationist top and a lower level tourist-oriented business group that was more flexible because of monetary concerns, allowed Manucy, through irresolution, to become the spokesman for the community. The power structure passively accepted the terrorists. As policemen and Klansmen stood shoulder to shoulder, moderates continued to refrain from interfering. Gradually, the vigilantes took over the town in a move that resulted in, despite the contradiction, institutionalized anarchy. The segregationists had created a monster; a convenient tool grew up and threatened all. Ultimately, the segregationists tolerated violence because they thought they could beat back integration.

A third Community Acceptance interpretation is Watter's "The American Middle Ground in St. Augustine."[7] Gangs of white toughs, who were Klansmen to the marchers, were not strictly restrained by police. The alliance of police with lawlessness is the "classical outline [of] the processes by which the protections of a free society collapse." With a right-wing mayor and right-wing speakers flowing through the city, St. Augustine found itself being forced to the logical conclusion of its "public anti-Negro big talk." The consequent slide to the right left the integrationists standing on moderate ground for *all* Americans' liberties against the threat of right-wing violence against liberties.

Militant segregationists generally belong to the We Really Won school of interpretation. Willie Eugene Wilson, Jacksonville Klansman and National States Rights Party member, assessed the significance of the integration threat for his National States Rights Party readers of *The Thunderbolt*: "As was clearly demonstrated in St. Augustine in the Summer of 1964, Protestants and Catholics can and did work together to deal Martin Lucifer Koon and his black mobs their most crushing defeat."[8] To Manucy, the fruits of victory were plucked from the militant segregationist's mouth by the "constitution of 1964," which was just for black people. Thus, the integrationist gained nothing from St. Augustine. Manucy attributed the success of militant segregationists to effective communications—"When they went to the beaches, we knew it even before they got there"—thorough organization (the militant segregationist marches were more effective than integrationist marches were because the former proved "anything they could do, we could do,") and community solidarity.[9] Stoner saw the crucial turning point to be the Chamber of Commerce's support of compliance with the Civil Rights Act. Had not the business elite taken this position, Stoner believed that "all the niggers would have moved out of St. Augustine."[10]

A third school of interpretation is the conspiracy school. the Florida Legislative Investigation Committee saw the quaint Ancient City, with its harmonious history of race relations, being invaded by outside agitators. Chosen for the publicity value of its 400th birthday, St. Augustine was the site for the "pilot project for a new form of political warfare, so called—'non-violent direct action.'"[11] Stoner and Lynch, also outsiders, inflamed the problem. Strangely enough, the press always knew, well in advance, where the communist King's non-violent army would go next. Federal District Court Judge Bryan Simpson tyrannically worked hand-in-glove with King's men. Had Simpson's harassment been avoided, and had state officers not themselves become tyrannical, the local police could have easily handled the situation.

Heinsohn, in his "Rape of the Ancient City," broods over this problem of tyrannical state officers. With Governor Bryant's untimely intervention and brutal state police, the local citizens gradually realized they were being subjected to a police state. Otherwise, the local police had the situation nicely in hand. Mrs. Peabody, whose husband had thirteen communist front affiliations, was an outsider; the nefarious, communist King was an outsider. Judge Simpson was biased in favor of King's hoodlums. To Sheriff Davis, the Negroes refused to eschew violence, played upon the racial prejudices of their opponents, and were led by law-breaking, communist King. The militant segregationists were not out to kill anyone, but merely ". . . to have a good time and beat the tar out of people."[12] Judge Simpson first favored the town but then suddenly reversed himself. Later, he became an Appellate Court Judge. Dr. Hayling came to specifically stir up trouble and prepare the way for King, whom Sheriff Davis will never forgive.

The Klan's Militant Backlash

In its hour of crumbling institutions, segregationist St. Augustine moved toward militant backlash as a solution to the crisis. St. Augustine turned to the Ku Klux Klan, an inextricably American group with a working and lower middle class base, which found itself playing a leading, but sometimes exaggerated, role in militant backlash. The Klan's activities were varied. What, then, were these activities?

Support

St. Augustine Klansmen and quasi-Klansmen were fortunate to have the hotbed of Klan activity in Jacksonville, just thirty-eight miles to the north. One Klan activity in St. Augustine was the succoring of local Klansmen by their out-of-town brethren. Of the three important militant segregationist leaders, Connie Lynch, Holstead Manucy, and J. B. Stoner, two of them,

Lynch and Stoner, were not native St. Augustinians. Stoner is a lawyer in Marietta, Georgia, and Connie Lynch, who died in the early 1970's, hailed from California. Not only did out-of-towners provide leadership, they also swelled the ranks. Many Jacksonville Klansmen attended the September 18 meeting. Sheriff Davis arrested four Klansmen from Jacksonville there.[1] According to Stoner, Jacksonville Klansmen helped out the local Klan. Indeed, Stoner involved himself in St. Augustine because his Jacksonville Klan friends were active in the Ancient City.[2] Sheriff Davis observed that Klansmen from Jacksonville, Starke, Palatka, Vernelle, Ocala, and Lake City would drive to the Ancient City after work for an evening's entertainment.[3] Manucy admitted that several Jacksonville Klansmen came down to help.[4] Beset by revolutionary forces, St. Augustine's militant segregationists could count on aid from Klansmen from around northern Florida. A few hardy souls even came down from Georgia to help.

Frequent Klan rallies and marches in Jacksonville provided inspiration and moral support for St. Augustine. Just prior to the rallies in St. Augustine in September, 1963, Klansmen held several membership drive rallies in Jacksonville. The "South's Oldest Secret Society" greeted prospective members with a sign reading "Welcome—Florida Ku Klux Klan," and with soft drinks.[5] In March and May, 1964, the Klan held rallies in Jacksonville. Often, the featured speaker would be either Stoner or Lynch, just as they would orate in St. Augustine in July, 1964.[6] These rallies kept spirits up in St. Augustine since St. Augustine's militant segregationists often attended.

Recruitment

The rallies in September were organizational rallies, which constituted an important role of the Klan—increasing the size of itself which represented organized militant backlash. At the September 18 meeting, Reverend Lynch extolled the virtues of the Klan and provided reasons for his audience to sign up.

We've got guts enough to do something about the situation and no other organization has. We need a good strong group in St. Augustine. You come and sign. But don't come if you are weak or a coward. This ain't no peaceful organization. We aim to do whatever is necessary to put the Nigger back in his place, preferably in his grave.[8]

Apparently, St. Augustinians were convinced that this was not a peaceful organization after seeing what the Klan did to Dr. Hayling and friends. Apparently, St. Augustinians liked what they saw. The Klan scheduled a rally for the day after the September 18 rally, which had drawn about 400 people. Over 500 cars with over 2,500 persons streamed out to the rally at the outskirts of St. Augustine. Even though rain hampered the activities, Klan spokesmen reported a large number of recruits.[9] Sheriff Davis reasoned that the Klan came to St. Augustine because it thought St. Augustine to be a good place to gather in new members.[10] Stoner conceded that St. Augustine was good for the membership rolls. The Klan attempted to organize militant backlash by enrolling those empathetic to militant backlash in the Klan.

Rallies

Klansmen organized and led rallies that aired the views and the frustrations of racists and that coalesced the militant opposition of the egalitarian revolutionaries. Klansmen took advantage of two types of rallies: the traditional cross-burner and the nightly Slave Market harangue. Klansmen conducted the former on private property outside of town. Both Davis and Manucy helped to secure permission to hold these meetings; handbills advertising the meetings were not subject to the city ordinance prohibiting distribution of handbills that integrationists' handbills were subject to.[11]

Lynch was the featured speaker at the rallies[12] in the fall of 1963, which were held off of U.S. Highway One near the bowling alley. In addition to the meetings of September 18 and 19, the Klan rallied on the 27 and 28 of September and on the 11, 12, and 13 of October.[13] In 1964, Stoner and Lynch shared the oratorical duties, although Stoner did most of the speaking until Lynch returned in the latter part of June.[14] Thus, Stoner probably spoke at the rally on the 15 of May at the point of Vilano Beach. The cross burned brightly enough to be seen across Matanza Bay.[15] McMillan reported that Klansmen met weekly at a large paved parking area near St. Augustine's civic center, [16] but the only other evidence of the Klan meeting there was when they used the parking lot as a staging area of their July 4 parade.[17]

From the 17th to the 24th of July, the Klan held nightly rallies on property of the City Baking Company just across the railroad tracks on State Highway 207. St. Augustinians knew about the rallies since robed Klansmen directed traffic off the highway and announced "all white people are welcome."[18] At the rally on July 19, which had a twenty-foot cross, Stoner urged the crowd of 2,000 to sign a petition that would put the National States Rights Party on the ballot in Florida for November. The platform of the NSRP, Stoner explained, was segregation forever. Political action was necessary since the way to achieve white supremacy was to expel from Congress those who had voted for the Civil Rights Act. To prove his point, Stoner touched a match to a copy of the Civil Rights Act and held it while it burned.[19] The meeting of the 22nd featured speakers who denounced the Civil Rights Act and integration and vowed to uphold state's rights, the white race, and the constitution.[20] After the Monson Motel received the fruits of General Molotov's genius on the night of the 24, police cracked down and arrested Stoner, Lynch, Paul Cochran of Jacksonville, and Barton Griffin of Jacksonville for burning a cross on the Baking Company's property without permission (they had been doing it for a week) and Bill Coleman of St. Augustine for helping with the cross burning and for violating the state's anti-mask law by wearing a hood.[21]

Although militant segregationists gathered to heckle and to attack integrationists in the Plaza since they had started to march in late May, the first evidence of a Klan-organized rally there was when Stoner gave a pep talk before a militant backlash march June 12 (the marches will be discussed below.) Thereafter, the Klan held rallies in the Slave Market regularly until the end of June. The regular speakers were, again, Lynch and Stoner, who voiced repeatedly such themes as "anyone who thinks blacks and whites are equal is a fool," "Hitler was a great man," "Americans should ship blacks back to Africa," and "the American government was intended to be of, by and for white people."[22] Violent militant segregationists would often peel off from the crowd to attack demonstrators, but that fact does not necessarily lead to Hartley's conclusion that Lynch and Stoner and thus the Klan perpetrated "much of the violence."[23]

No evidence that Lynch and Stoner themselves attacked demonstrators exists. Further, the crowds were not just Klansmen and Huntsmen. Rather, "local white people" who felt attracted by militant backlash attended the rallies. Stoner argues that it was "just local white citizens that the niggers would come uptown and provoke." Stoner added that when the integrationists came and provoked, "why everybody that could hit niggers did."[24] On the other hand, only very rarely did Stoner and Lynch try to prevent violence.

On June 14, 200 persons turned out to hear Stoner advocate the firing of Negro workers and to lament that "we will not march through niggertown tonight because there are too many coons out there swinging by their tails."[25] The Klan rally on the 16th drew only about 100,[26] but a respectable 500 turned out for the rally on the 19th. Klansmen Cochran and Stoner took turns attacking (verbally) the Civil Rights Act and the integrationists, warning against Trojan Horse bi-racial committees, advocating the firing of Negroes, and predicting a race war. When a nearby integration march headed for a white neighborhood, a shout of "kill the black apes" went up from the crowd and 200 persons peeled off from the audience to attack the marchers. The police repelled the attack; militant segregationists sullenly returned to the rally.[27] Saturday the 20th was a large rally in the plaza. Six hundred to seven hundred persons brought their confederate flags to a rally Sunday the 21st after the *Record* reminded folks that the rally would be at 6:30 prompt. Some brought their own picket signs, one of which urged: "Let's get rid of the niggers. Then we won't have to integrate with them." The speaker condemned race mixing, urged the firing of blacks and the formation of a quick parade. One of the marching integrationists astonished an old lady in the crowd enough to exclaim "Look at that red-haired nigger!" After their march, the segregationist speaker reasoned that the integrationists and the federal government were trying to outlaw the white race and pretty white girls.[28]

About 1,000 people attended the rally of the 24th.[29] The 25th's rally of around 900 exploded into violence, as has been discussed. There was a large rally the 26th, and 2,000 turned out for the Klan's production of the 27th. The speaker felt obliged to thank a newsman for a ten dollar contribution.[30] Part of the crowd that was listening to Lynch orate on the 29th took off after a truck when a woman screamed "get that nigger."[31] The evening of the 30th, "White segregation leaders, who have been battling King's 'non-violent army' toe to toe," canceled rallies for two weeks in compliance with Governor Bryant's truce. The Klan had put on an impressive schedule of rallies, which concentrated and encouraged militant backlash.

Marches

On June 11, 1964, in an apparently impromptu venting of frustration, a group of 100 to 200 militant segregationist youths fell into line at the Plaza and began marching toward a group of integrationists. An "army" of police stopped the marchers, who milled around and eventually dispersed, but the idea of a militant backlash march had been planted.[32] Klansmen liked the idea and got into the march-organizing business. Who marched? Who led the parades? Of course, Klansmen trod the streets; they were joined, however, by many non-affiliated St. Augustinians who turned out to express their outrage.[33] The Klan worked closely with the Ancient City Hunting Club to organize the marches, which were led by Stoner, Manucy, Dixon Stanford, and occasionally Sheriff Davis in his official capacity. Holstead Manucy would trail along behind the marchers to make sure everybody stayed in line.[34] After Police Chief Stuart refused permission for the marches, the Klan secured it from Sheriff Davis, who felt obliged to permit the marches since the integrationists were marching—a matter of fair play.

After a preliminary speech that featured a plea for non-violence by Stoner, on the evening of the 12th 200 to 300 militant segregationists stepped off in a "brash parade" through Lincolnville, "the colored section of town." Led by Stoner, Bubber Manucy, and Stanford and protected by Sheriff Davis, 200 officers, and five Negroes who scouted ahead of the march for trouble, the two-abreast marchers shuffled past signs proclaiming "Welcome. Peace and Brotherhood to you" and curious stares from porches. At one point in the twenty-block trek through Lincolnville, thirty-five patrons of Big Daddy's Blue Goose Lounge poured out and heckled the marchers. When a couple of drunks became abusive, Davis persuaded them to go back inside, arguing that the marchers were too numerous to handle. Towards the end of the march, which the *Tampa Tribune* thought "took the steam out of the anger" that had been building in the white community, several integrationists, behind an old house, heaved some stones at the march and, according to Davis, "bricked us pretty good." At the time, a leader of the march gave thanks to the cordon of police "for protecting us from these black savages." On reflection, however, Stoner said the police were really protecting the spectators. Otherwise, the "whites would have cleaned out niggertown."[36]

About the same number of militant segregationists marshalled the next evening, Saturday night. They marched towards Lincolnville behind a banner that was carried by a man and his wife and that warned "Don't tread on me." Once again, Stoner, who explained that the march was the militant segregationists' way of celebrating St. Augustine's quadricentennial, led the march that was dotted with American and Confederate flags and with militant backlash signs. Losing their shyness of the previous evening, 500 residents of Lincolnville lined the streets and sang, to the irritation of the marchers, "We love everybody." Protected by state, county, and city police, the marchers made it through Lincolnville without violence.[37]

On Sunday the 14th, the Klan declined to march into Linconville for reasons noted above and settled for a brisk step around the Plaza.[38] Sunday the 21st of June saw 300 to 400 militant segregationists march through Lincolnville. Waving confederate flags and signs and screaming rebel yells, the militant segregationists walked along the north side of King Street as 120 integrationists passed them on the far side of a wall of police.[39] June 24th, Lynch fired up the crowd by explaining that "King associates with communists," that "integration is communism," that "white men are the custodians of the old and new testaments," and that "white men wrote the constitution and, indeed, built civilization." Lynch and Stoner then led 400 to 500 high-stepping, Confederate flag waving, militant segregationists through Lincolnville. Returning to the Slave Market, the marchers found themselves halted by police, who were allowing 100 to 150 integrationists to pass. Angered, many militant segregationists broke ranks, rushed and surrounded the integrationists, but police prevented violence. Still, militant segregationists threw an occasional cherry bomb.[40]

Militant segregationists staged a different kind of parade June 28 when fifty cars, Confederate flags flapping, drove up and down the beach.[41] To cap off the marches and to express their abundant patriotism, Klansmen put on an all-Klan show July 4. Although calling in brothers from all of North Florida and Georgia, only 210 Klansmen, seventy of whom were in their robes, showed up for the march from San Marco Lot to the Slave Market and back. This number compares unfavorably with some of the marches that non-Klansmen marched in, but a good number of people spectated and listened to the Klan speaker question the constitutionality of the Civil Rights Act and vow that the rights of white people would be preserved.[42] Klansmen led militant segregationists through the streets of St. Augustine. In doing so, Klansmen provided St. Augustine a means of expressing its opposition to subversive integration in an orderly fashion.

Pickets

When the Civil Rights Act became law in early July, 1964, militant segregationists' relation to the law abruptly reversed itself: instead of staving off attacks on the legal order, militant segregationists had to try to dislodge integration from the new legal order. They grasped a model of protest from integrationists: picketing. When integrationists began testing compliance with the law July 8, Stoner, Lynch, and Manucy moved from store to store and sullenly watched the testers.[43] Picket signs, held by Klansmen, Huntsmen, and members of the National States Rights Party soon appeared in front of restaurants and motels that complied with the new law. In the face of signs such as "Delicious Food. Eat With Niggers Here" and "Niggers Sleep Here, Will You," James Brock resegregated his Monson Motel and Restaurant on July 10. Re-segregation followed pickets. After only one week of effort, picket leaders happily announced that only one restaurant stood "accused of not going along with the no-service agreement."

The community responded to the militant backlash pickets as the Klan leaders had hoped. As Brock put it, black pickets can hurt your business; white pickets can kill it. King's threats to renew massive demonstrations did not overturn the success of the pickets. Only Simpson's orders broke down re-segregation.[44]

Intimidation

Perhaps one reason that the militant backlash pickets were successful, other than the restaurateur's desire to re-segregate, was the Klan's reputation for intimidating opponents. In 1963, after the owner of a small grocery declined to allow the Klan to use his land for their rallies, persons harassed his children at school; vandals broke his car and store windows. Lynch's economic blockade of the grocery cost the owner eight thousand dollars in three months.[45] Dr. Hayling refused to go to court to testify against the Klansmen accused of pummeling him because the proceedings "have attracted heavy attendance from known Klansmen."[46] An *Alligator* reporter said that after following his car, a "known Klansman" got out of his own car with a chain in one hand and a club in the other.[47]

Conversely, many St. Augustinians credited Sheriff Davis and Manucy for preventing much violence by restraining overzealous youths.[48] The picketing went beyond picketing (and thus surely broke St. Augustine's picketing law).' Integrationists filed suit against the Klan, the Ancient City Hunting Club, and various individuals: "They do not comply with the provisions [of the Civil Rights Act] and they have conspired to undertake and have undertaken a course of action such that no one else complies with or receives the benefit of the Act."[49] Although they cannot be said to be Klansmen, several persons chased some testers and Simpson ordered a deputy who was a Huntsman to resign after he followed some testers. Simpson said the deputy followed to intimidate; the deputy said he followed to protect.[50] Tobias Simon, attorney for the SCLC, conceded that the problem was to "protect the rights of Negroes without throwing the restaurant owners to the wolves." [51] Nonetheless, one must wonder whether the Klan was included in the pack since Simpson dropped the Klan's name as defendants in the above suit.[52]

Other than the few acts of violence that can be traced to it, the Klan actively engaged in, and often led, militant backlash by support shown by out of town Kluxers, by recruiting new members into the Klan, by leading rallies, by leading marches, by organizing pickets, and by trying to intimidate the opposition. Although unsure whether they were doing the right thing or not, St. Augustinians accepted, permitted, and responded to the Klan's leadership in militant backlash. As the *Tampa Tribune* editorialized about "The Defenders," Lynch, Stoner and Manucy:

> These, then are the faces that stand out in the campaign to prevent St. Augustine from accepting the public accommodations laws . . . It is a campaign which professes to be waged in defense of local choice, Southern tradition and constitutional rights. Neither St. Augustine, Florida, the South, or the nation can be proud of such self-appointed defenders. The sooner they are removed from the scene, by law or by the force of public opinion the better for all.[53]

The force of public opinion did not remove the Defenders. St. Augustine, Florida, the South, and the nation had to wait upon the law.

Conclusion

As the crisis wore down in late August and early September—as the permanency of the integrationists' usurpation began to sink in, as people began to realize that the force of law through the Civil Rights Act of 1964 and through Judge Simpson was behind integration, as no marching integrationists appeared in the streets—the Klan's glory plummeted. The need to struggle against integration in the streets gave way to a need to remember the good old days, to persevere philosophically against integration, and to get tourists back into the streets of the Ancient City. Always disreputable, the lower and lower middle class Klan and its militant backlash gave way to the White Citizens Council and its tamer opposition.

Sharing their prejudices with Klansmen, Council members came from the solid middle class and formed the most respectable wing of the backlash movement.[1] Although Hartley suggests that St. Augustine had a Citizens Council throughout the crisis, he also notes that Mayor Shelley said there was not one during the "Spring Project."[2] The first evidence that I found indicating a Citizens council was on August 23, 1964, when the civic-minded *Record* informed readers that the Council would meet at the Holiday Inn. An overflow crowd of 350 showed up for the meeting. William Chew, an ex-manager of a motel and restaurant who refused to integrate, predicted a membership roll of 1,500 for the new Ancient City Citizens Council. Although Hurricane Dora postponed the Council's meeting slated for September 10, another overflow meeting elected Chew president on September 16.[3] As the respectable resisters gained in popularity, the Klan and the quasi-Klan withered. Manucy alone had to appear in federal court thirty-seven times; Simpson enjoined the Ancient City Hunting Club and all members from resisting the Civil Rights Act. St. Augustine's Klavern had such tenuous finances, and thus support from the community, that Exalted Cyclops Cooper bounced a check for eighteen dollars written on the Klan's account in September, 1965.[4] Times were bad.

For a while, though, many St. Augustinians turned to the lower and lower-middle class, genetically American organization, the Ku Klux Klan, to lead the struggle against a movement that had brought crisis down on St.

Augustine and that threatened to, and that indeed did, destroy an integral part of the St. Augustine way of life. Klansmen were gratified to find that they did not have to fight alone. Covertly and overtly, elements of the community responded to the Klan's leadership. Led by their youngsters, many St. Augustinians joined the Klan in militant backlash.

Table I

OCCUPATIONS
(122 total, 71%)

	A	B	C	D	E	F	G	H	I	J	K	L
1)	11	9	1	9	4	36	3	27	1	9	2	18
2)	25	20	1	4	6	24	6	24	5	20	8	32
3)	19	16	2	11	5	26	2	11	1	5	8	42
4)	28	23	0	0	10	36	7	25	1	4	9	32
5)	23	19	3	13	6	26	6	26	2	8	6	26
6)	16	13	1	6	6	38	4	25	1	6	4	25
Total no.			8		37		28		11		37	
Total %				7		30		23		9		30

EDUCATION
(70 total, 41%)

	A	B	C	D	E	F	G	H	I	J	K	L
1)	1	1	0	0	0	0	0	0	0	0	1	100
2)	12	17	0	0	3	25	3	25	0	0	6	50
3)	19	27	0	0	8	42	6	32	2	11	3	16
4)	23	33	0	0	7	30	4	17	2	9	10	43
5)	9	13	0	0	1	11	1	11	2	22	5	56
6)	1	1	0	0	0	0	1	100	0	0	0	0
7)	5	7	1	20	2	40	1	20	0	0	1	20
Total no.			1		21		16		6		25	
Total %				1		30		23		9		36

(continued)

153

Table I: continued

AGE
(124, 72%)

	A	B	C	D	E	F	G	H	I	J	K	L
1)	1	1	0	0	0	0	0	0	0	0	1	100
2)	26	21	2	8	8	31	6	23	2	8	8	31
3)	53	43	4	8	13	25	12	23	5	9	19	36
4)	26	21	2	8	8	31	8	31	2	8	6	23
5)	13	10	0	0	2	15	3	23	2	15	6	46
6)	5	4	0	0	1	20	1	20	1	20	2	40
Total no.			8		32		30		12		42	
Total %				6		26		24		10		39

EXPLANATION OF TABLE I

A—total number of Klansmen in category out of the group
B—total percentage of Klansmen in category out of the group
C—number of Imperial officers in category
D—percent of Imperial officers in category
E—number of Grand officers in category
F—percent of Grand officers in category
G—number of Exalted Cyclops in category
H—percentage of Exalted Cyclops in category
I—number of other local officers in category
J—percent of other local officers in category
K—number of non-ranked members in category
L—percent of unranked members in category

OCCUPATIONAL CATEGORIES

1. Skilled machinists, mechanics, carpenters, stone masons, (bricklayers, bonded warehousemen, electricians, printers, and journeyman plumbers added to Vander Zanden's category)

(continued)

2. Marginal small businessmen, small building trade contractors, proprietors of food stores, grills, gas stations, (farmers, self-employed house painters, small heating and air conditioning businesses, owners of auto repair shop and towing service, operator of a variety store, owner of a garbage collection business, operator of a cabinet shop added)

3. Marginal white collar workers, grocery store clerks, service station attendants, police, salesmen, (military, clerks in general, construction inspector for a city, assistant office manager, bank employees added)

4. Transportation workers, semi-skilled, unskilled workers in textiles, steel, automobiles, aircraft, and coal industries (worker for DuPont, mixer at paint co., workers at paper industries, bulldozer operator, employees of sewing machine co., shipbuilders, masonite corp., petroleum drillers, employees of Pullman plant, Westinghouse Electric, Florida Carbonic, General Motors added)

5. Those employed in higher prestige or better paying jobs than categories 1, 2, 3, or 4: co-owner of a gunworks, pensioned military, researcher, co-owner of garment works, all foremen, attorneys, a vice president of a school board, a principal, owner of a large sanitation business, assistant principal, all physicians, multi-business owners, and larger business owners, ministers, a wealthy farmer.

6. Those employed in lesser prestige or poorer paying jobs than jobs 1, 2, 3, 4: bartenders, employee insulation company, busboys, housewife, all full time Klansmen, employee of a clay co., those who cannot hold a steady job, criminals, loggers, city employee, employee of an implement co., painter for hire

EDUCATION CATEGORIES

1. No education
2. Eight years or less
3. More than eight years, but no high school diploma
4. High school diploma (or equivalency test) only
5. More than a high school diploma but no college diploma
6. Bachelor's degree
7. Degrees higher than bachelors

(continued)

AGE CATEGORIES
(as of 1965)

1. Ten to twenty years old
2. Twenty-one to thirty years old
3. Thirty-one to forty years old
4. Forty-one to fifty years old
5. Fifty-one to sixty years old
6. Over sixty years old

KLAN "TYPES" OR RANKS

Imperial Officers—those holding national office as designated by the rank "imperial"

Grand Officers—those holding state office as designated by the rank "grand."

Exalted Cyclops—the head of local groups, called Klaverns

Other local officers—less illustrious officers Kligrapps, Night Hawks, etc.

Members—Klansmen without formal rank

Table II

VANDER ZANDEN'S OCCUPATIONS OF KLANSMEN
COMPARED TO TABLE ONE
(153 Klansmen)

(categories are the same as categories 1-4, occupation group, Table one)

(Table One for Comparison)

	Number of Klansmen	Percent of Klansmen	Number of Klansmen	Percent of Klansmen
1)	51	33	11	9
2)	11	7	25	20
3)	36	24	19	16
4)	55	36	28	23

Above figures combined

1)	62	23
2)	36	13
3)	55	20
4)	83	30
5)	23	8
6)	16	6

Figures are taken from: James W. Vander Zanden, "The Klan Revival," *American Journal of Sociology*, LXV:5 (March, 1960)

Notes

The following abbreviations are used in the notes.

FA   *Florida Alligator*
FS   *Florida Star*
FTU   *Florida Times-Union*
GS   *Gainesville Sun*
MH   *Miami Herald*
NYT   *New York Times*
SAR   *St. Augustine Record*
SPT   *St. Petersburg Times*
TT   *Tampa Tribune*
IN-D   Interview with L. O. Davis, St. Augustine, February 6, 1976 Tape
        deposited in the University of Florida Oral History Archives, Florida
        State Museum, Gainesville.
IN-M   Interview with Holstead "Hoss" Manucy, St. Augustine, February
        21, 1976. Tape deposited in the University of Florida Oral History
        Archives, Florida State Museum, Gainesville.
IN-S   Interview with Jesse B. Stoner, Jacksonville, April 6, 1976. Tape
        deposited in the University of Florida Oral History Archives, Florida
        State Museum, Gainesville.
ENC   *Encyclopedia of the Social Sciences*, New York, Macmillan Co.,
        1968.

Chapter One

1. IN-S.
2. U.S. Congress, House Committee on Un-American Activities *Activities of the Ku Klux Klan Organizations in the United States*. 89th Cong., 2nd sess. p. 3669.
3. NYT June 26, 1964. p. 14. Elsewhere in the article, the author, H. Bigart, incorrectly names Connie Lynch as the orator when the violence occurred in the evening.
4. SAR June 26, 1964.

5. IN-M.
6. SAR editorial June 14, 1964.
7. SAR Aug 2, 1964.
8. Manucy points out that the Hunting Club used high quality CB's: "no trash." IN-M.
9. SAR June 26, 1964.
10. SAR editorial July 2, 1963.
11 By speaking of the lower and lower middle classes, I am referring to the four categories set forth by James W. Vander Zanden in "The Klan Revival," *The American Journal of Sociology*, Vol. LXV No. 5 (March, 1960) p. 458, plus the additional category I had to add: (1) skilled workers—machinists, mechanics, carpenters and stone masons; (2) marginal small businessmen, small building trade contractors, proprietors of food markets, grills, gas stations; (3) marginal white collar workers—grocery store clerks, service station attendants, police, salesmen; (4) transportation workers, semi-skilled and unskilled workers in textiles, steel, automobiles, aircraft and coal industries; and (5) workers whose jobs have less prestige or less pay than the above jobs.
12. Hayling ". . . bought guns for his group and trained these young blacks in their use." Robert Hartley, "A long hot summer: the St. Augustine Disorders of 1964" (M.A. thesis, Stetson University, May, 1972) p. 17.
13. SAR Nov. 26, 1964.
14. C. Vann Woodward "From the First Reconstruction to the Second," *Harper's,* April, 1965, p. 129.
15. SAR Sept. 22, 1964.
16. SAR July 17, 1963.
17. SAR July 23, 1963.
18. Hartley, see note 2.
19. "The American Middle Ground in St. Augustine," *New South*, Vol. 19, No. 9, (September, 1964).
20. IN-S; IN-M; W. Eugene Wilson, Exalted Cyclops of Robert E. Lee Klavern number 513 and member of the National States Rights Party, wrote in *The Thunderbolt:* "As was clearly demonstrated in St. Augustine in the Summer of 1964, Protestants and Catholics can and did work together to deal Martin Lucifer Koon and his black mobs their most crushing defeat." House Committee on Un-American Activities, p. 3698.
21. FS June 20, 1964.

CHRONOLOGY

1. The integrationist had cause to be concerned with the spirit of the celebration. An act of the Florida Legislature establishing the St. Augustine Historical Restoration and Preservation Committee began: "Whereas St. Augustine, Florida is the oldest community of the white race in the U.S. having a continuous history . . ." SAR March 11, 1963.

2. Hartley incorrectly reports that subsequent to this shooting Hayling said that "we are not going to die like Medgar Evers. I and others of the NAACP have armed ourselves and we will shoot first and ask questions later." Evers was shot on June 11. Hayling made the statement on June 19, 1963. Unless otherwise noted, I am relying on either Hartley or the Florida Legislative Investigation Committee for the chronology.
3. SAR Oct 1. 1963.
4. IN-D.
5. SAR Oct. 29, 1963.
6. Hartley is again mistaken in chronology. He reports the car's burning on January 11; the *Record* reports it on January 21. He reports the home burning on February 2 and the shooting of Hayling's home in January. The *Record* reports the home fire an February 7 and the shooting of Hayling's home on February 8. The Investigation Committee concurs with the later date for the shooting. Hartley, p. 43; SAR Jan. 22, 1964; Feb. 9, 1964; FLIC p. 33.
7. SAR Feb. 28, 1963; Feb 26, 1963; Feb. 27, 1963; Feb 9, 1963; Feb. 16, 1963.
8. The FLIC says on p. 37 that they began May 28; Hartley on p. 58 says May 27; the *Record*, May 28, 1964, reports marches on May 26; Watters, p. 7, says May 26.
9. Hartley, p. 58, states that the bombs went off July 21.

Chapter Two

MEMBERSHIP BASE

1. IN-D.
2. Indeed, the House Committee on Un-American Activities considered the Ancient City Hunting Club to be Klavern number 519 of the United Florida Ku Klux Klan, p. 1594.
3. SAR June 22, 1964.
4. Vander Zanden, see note 11 of the Introduction.
5. Vander Zanden, p. 458. I should note that Vander Zanden and I emphasize different aspects of the Klan. He argues that, although that the Citizens Council was a "countermovement, " the Klan's viability was not dependent on integregation efforts, p. 457. The Klan's existence, perhaps, was independent of the immediate threat of integration. Nonetheless, the Klan's re-emergence in the late 1950s and early 1960s was predicated on the rise of the integration movement. David Chalmers, *Hooded Americanism* (New York: Doubleday & Co., 1965: Quadrangle Books, 1968) p. 6. I am studying, however, the Klan's actions when that immediate threat of integration did arrive; obviously, Klansmen actions were then shaped by the presence of integration. Two possible arguments against my drawing statistics from the House Committee are (1) that the Committee may have concentrated on the leadership and thus

ignored the "average" Klansman and (2) that those indiscreet enough to be forced to appear before a public hearing surely could not be representative of the membership of a secret society. These Klansmen may have been bunglers and those who could not keep a secret. However, the great majority declined to testify either altogether or here and there; the appropriate incantations for refusing to testify sear into the reader's mind. The objection to the proportion of members to officials rests on an unknown: the actual proportion of members to officials. To determine this is impossible, though, given the bewildering array of offices—Imperial, Grand, and local—one suspects that there are more generals than privates. Anyway, as table 1 indicates, the membership was well represented. In the group of occupations, non-official members were thirty percent—only one other group was that high. In education, members had thirty-six percent of the total, as compared to the next highest thirty percent. In age, non-official members had thirty-nine percent as compared to thirty-two percent for all Grand officers.

6. Vander Zanden, p. 458.
7. Vander Zanden, p. 462.
8. A rather obvious assumption is that they do desire to rise on the social scale.
9. See David Fischer, *Historians' Fallacies* (New York; Harper Torchbook, 1970) p. 127.
10. House Committee on Un-American Activities, p. 3008.
11. The same argument used in note 5 concerning the distribution of non-officer members in the sample applies to the objection that youths would not appear before the Committee because most of the officers are probably older. Members made up thirty-nine percent of the age group sample.
12. Kenneth Jackson, *The Ku Klux Klan in the City, 1915 to 1930* (New York: Oxford University Press, 1967) pp. 240, 245.
13. Chalmers, pp. 354, 352.
14. TT June 15, 1964.
15. FA June 17, 1964. Interestingly enough, both this article and the preceding article were mistaken on the presence of Klansmen. The *Tribune* thought there were no Klansmen; the *Alligator*—in keeping with their policy of journalistic exaggeration—found all Klansmen. The marchers were, rather, a mixed bag.
16. IN-M.
17. Francis M. Wilhoit, *The Politics of Massive Resistance* (New York: George Braziller, Inc., 1973). Wilhoit calls backlash "Massive Resistance," which he terms counterrevolutionary. Indeed, militant backlash is counterrevolution if one considers integration revolutionary and if one considers taking to the streets to oppose the revolution as counterrevolution.

VIOLENCE

1. *Life* Feb. 7, 1964, p. 72.
2. Wilhoit, p. 109.
3. *The Klan Ledger,* July 4, 1964, House Committee on Un-American Activities, p. 2757.
4. Wilhoit, p. 50.
5. NYT May 13, 1963 p. 1.
6. NYT Sept. 16, 1963.
7. Reverend Irwin Cheney, "St. Augustine Ku Klux Klan Meeting" (typewritten) p. 4. I am indebted to Professor Chalmers for making his copy available to me.
8. IN-M.
9. House Committee on Un-American Activities, pp 1542, 3716.
10. House Committee on Un-American Activities, p. 3668.
11. Cheney, p. 9.
12. IN-D; Stoner wistfully sighed: "I wish I'd been there." IN-S.
13. House Committee on Un-American Activities, p. 3712.
14. SAR Feb. 6, 1964.
15. SAR Feb. 17, 1964.
16. SAR March 4, 1964; House Committee on Un-American Activities, p. 3704; IN-D.
17. FS July 18, 1964; FTU Nov. 26, 1964.
18. TT June 12, 1964.
19. NYT June 21, 1964.
20. IN-D.
21. IN-S.
22. SAR editorial, May 29, 1964.
23. NYT May 31, 1964, p. 50.
24. George McMillan, "The Klan Scourges Old St. Augustine," *Life,* June 26, 1964, p. 21.
25. SAR May 29, 1964.
26. GS July 6, 1964; SAR July 10, 1964.
27. Hartley, p. 58.
28. Heinsohm reports that Dr. Norris of the Florida Coalition of Patriotic Societies went so far as to assert that, prior to June 15, 1964 ". . .there was no strife in St. Augustine." A.G. Heinsohm, Jr., "St. Augustine: Rape of the Ancient City," *American Opinion,* October, 1964, p. 3.
29. SAR June 12, 1964.
30. IN-D.
31. IN-D.
32. IN-S.
33. SAR May 29, 1964; June 2, 1964; TT June 11, 1964; SPT June 21, 1964; IN-D.
34. Florida Legislature, Report of the Legislative Investigation Committee, Feb., 1965, *Racial and Civil Disorders in St. Augustine,* p. 42.

35. IN-D; SAR June 18, 1964; TT June 20, 1964.
36. SAR Jan. 12, 1963; Southern Christian Leadership Conference Newsletter, p. 12.
37. Hartley, p. 22; FTU Oct. 18, 1963; SAR Oct. 22, 1963; FS Sept. 7, 1963.
38. IN-D.
39. FA June 12, 1964.
40. IN-D.
41. FTU June 11, 1964.
42. L. Goodwyn, "Anarchy in St. Augustine," *Harper's* (January, 1965) p. 79; SAR June 25, 1964.
43. IN-S.

NATIVISM

1. SAR July 1, 1964.
2. SAR May 15, 1963.
3. SAR Jan. 6, 1963.
4. House Committee on Un-American Activities, pp. 2389, 2747.
5. Otto Klineberg, "Prejudice: The Concept," ENC, Vol. 12, p. 443.
6. Florida Legislative Investigation Committee, p. 59.
7. IN-M.
8. TT June 12, 1964.

FRATERNALISM

1. Frank Tannenbaum, "The Ku Klux Klan: Its Social Origin In The South," *The Century Magazine*, Vol. 105, No. 6 (April, 1923) p. 879.
2. SAR Sept. 5, 1963.
3. NYT March 23, 1964, p. 1.
4. IN-M.

ANTI-COMMUNISM

1. Chalmers, p. 377; Hartley, pp 2-3.
2. SAR March 5, 1963.
3. SAR Sept. 25, 1963.
4. SAR May 17, 1963; Nov. 17, 1963.
5. SAR July 5, 1964.
6. SAR March 3, 1964.
7. SAR Jan. 26, 1964.
8. SAR July 5, 1964; Aug. 14, 1963; Aug. 23, 1963.
9. SAR April 24, 1964; March 28, 1963.
10. SAR May 19, 1963; July 2, 1963.

11. SAR March 23, 1964.
12. SAR May 24, 1964.
13. SAR March 13, 1964.
14. U.S., Congress, House Committee on Un-American Activities, *The Present Day Ku Klux Klan Movement*, 90th Cong., 1st sess., 1967, (Washington D.C.: U.S. Government Printing Office, 1967) p. 76.
15. Chalmers, p. 352.
16. Chalmers, p. 322.
17. *The Klan Ledger*, House Committee on Un-American Activities, *Activities of the Ku Klux Klan in the U.S.*, pp. 2756-2757, 2747.
18. SAR June 7, 1964.
19. *Clay County* (Green Cove Springs, Fla.) *Crescent*, Feb. 27, 1964.
20. SAR July 24, 1964.
21. SAR June 14, 1964.
22. FA June 17, 1964.
23. SAR June 11, 1964.
24. SAR June 2, 1964.
25. FA June 17, 1964.
26. NYT July 8, 1963, p. 19.
27. Sheriff Davis was kind enough to lend me his copy.
28. "Communism and the NAACP," pp. 10, 22, 42.
29. *Gibson v. Florida Legislative Investigation Committee*, 372 U.S. 539 (1963).
30. Florida Legislative Investigation Committee, pp. 50, 55.
31. SPT Aug. 1, 1964.
32. David Bartholomew, "An Analysis of Change in the Power System and Decision-Making Process In A Selected County," (Ed.D. dissertation, U. of Florida, 1971) p. 38.
33. SAR Aug., 1, 1964.
34. Hartley, pp 69-70; IN-D.
35. NYT *Magazine* July 5, 1964, p. 30. As Chalmers notes: "When Southern Governors denounced the Negro revolt as the product of communism and troublemaking outsiders, surely the Klansman was justified in adopting similar theories of his own." p. 352.
36. NYT March 23, 1964, p. 16.
37. NYT May 4, 1964, p. 25.
38. SAR June 25, 1964.
39. NYT July 3, 1964, p. 8.
40. IN-S.
41. IN-M.

RACISM

1. Jacques Barzum, *Race: A Study in Superstition* (New York: Harper and Row) revised edition, 1965, p. 5.

2. James W. Vander Zanden, "The Ideology of White Supremacy," *Journal of the History of Ideas*, Vol. XX, No. 3 (June-Sept. 1959) p. 397.
3. Klineberg, p. 444.
4. TT June 21, 1964, see picture p. 18-A; IN-D.
5. IN-D.
6. IN-D.
7. SAR June 19, 1963.
8. *Clay County Crescent*, Aug. 1, 1963.
9. TT July 31, 1964.
10. In-D.
11. Hartley, p. 115.
12. SAR July 28, 1964.
13. SPT July 23, 1964; TT July 9, 1964.
14. SAR June 2, 1964; TT June 18, 1964.
15. Hartley, p. 112; SAR July 16, 1964; TT July 24, 1964; FTU July 16, 1964; SPT June 21, 1964.
16. SAR July 8, 1964.
17. TT July 9, 1964; SAR Aug. 11, 1964.
18. IN-S.
19. Hartley, p. 52.
20. SAR July 7, 1963.
21. SAR July 18, 1963.
22. SAR June 17, 1963; June 30, 1963.
23. Cheney, p. 4.
24. SPT June 28, 1964.
25. Watters, p. 8; GS June 29, 1964.
26. NYT May 4, 1964, p. 25.
27. Hartley, p. 78; Watters p. 19.
28. House Committee on Un-American Activities, *The Present Day Ku Klux Klan Movement*, p. 75.

BROTHERS IN ARMS

1. Plato, *Phaedo*, p. 99b.
2. Chalmers, p. 381.
3. IN-D.
4. SAR Sept. 14, 1964.
5. Hartley, p. 56.
6. IN-D; IN-M.
7. Hartley, p. 56; SAR Sept. 14, 1964.
8. IN-M.
9. SAR Sept. 14, 1964.
10. IN-D.
11. NYT June 21, 1964 p. 69.
12. SAR Oct. 29, 1963.

13. House Committee on Un-American Activities, *Activities of the Ku Klux Klan Organizations in the U.S.*, p. 3703; SAR Oct. 18, 1963.
14. NYT June 21, 1964; IN-M.
15. House Committee on Un-American Activities, *Activities of the Ku Klux Klan Organizations in the U.S.*, p. 3690.
16. IN-D.
17. TT June 15, 1964; Bubber Manucy; "We wanted to see if the white people would be offered the same rights"; IN-M.
18. IN-M.
19. IN-M; IN-S.
20. IN-S.
21. IN-S.
22. IN-M; see Hartley, p. 57 for a different view.
23. IN-S.
24. Hartley, p. 105.
25. TT June 28, 1964; SPT June 28, 1964.
26. McMillan, p. 21.
27. IN-D.
28. Chalmers, p. 280; House Committee on Un-American Activities, *Activities of the Ku Klux Klan Organizations in the U.S.*, p. 3669.
29. IN-D.
30. IN-D.

Chapter Three

CRISIS

1. IN-S.
2. *Southern Christian Leadership Conference Newsletter*, p.4.
3. SAR Aug. 7, 1964; Chalmers, p. 381.
4. SAR April 15, 1964.
5. IN-M.
6. Chalmers, p. 382.
7. SAR June 3, 1963; June 4, 1963.
8. FTU June 4, 1963.
9. SAR Jan. 10, 1963.
10. SAR July 7, 1964; July 23, 1964. Nearby Flagler County had a different kind of crisis. Both State Senator Pope and Congressman D.R. "Billy" Mathews supported the use of concrete in I-95 so that the Lehigh Portland Cement Co. could re-open and relieve some of the county's unemployment.
11. FS March 14, 1964.
12. FS March 21, 1964.
13. FS March 18, 1964; Aug. 11, 1964; March 22, 1964; SAR March 23, 1964.
14. FTU March 13, 1963.

15. FS July 27, 1963.
16. *Flagler* (Bunnel, Fla.) *Tribune*, April 11, 1963.
17. SAR Feb. 27, 1964; March 1, 1964.
18. Stoner considered the effect of the FEC strike insignificant. As one might expect, the most important factor to Stoner was race. IN-S.
19. Bartholomew, pp. 23-24.
20. IN-D; see also Hartley, p. 55.
21. IN-D.
22. SPT July 23, 1964; Bartholomew, p. 23.
23. The figures are from the Chamber of Commerce as reported in the *Record*.
24. *Southern Christian Leadership Conference Newsletter*, p. 9.
25. FTU Oct. 31, 1963; SAR Oct. 30, 1963.
26. SAR March 31, 1964.
27. GS June 22, 1964.
28. FTU Nov. 5, 1963.
29. SAR June 5, 1964; June 7, 1964.
30. SAR Sept. 20, 1963.
31. SAR Oct. 1, 1963.
32. SAR July 1, 1964; June 28, 1964.
33. SAR May 29, 1964; May 31, 1964; June 8, 1964.
34. SAR June 13, 1964; July 28, 1964.
35. FS June 13, 1964; NYT June 11, 1964, p. 23.
36. SPT Aug. 19, 1964.
37. My purpose in tracing the integrationists' violence is to present an important factor in the community's turning to the Klan and to show an ugly side of integration not usually presented. Certainly, by omitting a detailed examination of militant segregationist violence, I am not denying its existence. If anything, it was more prevalent than integrationist violence—at any rate, militant segregationist violence was more publicized than integrationist violence.
38. Klineberg, p. 445; IN-D.
39. Hartley, pp. 18, 19; SAR July 2, 1963; NYT July 4, 1963; FS July 6, 1963.
40. Hartley implies he should not have by noting that police had the gun. Seven witnesses failed to identify who did the shooting, Hartley, p. 19; SAR July 17, 1963.
41. SAR July 18, 1963; Aug. 7, 1963.
42. SAR Oct. 24, 1963.
43. SPT June 21, 1964.
44. SAR June 8, 1964; June 25, 1964; TT June 10, 1964.
45. Quote from Hartley, p. 24; SAR July 27, 1963.
46. SAR June 29, 1964; Aug. 2, 1963.
47. IN-D.
48. Hartley, pp. 90-91.
49. IN-D; SAR June 26, 1964; See also Chapter II: Racism, for the deliberate provocation of militant segregationist by integrationists.
50. Vander Zanden notes in a footnote on p. 459: "At times such excessiveness may be condoned if not actually welcomed by the population at large, which

sees it as a temporary expediency arising from a definition of the situation as unusual and frequently threatening. Means normally proscribed are seen as effective for accomplishing the task at hand, and their employment is justified by the atypical situation and this temporary character. At the same time, those more inhibited by a greater internalization of the prevailing societal norms are 'saved' from violating the norms and consequent anxiety." "The Klan Revival.".

51. SAR July 7, 1963.
52. SAR July 9, 1963.
53. SAR Oct. 28, 1963.
54. SAR Dec. 17, 1963.
55. SAR Feb. 9, 1964.
56. Acker, as quoted in Bartholomew, p. 78.
57. TT June 7, 1965. Mayer notes: "The fascist movement did its best to heighten and embitter this crisis situation. At the same time fascist leaders offered their shock troops as auxiliary forces to panic-stricken . . . elite." Arno J. Mayer, *Dynamics of Counterrevolution in Europe, 1870-1956* (New York: Harper, 1971) p. 22.
58. IN-M; IN-S.
59. TT June 20, 1964.
60. SPT July 26, 1964; Hartley, p. 57; see also below on the interpretations of Hartley, Watter, and Goodwyn.
61. Hartley, p. 83.
62. IN-S. When I interviewed him, he had two small Confederate flags in his breast pocket.
63. FTU July 3, 1964.

INTERPRETATIONS

1. See footnotes 2, 6, 8, and 9 in Chapter I: Chronology.
2. Hartley, p. 10.
3. Hartley, p. 20, 28, 42.
4. Chalmers, p. 376.
5. Obviously, Chalmers's right-thinking community and my turn toward militant segregation have much in common, as does the interpretation of the Americanism of the Klan. However, I was unable to find sufficient evidence to say with confidence that it was "Klansmen and Manucy's raiders" who daily and nightly assailed the integrationists. On the contrary, I did find evidence that questioned the Klan's personal, immediate role in violence, save for isolated occasions. The evidence, to my knowledge, simply does not exist to transform the Klansman-behind-every-rock stereotype into reality.
6. *Harper's* (Jan., 1965) p. 74.
7. *New South*, Vol. 19, No. 9 (Sept. 1964).
8. As quoted in House Committee on Un-American Activities, *Activities of the Ku Klux Klan Organizations in the U.S.*, p. 3698.
9. IN-M.

10. IN-S.
11. Florida Legislative Investigation Committee, p. 24.
12. IN-D.

KLAN'S MILITANT BACKLASH

1. SAR Sept. 19, 1963.
2. IN-S.
3. IN-D.
4. IN-M.
5. SAR Sept. 5, 1963.
6. SAR March 18, 1964; Aug. 8, 1964; May 3, 1964; NYT May 4, 1964, p. 25.
7. IN-M.
8. Cheney, p. 6.
9. SAR Sept. 20, 1963.
10. IN-D.
11. IN-M; SAR Oct. 3, 1963; MH Oct. 31, 1963, Cheney, p. 10.
12. IN-S.
13. SAR Sept. 27, 1963; Oct. 11, 1963.
14. IN-S.
15. SAR May 17, 1964.
16. McMillan, p. 21.
17. SAR July 5, 1964.
18. SAR July 23, 1964.
19. SAR July 20, 1964.
20. SAR July 23, 1964.
21. SAR July 26, 1964; SPT July 25, 1964.
22. GS June 29, 1964.
23. Hartley, p. 58.
24. IN-S.
25. NYT June 15, 1964, p. 23; SAR June 15, 1964.
26. SAR June 17, 1964.
27. NYT June 21, 1964; June 20, 1964; SAR June 21, 1964.
28. SAR June 21, 1964; SPT June 28, 1964.
29. SAR June 24, 1964; June 25, 1964.
30. SAR June 28, 1964.
31. NYT June 30, 1964, p. 20.
32. SAR June 12, 1964. The *Tampa Tribune* reported that the marchers assembled at the Ponce de Leon Hotel and were prevented from marching into Lincolnville. June 14, 1964. See also NYT, June 12, 1964, p. 17.
33. IN-M; IN-S.
34. IN-D; TT June 15, 1964; June 20, 1964; FTU June 13, 1964.
35. IN-D; IN-M; SAR June 3, 1964.
36. IN-S; Watters, p. 4; For the march on the 12th, see: FA June 17, 1964; NYT June 13, 1964, p. 21; FTU June 13, 1964; TT June 14, 1964; SAR June 14,

1964; Hartley, p. 78; IN-D. The *Alligator* reported that Klansmen walked with their guns flapping at their hips.

37. For the march on the 13th, see: TT June 14, 1964; SPT June 15, 1964; FTU June 14, 1964; SAR June 14, 1964; Hartley, p. 80; IN-M.
38. SAR June 15, 1964.
39. GS June 22, 1964; TT June 22, 1964; SAR June 22, 1964.
40. SAR June 25, 1964; TT June 25, 1964; Hartley, p. 98.
41. GS June 29, 1964.
42. SAR July 3, 1964; July 5, 1964; GS July 3, 1964.
43. TT July 9, 1964.
44. SAR July 10, 1964; July 12, 1964; July 16, 1964; FTU July 15, 1964; SPT July 18, 1964; July 25, 1964; IN-M; IN-S; Hartley, p. 107.
45. Hartley, p. 31.
46. MH Nov. 11, 1963.
47. FA June 12, 1964.
48. TT June 30, 1964; IN-M; IN-D.
49. SPT July 21, 1964.
50. SAR Aug. 18, 1964; Aug. 19, 1964.
51. TT July 24, 1964.
52. MH Aug. 6, 1964.
53. TT Aug. 3, 1964.

CONCLUSION

1. Neil R. McMillen, *The Citizens Council: Organized Resistance to the Second Reconstruction 1954-1964*, (Urbana, Ill., 1971) pp. ii, vii.
2. Hartley, pp. 2, 52.
3. SAR Aug. 23, 1964; Aug 26, 1964; Sept. 10, 1964; Sept 15, 1964; Sept. 17, 1964; FTU Aug. 27, 1964.
4. House Committee on Un-American Activities, *Activities of the Ku Klux Klan Organizations in the U.S.*, p. 3703.

Bibliography

BOOKS AND ARTICLES

Barzum, Jacques. *Race: A Study in Superstition*. New York: Harper and Row, 1937; revised ed., 1965.

Chalmers, David. *Hooded Americanism*. Chicago: Quadrangle Books, 1965.

Degler, Carl. "A Century of the Klans: A Review Article." *Journal of Southern History*, Vol. 31, No. 4 (November 1965): 435-443.

Fischer, David. *Historians' Fallacies*. New York: Harper and Row, 1970.

Goodwyn, Larry. "Anarchy in St. Augustine." *Harper's*, January, 1965: 259-261.

Harding, John. "Stereotypes." *International Encyclopedia of the Social Sciences*. Vol 15. United States of America: Macmillan Co., 1968: 259-261.

Heinsohn, A.G., Jr. "St. Augustine: Rape of the Ancient City." *American Opinion*, October, 1964.

Herbers, John. "Critical Test for the Non-Violent Way." *New York Times Magazine*, July 5, 1964: 30-31.

Jackson, Kenneth. *The Ku Klux Klan in the City, 1915-1930*. New York: Oxford University Press, 1967.

Jordan, Winthrop. *White Over Black*. Baltimore: Penguin Books, 1968.

Kirby, Jack. *Darkness at the Dawning: Race and Reform in the Progressive South*. Philadelphia: Lippencott, 1972.

Klineberg, Otto. "Prejudice: The Concept" *International Encyclopedia of the Social Sciences*. Vol. 12. United States of America: Macmillan Co., 1968: 439-446.

Kohn, Hans. "Race Conflict." *Encyclopedia of the Social Sciences*. New York: Macmillan Co., 1930: 36-41.

Laquer, Walter, ed. *A Dictionary of Politics*. revised ed. New York: Macmillan Co. 1974.

Mayer, Arno. *Dynamics of Counterrevolution in Europe, 1870-1956*. New York: Harper, 1971.

McMillan, George. "The Klan Scourges Old St. Augustine." *Life*, June 26, 1964: 21.

McMillen, Neil. *The Citizens Council: Organized Resistance to the Second Reconstrucgion 1954-1964*. Urbana, Ill., 1971.

Meusel, Alfred. "Revolution and Counterrevolution," *International Encyclopedia of the Social Sciences*. United States of America: Macmillan Co., 1968.

"Acid Test." *Newsweek*, June 29, 1964: 26-27.

Robertson, Wilmot. *The Dispossessed Majority*. Cape Canaveral, Fla.: Howard Allen, 1972.

Southern Christian Leadership Conference Newsletter. June, 1964. .

Smoot, Dan. *The Hope of the World*. Dallas: Tom Newman Lithography, 1958.

Tannenbaum, Frank. "The Ku Klux Klan Its Social Origin in the South." *Century Magazine*, April, 1923: 873-882.

Vander Zanden, James. "The Klan Revival." *American Journal of Sociology*. Vol. XV, No. 5 (March, 1960): 456-462.

Vander Zanden, James. "Resistance and Social Movements." *Social Forces*. vol 37 #4 (May, 1959): 312-316.

Vann Woodward, C. *Origins of the New South 1877-1913*. Louisiana: Louisiana State Press, 1951.

Watters, Pat. "The American Middle Ground in St. Augustine." *New South*, September, 1964.

Wilhoit, Francis. *The Politics of Massive Resistance*. New York: Braziller, 1973.

Yinger, J. Milton. "Prejudice: Social Discrimination." *International Encyclopedia of the Social Sciences*. Vol. 12. United States of America: Macmillan, 1968.

DISSERTATIONS

Bartholomew, David. "An Analysis of Change in the Power System and Decision-Making Process in a Selected County." Ed.D. dissertation, University of Florida, 1971.

Fox, James. "Comparisons of Civic Beliefs of Influential Leaders, Status Leaders, Educational Personnel, and Citizens in Two Selected Florida Counties." Ed.D. dissertation, University of Florida, 1971.

Hartley, Robert. "A long hot summer: The St. Augustine disorders of 1964." M.A. thesis, Stetson University, 1972.

PUBLIC DOCUMENTS

Florida Legislature. Report of the Legislative Investigation Committee. *Racial and Civil Disorder in St. Augustine.* February, 1965, Robert Mitchell, Chairman.

Georgia Commission of Education. *Communism and the NAACP.* Atlanta, Ga. In the collection of Sheriff L.O. Davis.

U.S. Congress. House Committee on Un-American Activities. *Activities of the Ku Klux Klan Organizations in the United States. Hearings before the Committee on Un-American Activities.* 89th Cong., 1st and 2nd sess., 1965, 1966. parts I-V.

U.S. Congress. House. Committee on Un-American Activities. *The Present-Day Ku Klux Klan Movement.* Report by the Committee on Un-American Activities. 90th Cong., 1st sess., 1967.

NEWSPAPERS

Clay County (Green Cove Springs, Fla.) *Crescent.* Jan. 1963-Dec. 1964.

Flagler (Bunnell, Fla.) *Tribune.* Jan. 1963-Dec. 1964.

Florida (Gainesville) *Alligator.* As in Dr. Chalmers's file on St. Augustine.

Florida (Jacksonville) *Star.* Jan. 1963-Dec. 1964.

Florida Times-Union. Jan 1963-Dec 1964.

Gainesville Sun. As in Dr. Chalmers's file on St. Augustine.

Miami Herald. As in Dr. Chalmers's file on St. Augustine; as filed under "St. Augustine" in the Florida Vertical File, Research Library, University of Florida.

New York Times. Jan. 1963-Dec 1964.

St. Augustine Record. Jan. 1963-Dec. 1964.

St. Petersburg Times. As in Dr. Chalmers's file on St. Augustine.

Tampa Tribune. As filed under "St. Augustine" in the Florida Vertical File, Research Library, University of Florida.

INTERVIEWS AND TYPESCRIPTS

Cheney, Irvin. "St. Augustine Ku Klux Klan Meeting." Eye-witness report. (Typewritten.) Again, in the files of Dr. Chalmers.

Davis, L.O., St. Augustine. Interview, Feb. 6, 1976. The tape is filed in University of Florida Oral History Archives, Florida State Museum, Gainesville.

Manucy, Halstead "Hoss." St. Augustine. Interview, Feb. 21, 1976. The tape is filed in University of Florida Oral History Archives, Florida State Museum, Gainesville.

Stoner, Jesse B. Jacksonville. Interview, April 6, 1976. The tape is filed in the University of Florida Oral History Archives, Florida State Museum, Gainesville.

Racial and Civil Disorders in St. Augustine

REPORT OF THE
Legislative Investigation Committee

FEBRUARY, 1965

R. O. Mitchell, *Chairman*

Leon C. Jones

William E. Owens

George B. Stallings Jr.

C. W. Young

Foreword

Racial strife and civil commotion last summer cost the economy of St. Augustine, Florida an estimated five million dollar loss of business. Lost business also means lost state taxes. Which means that all citizens of Florida indirectly paid for Martin Luther King's visitation to America's oldest city. In addition there is the more intangible factor of adverse publicity. Carefully edited TV camera and newsreel shots can zero in a devastating barrage of unfavorable publicity on any community, particularly a small city heavily dependent on tourist business. Purported "news accounts" as most sophisticated Americans have learned, can be so slanted, distorted, and biased as to make black come out white, and white seem to be black.

The damage to St. Augustine cannot be undone. Some valuable lessons, however, for other Florida communities and their law enforcement officers can be salvaged from last summer's riots and disorders. The Legislative Investigation Committee therefore decided that a study-report together which such recommendations as it might develop would perform an important service to the whole state of Florida as well as other American communities, which might be faced with a similar invasion in the near future.

All public officials in St. Augustine and some thirty or more other knowledgeable individuals were interviewed over a period of several weeks. All police and arrest records were scrutinized. A number of transcripts of testimony in various cases before Federal Judge Simpson in the U. S. District Court in Jacksonville were examined. In addition books by Martin Luther King, tape recordings of some of his press interviews, and other pertinent material were consulted.

iii

Racial and Civil Disorders in St. Augustine

Most Americans who have toured Florida are familiar with the quaint and unique city of St. Augustine. America's oldest city will celebrate its 400th anniversary this summer with appropriate cultural presentations and festive celebrations. That is, if the Quadricentennial of the city's founding by the Spaniards is not marred and disrupted by a performance similar to last summer's racial strife and commotion. In 1963 some 444,000 tourists thronged through the old Spanish fort in the heart of St. Augustine. Last year there were only 322,000—a sharp drop of 27%. This decline in visitors naturally depressed those businesses catering to and largely dependent on the tourist trade. St. Augustine's economic losses by the end of 1964 were estimated at over five million dollars.

Despite massive propaganda to the contrary, Negroes and whites have lived together amicably in St. Augustine for centuries. Two hundred and fifty years ago the old Spanish city was a refuge for fugitive slaves from the Georgia plantations. There has been no residential segregation as far back as anyone can remember. White patients made up more than half of the leading colored doctor's patients, two generations ago. The leading dentist for many years was a highly respected Negro. Both the city police force and sheriff's office have had one or more Negroes on their staffs for years. The Catholic Cathedral has been bi-racial for years. All city facilities were desegrated.

Only the privately owned hotels, restaurants and motels catering to tourists reserved the right to determine whom they would serve. Their defense was that tourists from out of state would pass them by if they catered to colored customers. Negroes comprise about 23% of the old city's 20,000 population. City officials assert that there never had been any serious racial disorders or even friction between the races prior to 1962.

1

Under date of February 23, 1963, the St. Augustine Branch of the N.A.A.C.P. addressed a letter to then Vice President Lyndon Johnson (who was to speak in St. Augustine) protesting that neither the welcoming committee nor the Quadricentennial planning committee had any Negro members. The Vice President was asked to reconsider his acceptance to speak at a dedication ceremony. Copies were sent to a number of prominent people and national circulation magazines and newspapers.

180

On May 7, 1963, the *St. Augustine Record*, a daily newspaper published the text of another N.A.A.C.P. letter, this time addressed to President Kennedy. It asked the President to withhold federal funds appropriated for the 1965 Quadricentennial unless and until the city of St. Augustine met certain Negro demands. On June 18, 1963, the Tallahassee Branch of CORE (Congress of Racial Equality) sent a telegram to President Kennedy urging that he block St. Augustine's request for $350,000.00 for the Quadricentennial because this money would be used "to celebrate 400 years of slavery and segregation in America's oldest city." Needless to say, these communications did not serve to help already deteriorating racial relations.

On June 19, 1963, Dr. Robert Hayling, a Negro dentist and St. Augustine spokesman for the N.A.A.C.P. was quoted as having said:

"Passive resistance is no good in the face of violence. I and others of the N.A.A.C.P. have armed ourselves and we will shoot first and ask questions later." Appendix No. 1

Hayling later denied having made this remark but a Jacksonville newspaperman filed an affidavit attesting to its authenticity.

On June 24, 1963, the St. Augustine branch of the N.A.A.C.P. addressed a letter to City Manager Charles Barrier asking for a meeting with the city commission in order to discuss a number of issues and grievances. (see Appendix 2 and 3) A very short session was held but since the city

2

commission lacked a quorum, because several members and the mayor were out of the city, nothing was accomplished. On August 3, 1963, the Youth Council of the St. Augustine N.A.A.C.P. sent a long protest letter to Vice President Johnson setting forth a number of grievances and charging the city of St. Augustine with using "police state tactics." (see Appendix 4)

The Widening Rift

The summer of 1963 saw a number of trial runs for bigger demonstrations to follow. Stores with lunch counters serving only whites were picketed or subjected to sit-ins, mostly by juveniles and teenagers. Some were as young as ten years. Juvenile Court Judge Charles Mathis issued an order prohibiting picketing or demonstrations by anyone under seventeen years of age. When picketing and other forms of harrassment continued, those under seventeen were escorted home and their parents summoned to juvenile court.

Police and sheriff's records from June to September, 1963, show a long list of inter-racial incidents. These ranged from threatening or obscene telephone calls to white women to rock-throwing between white and colored children. Strong racial feelings began to develop. They finally reached the felony stage in August when a white woman was robbed and raped at knifepoint by an unidentified Negro.

Enter the K.K.K.

On September 1, 1963, the Ku Klux Klan held a night meeting in the open country on a side road some three miles south of St. Augustine after having been refused a permit to hold their rally in the city. Dr. Robert Hayling and three colored companions attempted to observe the proceedings but were caught by Klansmen and severely beaten. Deputy sheriffs rescued the four Negroes and arrested four Klansmen from Jacksonville. The *St. Augustine Record* reported that this was "the first open meeting of its kind in this area in recent years." Some 400 people attended this meeting and a reputed 2,500 attended a meeting the following night.

Local authorities claimed that very few of them could be identified as citizens of St. Augustine.

The First Death

On October 25, 1963, four white youths drove a car through the Negro neighborhood. One, William David Kinard, age 24, carried a loaded shotgun on his lap. The car was fired on by Negroes and Kinard died almost instantly with a bullet through his head. There had been no gunfire from the car. Several Negroes living in houses nearby were arrested and charged with manslaughter. A fifteen year old colored girl, Joyce Green, was questioned as a material witness. She was later released because of her age. She subsequently disappeared and has been missing ever since. The FBI was asked to investigate her disappearance but to date no trace of the girl has been found.

Three nights after the Kinard slaying, unidentified whites fired from automobiles at two Negro night clubs, a market, and two private homes. Tension began to increase in America's oldest city.

On November 15, 1963, U. S. District Judge, William McRae, sitting in Jacksonville dismissed a suit filed by Hayling seeking an injunction against St. Augustine city officials. The N.A.A.C.P. official sought to enjoin the city from arresting demonstrators. In a 12-page order Judge McRae ruled that the plaintiffs had not submitted sufficient evidence to warrant judicial overriding of a city ordinance requiring a police permit to parade through the streets or to hold public meetings.

Judge McRae observed:

"The court is of the opinion that the plaintiff did not come into court with clean hands. Their leadership and particularly Robert B. Hayling have displayed a lack of restraint, common sense, and good judgment, and an irresponsibility which have done a disservice to the advancement of the best interests of all the plaintiffs and others in St. Augustine who are similar situated.

Problems which might well have been solved by intelligent

action have been handled with deliberate provocation and apparent intent to incite disorder and confusion."

On December 16, 1963, the St. Johns county grand jury handed up a presentment to Circuit Court Judge Robert Winfield blaming two outside militant elements, the Ku Klux Klan and Negro civil rights workers, as responsible for the worsening racial situation and disorders in St. Augustine. The grand jury found that Ku Klux Klan did not represent the majority view of the white citizens of St. Johns County. Four days later two local N.A.A.C.P. officials, Goldie Eubanks and Dr. Robert Hayling informed the United Press International that they had resigned from the N.A.A.C.P. in the hopes that "less militant" Negro leaders would be able to make more progress in restoring interracial harmony once more in St. Augustine. It was assumed that Hayling's "resignnation" was not voluntary but a culmination of the Judge McRae decision, the grand jury's presentment and other factors leading to a decision to change leadership. It was common knowledge that a majority of the more responsible Negro leadership in St. Augustine were not too pleased with Hayling's activities.

Nine weeks later four loads of buckshot were fired from an unidentified car at 1:25 in the morning into the home of Dr. Hayling. Dr. Hayling's dog was killed and his house and furnishings suffered considerable damage.

1964 Opens Stormy and Cloudy

On March 11, 1964, Dr. Hayling sent a form letter to the Massachusetts chapter of the Southern Christian Leadership Conference. See Appendix No. 5 (This organization will be discussed elsewhere in this report under Martin Luther King.) In this letter college students "from all over the nation" who normally headed for Florida's sunny beaches during their spring vacation were invited to St. Augustine to join a "struggle for human rights" in that city. Similar to the Mississippi "Summer Project" this effort was entitled "Florida Spring Project, SCM-SCLC." The initials stood for the two sponsoring organizations: Student Christian Movement and Southern Christian Leadership Conference.

Appended to the appeal was a short statement of just what the "Florida Spring Project" hoped to accomplish, an application form, and a set of guidance instructions on what to wear, what to bring, anticipated expenses, and instructions how to conduct oneself after arriving in St. Augustine. The letter frankly admitted that a "tense situation" existed in St. Augustine and that "our coming will increase this." *"General Qualifications"* then continued:

184

"Many have sought to dissuade us with predictions of violence. No one denies this possibility. *The advocate of non-violence does not deny violence.* The existing conditions of injustice results in great violence to the lives of people there. Non-violence direct action is a means of speaking and acting in the midst of a violent world, in a way that seeks to convert the world. Anyone who is not committed to non-violence should not go to St. Augustine. Workshops will be held for all participants when they arrive. In St. Augustine each participant must be prepared to follow the authority of the designated leader. Each participant must be willing to go to jail." (Appendix 5) (Emphasis ours)

City officials maintain that this statement was full of false charges and Mayor Joseph Shelley on March 22, 1964, issued the city's reply. (see Appendix 6)

The "Florida Spring Project"

On March 12, 1964, Mayor Shelley received a long distance telephone call from a St. Augustine student at a New England college warning that a mass invasion of civil rights demonstrators was being mobilized in the New England area. About the same time a Boston radio commentator advises Mayor Shelley by phone that Mrs. Malcolm Peabody, mother of the governor of Massachusetts, was coming to St. Augustine and asked the mayor what he would do if she violated any local laws? Mayor Shelley replied that he would do nothing as long as Mrs. Peabody broke no laws. If she did, the police would have no choice but to arrest her just like any other lawbreaker.

6

This simple and matter of fact statement was promptly distorted in the headlines to read that Mayor Shelley had threatened to arrest the mother of the Governor of Massachusetts. *That same day* between 150 and 175 reporters, photographers, and TV cameramen began arriving in St. Augustine from all over the United States. Local authorities naturally surmised that "something big" was about to break to justify such a massive invasion of news-gathering services.

The first contingent of the New England demonstrators, some thirty strong, arrived by bus and plane on March 23, 1964. Several appeared to be university faculty members and chaplains. They told newsmen that they would stage sit-ins at segregated restaurants, picketing, and pray-ins at local churches which barred Negroes. During the next few days a steady stream of white "civil rights workers" continued to arrive in St. Augustine. On March 28, 1964, 26 of these Negro and white demonstrators, led by a Yale University chaplain, were arrested after being warned against trespassing and conspiring to commit a misdemeanor.

Easter Sunday and Mrs. Peabody

St. Augustine's traditional Easter Sunday parade was held without incident. The local negro high school band was applauded by some 20,000 spectators. Mrs. Malcolm Peabody arrived late that afternoon. City officials claim that she made no effort to contact them or make known the purpose of her visit. A communion service set for 10 A.M. March 31, 1964, at the Trinity Episcopal Church was hastily cancelled when it was learned that Mrs. Peabody, the wife of a Bishop, might try to integrate the service with some 75 colored students from Murray High School who were marching into the city. Mrs. Peabody entered the church about 9:45 A.M. and held a brief discussion with the vestrymen. She denied any intention to demonstrate inside the church. She said she merely wanted to "integrate" it. Bishop Hamilton West of Jacksonville had appealed to Bishop Malcolm Peabody in Boston to persuade his wife not to disrupt the communion service.

Mrs. Peabody was arrested the following day charged with trespass and conspiracy to commit a misdemeanor when she participated in a sit-in demonstration in the Ponce de Leon Hotel. She refused to make bail and elected to remain in jail. After spending two days in jail Mrs. Peabody posted $450 bond and departed by plane from Jacksonville. The arrest and jailing of the wife of a Bishop and mother of a governor naturally received tremendous nationwide newspaper, radio and TV attention. Interviewed in jail Mrs. Peabody said, "I am afraid it is pretty much of a lark. Everyone is so nice. My cell is quite comfortable and clean with running water and showers." She readily conceded that she had intentionally broken a state law and had fully expected to be arrested.

186

The tactic of inducing socially prominent and elderly ladies to act as "catspaws" in order to win sympathy and wide publicity has long been a Communist and radical technique. When the Communists some years ago anticipated that their daily newspaper, *THE WORKER*, might be seized or involved in litigation, ownership papers were quickly drawn up listing three ladies of advanced age and social position as sole owners. One was a lineal descendant of a Revolutionary War hero and member of an old Philadelphia family. See Appendix 7

With the departure of Mrs. Peabody some 128 white and Negro demonstrators arrested during the hectic Easter Week disorders, posted bonds and were released. Mayor Shelley issued a public statement deploring the fact that the mother of a governor of another state had journeyed more than a thousand miles to Florida for the self-admitted purpose of flouting the law. The mayor also charged that some of the news media were deliberately misquoting him and distorting the true picture of just what was happening in the oldest city.

The St. Augustine City Commission considered one national network program so biased and distorted in relating what happened in St. Augustine that they requested the network to give Mayor Shelley equal time in order to present a true and factual picture of developments in America's oldest city.

City Manager Barrier later charged that "It was very evident that Martin Luther King and the newsmen were working together in demonstrations. Newsmen were notified of when, what, and where everything was to happen." (see Appendix 8)

By the 5th of April, 1964, the whole civil disobedience campaign was at a low ebb. Hosea Williams, one of King's chief lieutenants, was able to muster only ten volunteers from an audience of 200 for a sit-down and possible arrest. Nearly all the northern demonstrators had departed and local St. Augustine negroes, excepting juveniles, apparently did not care to support the "negro revolution." Williams warned: "If segregation barriers remain up in St. Augustine it will be because the people here did not support the movement." A week later five Negroes attended services at Trinity Episcopal Church without incident. North Florida Diocese Bishop West had ordered all diocesan churches to admit anyone without regard to race or color.

King Threatens a "Long, Hot Summer"

On May 18, 1964, Martin Luther King arrived in St. Augustine. He left the next day promising that he would soon return with his "Non-violent Army." In a press statement he charged that St. Augustine "was a small Birmingham." Two of King's assistants, Andrew Young and Harry Boyte, arrived in St. Augustine on May 25, 1964. They conferred with Mayor Shelley at some length but made no specific demands or requests. Asked why St. Augustine had been selected by King for a visitation by his "Non-violent Army" they frankly admitted that as America's oldest city, St. Augustine was symbolic and "we feel that we can get better publicity out of St. Augustine." (see also first two paragraphs of statement by the General Manager of the *St. Augustine Record* in Appendix 9.)

King returned on May 26, 1964, and the following day announced that his "Non-violent Army" was being mobilized and would soon be in St. Augustine. He promised the ancient city "A long, hot summer" but piously added that he hoped it

187

would be a "long hot non-violent summer." King's "Non-violent Army" began arriving on May 28, 1964. See Appendix No. 10. Some 300 of King's demonstrators marched on the "Old Slave Market," and a large group of young whites gathered, armed with clubs and tire irons arrived on the scene. City police, with trained dogs, county deputy sheriffs, and Florida Highway patrolmen prevented contact between the two hostile groups.

The cameramen suddenly turned on blinding floodlights while at the same time training their lens on the crowds. These lights in turn excited the police dogs who leaped and barked. Angered at having cameras trained on them, some of the young toughs attacked the cameramen, injuring one of them. There also were reports that some cameramen had complained of the high cost of keeping their expensive TV equipment in St. Augustine for days without too much "action," and that they had incited both sides to "get things going." (The Committee's observations on this development may be found in the Summary-Conclusion of this report.)

Coincident with the Mayor's appeal to all parents, colored and white, to keep their children away from the downtown area at night, Chief of Police Virgil Stuart instructed Negro demonstrators to stay away from center of the city after dark. Stuart also called upon all white people to stay away from the downtown area after dusk. Chief Stuart believes that some Black Muslims had come to St. Augustine from Jacksonville to stir things up. He also stated that most of the white men engaged in violence were not local people and that some were known Klansmen from nearby cities. *King was in California when the violence broke out.* He wired President Johnson asking for Federal protection for his "non-violent" demonstrators.

Flood the Jails

On May 30, 1964, a new tactic was unveiled by King's demonstrators. Nearly 200 defied a police order and began another march on the center of the city. Fifteen were arrested but refused to post bond, electing to remain in jail ten to twelve days in lieu of fines. During the following days a number of demonstrators courted arrest and accepted jail sentences rather than pay small fines. "Flooding the jails and clogging the courts" was a technique devised to attract the greatest publicity to a civil disobedience show that had started to taper off and to collapse.

On June 1, 1964, the City Commission adopted an emergency measure prohibiting minors under 18 to be on the streets or in public places between the hours of 9 P.M. and 5 A.M. Parking also was banned on some 42 downtown streets during the same hours. This was done to prevent large crowds from gathering in and around the main square downtown where all the rioting and disorders tended to ignite. It worked a hardship on the business firms and a movie house located in the area. King's lawyers immediately petitioned the Federal Court in Jacksonville for a restraining order against St. Augustine's city and county officials. The City Commission repealed the two emergency orders five days later.

Federal Court Enters the Picture

All demonstrations were suspended for several days while District Court Judge Bryan Simpson held extensive hearings on the injunction petition. The Court sought to determine if Sheriff L. O. Davis was a member of the K.K.K. Davis denied under oath that he was. The Judge also questioned Davis as to whether or not any of his deputies were or had been Klansmen.

King returned to St. Augustine and denounced that city as "the most lawless he had ever visited." He states that President Johnson was closely watching developments in St. Augustine.

On June 9, 1964, Federal Judge Simpson ordered the city officials of St. Augustine to permit demonstrations "anyhow in the nighttime" and not to restrict or restrain such marches under pain of contempt. (There had never been any ban on daytime marches.) Night marches were resumed within a matter of hours. Meanwhile Martin Luther King had returned to St. Augustine threatening "massive demonstrations" unless all integration demands were promptly met. It

189

11

was reported that he had boasted that he would bring the city of St. Augustine to its knees within ten days. Racial feelings naturally tended to harden still further.

On June 10, 1964, Governor Bryant announced at Tallahassee that he would not hesitate to use every power at his command to preserve law and order in the ancient city. At a news conference in St. Augustine King announced that he would go to the well kown Monson Motor Lodge (one of the largest in the city) the next day and commit an "act of civil disobedience." Busloads of King's "Non-violent Army" continued to roll into St. Augustine from the eastern seaboard.

190

The Motel Pool Incident

"Testing" the Monson Motor Lodge, on June 11, 1964, King and two of his associates, Ralph Abernathy and Robert England, were arrested for trespassing on private property and conspiring to commit a misdemeanor. King's attempt to integrate the motor lodge made a fine TV and newsreel show for millions of viewers but it was overshadowed by what may have been intended to be a mere sideshow.

Two white northern integrationists, who had secured accommodations at the motor lodge, jumped into the swimming pool. They were immediately followed by several negro men and women. The whole group congregated in the middle of the pool where police officers could not reach them. The white integrationists insisted that the Negroes were their "guests" and hence not guilty of trespassing. An off duty city patrolman finally jumped into the pool and the whole group was dragged out and arrested.

The manager of the motel, apparently under great stress and excitement, poured a bottle of muriatic acid into the pool hoping to scare the demonstrators into leaving. Muriatic acid is commonly added to swimming pools as a disinfectant, a fact well known to one of the white demonstrators. He calmed the apprehension of the negroes by offering to drink some of the water to prove it was harmless. The TV and news cameras picked up the whole bizarre scene for millions of viewers all over the United States. These pictures were flashed to Europe and the rest of the world affording unlimited propaganda opporunity for anti-American elements to offer as another "typical example of American barbarism and racism."

For his own protection and safety, King was removed from the St. Johns County Jail to the Duval County Jail in Jacksonville. Tension was mounting in St. Augustine and some TV cameramen and reporters hired bodyguards to protect them against possible attacks. Busloads of negro and white demonstrators continued to arrive in the ancient city. *The N. Y. Times,* reporting from the scene, admitted that "Dr. King has appealed for outside help to fill up the jails and to put more people in the streets." *The news account added that most St. Augustine Negroes "are not taking part in the movement."* By this time Governor Bryant had ordered some 145 State highway patrolmen and armed Conservation and Beverage Control officers to St. Augustine. In addition Tallahassee had dispatched several investigators and assistant states' attorneys to the city as observers. See Appendix 11

191

New incendiary elements had now been added to an already highly volatile situation. Conrad Lynch and an Atlanta lawyer, J. B. Stoner, arrived on the scene. Both represented the National States Rights Party, which has already been made the subject of a separate report by this committee. Stoner and Lynch held forth at nightly meetings in the main Plaza, which had erroneously been dubbed the "Old Slave Market" many years ago presumably for tourist publicity purposes. Trained rabble-rousers, Lynch and Stoner, while ostensibly defending the Constitution and Christianity, managed to work on the latent racial prejudices held by some of their listeners.

One of St. Augustine's leading physicians, Dr. Hardgrove Norris, writing in a small publication entitled *FOCUS* under date of July 7-14, 1964, had this to say:

"A lawyer, J. B. Stoner, from Atlanta, Ga., and a California preacher, Connie Lynch, materialized to harangue the restless crowd. These men are well schooled in agitational techniques; and, although theoretically well educated,

13

speak in the rhetoric of the mass. They merchandize a doctrine of hate only. Their sole objective seemed designed to divide the community into quarreling factions and to agitate the more volatile elements of the Whites to overt aggression against the Blacks. They proved to be one of the most helpful factors in Martin Luther King's invasion. Without their appearance it is quite probable that Martin Luther King would have met total failure—even with the other pressures that were brought to bear. This must be noted. In analyzing the situation as it occurred in St. Augustine King's appearances and Stoner's appearances were always perfectly co-ordinated. Whenever King was in town, Stoner was almost certainly to be. Martin Luther King divided the negroes and whites; Lynch and Stoner successfully divided the whites. These two, by operating under an organization with the high sounding name, National States Rights Party, sought to gain an aura of respectability. The literature of this party can serve but one purpose: fragmentation of the community and discreditation of worthwhile patriotic organizations."

On June 12, 1964, an entirely new development occurred. Whites organized a counter-demonstration, marching into the predominately colored section of Lincolnville only a few blocks from the center of the city. Police requests that they refrain from further inflaming an already dangerous situation were answered with quotations from Federal Judge Simpson's order enjoining the city officials of St. Augustine from interfering in any way or at any time with Martin Luther King's "civil rights" marchers. In effect, "What's sauce for the goose, is sauce for the gander."

These counter-demonstrations were heavily guarded on all sides by almost as many law enforcement officers as there were marchers. Negro leaders were able to control the colored community so that there was no violence or provocation to violence. A large sign at a street corner read: "WELCOME! PEACE AND BROTHERHOOD TO YOU." Several hundred Negroes either carried signs reading "We Love Everybody" or chanted the words. Martin Luther King was released from jail under bond and hurried to Yale University to pick up an honorary degree.

192

14

By June 14, 1964, the demonstrations and counter-demonstrations had simmered down. Andrew Young, a King lieutenant, told newsmen that nighttime marches would be resumed as soon as new forces were mustered and *brought from other states*. He had previously been quoted as saying that if the townspeople would not come down to watch the demonstrations "then we'll take it to them." Judge Simpson's order gave the Negro demonstrators the right to parade at will through any part of the town. The marches now rambled through the private residential sections of the old city shouting and singing until 11 P.M. This aroused a number of citizens to sign a petition to Judge Simpson praying for relief from these noisy demonstrations. (See Appendix 12)

193

Apprised of this situation Governor Bryant on June 15, 1964, invoked the emergency powers of Sections .021 and .022, Chapter 14, of the Florida Statutes. Five days later, Governor Bryant signed Executive Order No. Two banning all demonstrations and marches between the hours of 8:30 P.M. and sunrise. The Governor also found that the law enforcement detail at St. Augustine had been strengthened to its maximum and that additional officers "would not in any way alleviate the circumstances creating the danger to peace and order." (See Appendix 13)

Law enforcement officers in St. Augustine were positive that they could control demonstrations and protect both demonstrators and peaceful citizens if the marches were confined to daylight hours. The reason for this insistence on daylight hours was the peculiar nature of many of St. Augustine's downtown streets. Laid out by the Spaniards 300 years ago many streets are extremely narrow and bordered by low stone walls or hedges. There are numerous alleyways and narrow passages between buildings. Reconstruction of old Spanish and British buildings had left piles of rubble, bricks, and other material ideally suited for missiles, ready at hand. Lighting in some of the narrower streets was poor.

In short, young toughs able to leap low walls and hedges and dodge down dark passageways had little difficulty in evading the police after throwing brickbats at demonstrators. In the daytime most of them would be in school or working.

15

Daytime demonstrations would also limit participation mainly to local people and such professionals from other states already ensconced in the old city. Judge Simpson's order on the other hand gave trouble-makers on both sides ample time to drive to St. Augustine after work from a radius of 100 miles or more.

Daily arrests for violating Florida statutes ran from 18 or 20 to as high as ninety in a single day. *Many were juveniles as young as fourteen years who gave their home addresses as being a thousand or more* miles form St. Augustine. Individuals arrested came from as far away as Maine, Seattle, and San Diego. Local law enforcement officers were impressed by King's remarkable ability in mobilizing his "Non-violent Army" from the far corners of the United States.

194

After four days of hearings, the grand jury returned a presentment on June 18, 1964, calling on King and all others to demonstrate good faith by declaring a 30 day moratorium on all sit-ins, wade-ins, demonstrations and counter-demonstrations. For over two hours, it heard over 25 witnesses including King.

At the expiration of this thirty day cooling off period the grand jury would reconvene and name a ten-man bi-racial committee to work with the grand jury in trying to solve local problems and restoring racial harmony as it had existed in the past. It blamed "sensational news reporting" as having libelled St. Augustine as being "the most segregated city in America. This is not true." The grand jury, *of which two members were colored* then reported:

"Unlike many cities, Negroes have not been excluded from jury duty. They have served on juries, both petty and grand, for many years, including this Grand Jury. Unlike many cities, no voter test is required nor has one ever been required to the knowledge of this Grand Jury. In fact, by looking at the registration card itself, no classification is made as to race, color or creed. Unlike many cities, Negro homes are now and always have been interspersed throughout the mainland portion of the City, and, the inhabitants have lived in harmony. The 13 internationally known tourist attractions are integrated. In law enforcement, Negroes have served in the past, and are serving now in this capacity. The City has desegregated all municipal owned facilities. The county school system is integrated, and was integrated without incident. At the present time, two, and perhaps, more of the modern, luxurious motels have integrated. Two downtown lunchrooms have integrated. The City has revised its Code to eliminate racial restrictions against the hiring of Negroes in civil service positions." See Appendix 14

195

King refused the grand jury's suggestion that he remove himself from St. Augustine for thirty days and countered with a demand that the grand jury appoint a bi-racial committee immediately. (See Appendix 15.) The grand jury replied by issuing a statement charging that King had rejected the jury's good faith attempt to find a solution to the current disorders and racial strife, adding:

"Further, he has apparently made efforts to embarrass this Grand Jury by staging demonstrations within earshot of the St. Johns County Courthouse, where our deliberations were conducted. At almost the very hour we were to issue our presentment, Dr. King fostered a demonstration which could only have been planned to divert the attention of the public away from our good faith effort to reach accord in these matters. On the day when it appears a sweeping civil rights bill will pass the U.S. Senate, Dr. Martin Luther King stands accused of bad faith and insincerity. It would appear he has no desire to actually achieve the goals he publicly espouses. Dr. King apparently chooses to ignore the fact that in such things as labor troubles there are provisions available to the President of the United States to call for a ninety day cooling off period. In a good faith effort to be fair, we seek a thirty day period. The plan devised by this Grand Jury could, if properly implemented, provide a guide to the peaceful implementation of the civil rights bill, not only in St. Johns County, but in the State of Florida as a whole. This Grand Jury will not be intimidated. We will not negotiate. We will not alter our Presentment."

17

Final Conciliation Effort Fails

The grand jury presentment reflected a marked change in attitude on the part of many St. Augustinians. A representative group of businessmen had met and agreed to abide by all present and future laws, including the pending Civil Rights Act of 1964. The late marches by several hundred singing and shouting Negroes through residential areas merely served to harden feelings and to reduce the influence of so-called "moderates" trying earnestly to find some mutually acceptable solution to the racial problem. King's summary rejection of the grand jury's suggestion for a thirty day "cooling off" period merely strenghtened the position of the more obdurate defenders of the status quo. State Senator Verle Pope, a citizen of St. Augustine, presumably summed up the position of most white residents and businessmen of the city when he said: "The people of St. Augustine will never yield to stipulations set forth by outside groups."

With this hardening of feelings and rising tension in the strifetorn community an already bad situation was still further bedevilled by another unfortunate development. A widening rift was developing between the local law enforcement officers and the special task force of state highway patrolmen, conservation, and beverage control officers. Under the governor's order this special detachment had superseded and in effect assumed supreme law enforcement control for St. Johns County and the city of St. Augustine.

At a conference with nine of the city's doctors, Major Simmons, then in charge of the state's special task force, was quoted as having stated that his orders were limited to protecting the Negro demonstrators against violence. One of the state highway patrolmen, not identified, was alleged to have said: "We have the power to do anything we want. We do not need a warrant—complete law enforcement is in our hands." Whether authorized and correct or merely an offhand remark, the repetition of such a statement under the flash-point tension then prevailing in St. Augustine could have nothing but unfortunate effect.

The state troopers had cordoned off a number of streets in the heart of the city. Cars were searched indiscrimately and all objects which could possibly be used as weapons or missiles were removed and confiscated. Even a child's popgun apparently fell under the category of "dangerous weapons." A respected and well-known local physician, Dr. Raymond Cafaro, returning from a house call, was searched in front of a crowd even though he had identified himself. The doctor was forced to leave his car in the middle of the street and taken to jail. When some respectable citizens objected to the trooper's arbitrary action, they were told to shut-up or they, too, would be arrested.

The wife of another doctor, Mrs. Gladys N. La Rosa delivering some medicine to a friend, was similarly stopped for "Failure to obey a lawful command." She had mistaken a waving flashlight as a signal to proceed with caution. Mrs. La Rosa was arrested and removed to jail, the first jail experience in her life, and her husband had to effect her release by posting a $25.00 bond. See Appendix 16.

197

A St. Augustine policeman, Chessley G. Smith, with the police force for seventeen years, was arrested by a State Highway patrolman and charged with carrying a concealed weapon. Smith was carrying a ten inch length of pipe. A store manager had found it on his premises, and the officer was taking it to the local police headquarters for possible fingerprints. Without bothering to establish Smith's identity (he was in plain clothes) the highway patrolman and a Conservation officer whisked Smith off to jail. (See Appendix 17)

These and other incidents moved the *St. Augustine Record* of June 18, 1964, to publish a front page editorial criticizing the state's special task force in St. Augustine. It states that while St. Augustine was grateful for their presence, there "was an increasing feeling among citizens here that the rights of white citizens are being abridged to give Negroes unlimited freedom of movement." (See Appendix 18)

It is almost inevitable that untrained officers hastily pressed into riot control duty are bound to make some errors under conditions of super-charged tension and excitement. To the local townspeople accustomed to years of tranquillity and peace, such galling personal indignities could easily assume major if not sinister proportions.

Maneuvering law enforcement officers into situations which involve them in friction and antagonism with the majority of the population, is, needless to say, always a hoped for dividend by the planners of alleged "non-violent" civil disobedience demonstrations. "Police brutality" seldom means much to the average citizen until he or his family feel the bite of a policeman's club.

It should be noted that the consensus of opinion by most of those interviewed is that the overwhelming majority of the older and more responsible Negro citizens not only stayed at home but gave little indication that they supported the wild goings-on whipped up by non-residents.

198

The Battle of the Beaches

The battle now shifted to the world famed St. Augustine beaches, several miles east of the city proper. Here again violent clashes between negroes seeking to integrate the beaches and whites opposing them supplied "made to order" footage for the TV and news camera. *The fact that cameramen always arrived on the scene well ahead of the "non-violent" demonstrators more or less gave away the whole show as a planned and stage-managed propaganda production for nationwide consumption.* At one point, when they found their way into the surf barred by segretationists, the demonstrators kneeled on the wet beach to conduct prayers. State officers were vigorous in using their clubs on the heads of the white counter-demonstrators. Several were severely beaten on the head and required hospital attention.

The State Highway Patrol now has a training film on riot control composed of motion pictures taken during some of the worst of the St. Augustine riots. The commentary that accompanies this film is Appendix 19.

What the newspaper columnists, radio commentators and TV cameras did not reveal was that very few Negroes ever used their own beach, the Frank Butler State Park. This beautiful sandy Atlantic beach is over a mile long and adjoins the other ocean beaches and is therefore identical in attraction and desirability. This beach is named for a re-

20

spected and prominent St. Augustine Negro, Mr. Frank Butler, who has been in the real estate business for many years. While these "stage managed" wade-ins continued for several more days, making good TV shows, the scene shifted to the dignity and decorum of a Federal court in Jacksonville.

Governor Bryant Enjoined By Federal Court

Two days after Governor Bryant had signed his Executive Order No. Two. Federal Judge Bryan Simpson, sitting in Jacksonville ordered Governor Bryant, Attorney General James Kynes, Major Jourdan of the State Highway Patrol, Mayor Joseph Shelley, Chief of Police Virgil Stuart and Sheriff L. O. Davis to appear before him on June 26, 1964, to show cause why they should not obey, conform to and abide by the court's preliminary injunction of June 9, 1964, and a later order of June 15, 1964, or, in the alternative why they should not be held in contempt, etc. (See Appendix 20.) This order was signed on June 22, 1964, and the same day that lawyers for Andrew Young of the Southern Christian Leadership Conference had filed their petition!

199

Two days later on June 24, 1964 Governor Bryant stated that he would stand on his constitutional rights as the governor of a sovereign state and that he would ignore Judge Simpson's order. The Attorney General was delegated to represent the governor. Instead of appearing in Judge Simpson's court, the governor made a hurried trip to St. Augustine on June 26, 1964, to confer with such state and local officials that were in the city. Most of them were in Judge Simpson's court in Jacksonville for long-drawn out hearings on various petitions filed by a battery of civil rights lawyers brought in from as far away as New York and Chicago.

The previous night had been one of the most violent and potentially dangerous thus far. The Governor, on returning to the Capitol, said that he had found St. Augustine facing a "very explosive and very tense situation." He ordered 80 more highway patrolmen and other state officers to the ancient city bringing the total there to 235.

Lynch and Stoner had again harangued about 500 white segregationists already angered by the severe clubbing suffered by one of their number at the beach. When another demonstration appeared, the inflamed whites broke through the heavy police guard and scattered the Negro demonstrators. Fifteen persons were arrested. Thirty, mostly colored, had to be given emergency first aid treatment at the Flagler Memorial Hospital. Some were merely hysterial and required only sedation. Although Martin Luther King was in town at the time he did not take part in the demonstration. In fact, there is no record that he ever actually participated in any of the marches on the central Plaza. While he exhorted his colored listeners to be prepared to suffer and "if we must, offer our bodies as sacrifices" there is no record that he *himself ever "offered his body" or did any suffering.* Instead, he appears to have been on the phone trying to get the White House to send in federal marshals.

On July 1, 1964, Governor Bryant announced that he had appointed a four man bi-racial committee of St. Augustine citizens to try to restore communication between that community's white and colored citizens. The committee was to serve only until the St. Johns county grand jury was able to appoint a permanent committee as it had suggested in its June 18, 1964, presentment. The governor declined to identify the members of his bi-racial committee in order to spare them embarrassment. There is no record that it ever met or that the identities of the committee members were ever made known to anyone.

Immediately, Martin Luther King called a hurried press conference to announce a 12 to 15 day "truce" on all demonstrations. The Associated Press had previously quoted him as saying that "The purpose of our direct action was to create a crisis." President Johnson signed the Civil Rights bill the following day radically altering the whole legal situation as far as the St. Augustine "crisis" was concerned. St. Augustine businessmen met and told a press conference that while they had strong personal objections to the new law they would comply with the public accomodations section of the statute.

22

Peace and quiet prevailed in the old city for a few days but on July 4, 1964, some 200 robed Klansmen arrived to stage a provocative parade. The racial truce was further marred by a gang of white toughs attacking six Negroes fishing from a bridge. The police later arrested nine of them and charged them with assault and battery. Mayor Shelly issued another appeal to all citizens urging restraint and respect for the new law. Out of town and local Negroes began "testing" some 29 motels and restaurants to ascertain whether or not the public accommodations section of the new Civil Rights Law was being observed.

201

Those public eating places and motels which complied now found themselves picketed by white segregationists seeking to discourage patrons from entering because they served negroes. Several St. Augustine businessmen were summoned before Judge Simpson under the new Civil Rights Act or appeared as witnesses. They testified that they were "caught in the middle" and feared mob violence if they complied with the new law and served negroes. Two flaming "Molotov cocktails" were hurled through the front window of a leading complaint motel at an early hour in the morning. Damage was set at $3,000. Connie Lynch and J. B. Stoner returned to the ancient city and with three others were arrested for burning a K.K.K. cross on private property with the owner's consent.

By this time an interminable series of injunctions and orders issued by Federal Judge Simpson had established de facto control by the Federal court over the public order administration of St. Augustine. Duly elected city and county officials found their Constitutional powers and duties preempted by a stream of hastily issued court orders. A tireless corps of Southern Christian Leadership Conference lawyers, many from New York City, ground out a torrent of petitions, appeals, and suits against state, county, and city officials of Florida. Many were of such a frivolous and flimsy character that legal harrassment and not justice seemed to be their real motivation.

With the beginning of school in September most of the northern demonstrators and agitators had departed. The battle of the streets was transferred to the more sedate atmosphere of the courtroom. On November 19, 1964, the Attorney General filed a motion to dismiss Judge Simpson's injunction against Governor Bryant. A dismissal order was signed six days later conceding that all issues in the St. Augustine case were now resolved. St. Augustine returned to the peaceful and quiet life its citizens had enjoyed until it was selected as a pilot project for a new form of political warfare, so called —"non-violent direct action." Martin Luther King's "peaceful" and "non-violent" visitation had cost the city an estimated five million dollar in lost tourist trade. Negroes naturally shared in this loss as employees of those businesses catering to tourists.

202

It will probably require years to restore the amicable relations once existing between the two races in America's oldest city. In the wake of economic catastrophe, riots, violence, physical injury, property damage and much human suffering, Dr. Martin Luther King, Nobel Peace prize winner and his "Non-violent Army" departed for other pastures. The Negro community of St. Augustine is divided and bewildered. No effective voice speaking for the whole colored community remained since the Ministerial Alliance of many years standing broke up over whether or not to support the King enterprise. Unfortunately there is no civic or business association of colored St. Augustinians, leaving the field wide open for any small special interest group with little local support, to move in and claim to speak for the entire Negro community.

In November the N.A.A.C.P. held its state convention in Tallahassee. Roy Wilkins, from New York, executive secretary of the organization, expressed the hope that "the new governor of Florida and others concerned with the image of the state will get together and reason with St. Augustine." He said that the nation's oldest city "has the oldest ideas on race relations in the United States and that the "economic screws should be tightened on St. Augustine." (UPI Nov. 16, 1964.)

St. Augustine in Federal Court

All city and county officials of St. Augustine and St. Johns County who were interviewed were unanimous in their opinion that the state of Florida could have handled the St. Augustine situation decisively but for the intrusion of Federal Judge Bryan Simpson of Jacksonville. While the city of St. Augustine is still bitter over the distorted and biased picture which some of the news media and particularly the TV camera crews broadcast over the United States, their deepest resentment is directed at Judge Simpson. There is no doubt that some bizarre and extraordinary rulings, interrogatories, observations, orders, and open coaching of S. C. L. C. lawyers occurred in this court.

A Federal Judge Assumes Jurisdiction

Lawyers appeared as attorneys of record for scores of defendants or plaintiffs whose names they did not even know. Municipal and county officials, already worn out by weeks of violence and disorder, now were forced to spend a great deal of their time in Judge Simpson's court or travelling back and forth in connection with frivolous and trivial cases which properly belonged in a court of the justice of the peace. Cases involving civil rights demonstrators, regardless of how petty or trivial, were arbitrarily ordered out of St. Augustine by Judge Simpson to his own jurisdiction.

Without bothering to go to trial, the S.C.L.C. lawyers alleged that their clients could not receive a fair trial in any court in St. Johns County. Judge Charles Mathis, County Judge of St. Johns County, charged that over 490 cases had been removed from his jurisdiction and transferred to the Federal court in Jacksonville. See Appendix No. 21&22. Normal filing charges of $25 were waived so that such transfers cost Martin Luther King's lawyers nothing. Petitions for orders filed for the S.C.L.C. by Tobias Simon, a Miami lawyer, by mail or phone from Miami were acted on by Judge Simpson with alacrity. Lawyers appearing for city and county officials or white plaintiffs or defendants felt they received scant courtesy from Judge Simpson.

Judge Simpson, for example, ordered Sheriff L. O. Davis to bring to court a complete list of all his deputies including special and honorary deputies. Davis was grilled for hours over this list. Simpson ordered deputy sheriff Charles Lance to "resign his commission, or turn in his badge, or whatever it takes to get off the sheriff's department." This moved Senator Strom Thurmond of South Carolina to comment in Washington:

204

> "When a federal judge can order a deputy sheriff, a local law enforcement officer, to surrender his star, we certainly have reached the point approaching judicial tyranny."

Judge Simpson frankly admitted he had no legal authority for his action but did so because he considered this a "special case."

On another occasion after listening to charges that Negro demonstrators had seen "armed men" in the Plaza as they marched past, Judge Simpson observed:

> "I accept the testimony of the marchers on this point and reject that of the police. The police testimony is negative. —They saw no weapons! The police had made no close inspection to see if the whites were armed." (The Negroes had testified that the Plaza was dark yet they saw "armed" men.)

> "It is my finding that the group on Wednesday, as well as on the following night, Thursday, May 28, was composed of armed thugs and hoodlums predominantly youthful but with a sprinkling of older leaders." (Transcript Young vs. David 64-133J)

Judge Simpson was also deeply interested in the Ancient City Hunting Club operated by Halstead "Hoss" Manucy. There was no evidence before the court that this club had any connection with the K.K.K. but Judge Simpson, indicated his belief that the K.K.K., the Ancient City Hunting Club, and Citizens Band Radio "were one and the same thing."

> "Well, you know what everybody knows and what the newspaper prints everyday for weeks, there comes a time

26

when, as insulated and as cottonwrapped as Courts are, that Courts almost get to know it. I mean, there comes a point when general knowledge may be equated with judicial knowledge, or the other way around, and I think there's no real secret involved as to the source of what have been called the anti-demonstrations or counter-demonstrations, whether you call them the Klan, the Ancient City Hunting Club, the Citizens Band Radio, or Manucy's Raiders, or whatever name you give them."

The Citizens Band Radio is a radio frequency of 27 megacycles granted by the Federal Communications Commission all over the United States for short wave radio communication use in cars and mobile vehicles generally. Business houses use the C. B. Radio to communicate with delivery trucks. It is estimated that there are at least 250,000 Citizens Band Radio licenses in the United States.

Lawyers and lower court judges are traditionally reluctant to criticize, at least publicly, higher courts for understandable ethical and practical reasons. Nevertheless Judge Charles Mathis felt constrained to make the following comment on Judge Simpson's judicial conduct:

"The faith and confidence of the lawyers, laymen, and law enforcement officers in the Federal judiciary system, has been shaken, if not destroyed, by the action of the Federal District Court in Jacksonville in cases entertained and considered as civil rights cases. The citizens of St. Johns county now see this court as a threat to their freedom rather than as a guardian of their rights."

Justice of the Peace, G. Marvin Grier, was even more direct and blunt. He commented:

"I do not believe that recent decisions of Judge Simpson are in keeping with the best traditions and ethics of American jurisprudence."

On September 27, 1964, the *St. Augustine Record*, the daily newspaper in St. Augustine, devoted four columns of its front page to a general summary of Federal Judge Simpson's rulings during the preceding "long hot summer" in St. Augustine. (See Appendix 23.)

Chronology of Significant Racial Incidents

In St. Augustine, Florida, 1962-64

1962

206 April 6 — Negro residents of St. Johns county and St. Augustine file suit in Federal court to force racial integration in the public school system.

The Widening Rift

1963

Feb. 23 — The St. Augustine branch of the National Association for the Advancement of Colored People addressed a letter to Vice President Lyndon B. Johnson, requesting that he cancel an appearance as principal speaker on March 11, 1963, at a local dedication ceremony. The letter charged that not a single Negro was on the welcoming committee, and that the city government practiced segregation.

May 7 — *The St. Augustine Record* published the text of a letter sent by the St. Augustine Branch of the N. A. A. C. P. to President John F. Kennedy, asking him to block the granting of any Federal funds for the 1965 Quadricentennial celebration of the founding of St. Augustine unless certain demands by the Negro community were granted by the city government.

May 10 — A number of Negroes made application to transfer their children to previously all white schools.

June 3   Dr. Joseph A. Shelley, an M.D., elected mayor.

June 16   City Commission of St. Augustine held a special meeting with Negro leaders to discuss "mounting racial problems."

June 18   Tallahassee Branch of the Congress of Racial Equality (CORE) sent a telegram to President Kennedy, asking that he deny a St. Augustine Quadricentennial request for $350,000, because the money would be used to "celebrate 400 years of slavery and segregation in America's oldest city."

207

June 19   Dr. Robert Hayling, Negro dentist and St. Augustine spokesman for the N.A.A.C.P., was quoted in the *St. Augustine Record* as saying that "passive resistance is no good in the face of violence. I and others of the N.A.A.C.P. have armed ourselves and we will shoot first and answer questions later." (Dr. Hayling later denied making the remark.)

July 3   Three Negroes and one white youth arrested in connection with two shooting incidents on July 1. Four Negroes were hit by shotgun pellets fired from a car driven by white youths.

July 7   Mayor Joseph A. Shelley issued a long statement on the racial situation in St. Augustine. (See Appendix 6.)

July 17   County Court Judge Charles C. Mathis dismissed charges against three Negroes and one white youth for lack of evidence in connection with the July 1 shooting affray.

July 18   Picketing and sit-downs began in front of or inside certain stores downtown with lunch counters which did not serve Negroes. While some 200 or more Negroes and whites participated in these demonstrations, only sixteen arrests were made for trespassing—six of them being juveniles.

The Breach Widens

July 22-23   Eight more juveniles arrested for picketing or demonstrating. When the parents of four of these juveniles refused to sign stipulations to restrain their children from further picketing, the children were remanded to the Juvenile Court. Later these four minors, two boys and two girls, were sent to reform schools at Ocala and Marianna. This caused considerable resentment in the Negro community.

Juvenile Court Judge Charles Mathis issued order prohibiting picketing or demonstrating by juveniles under seventeen years of age. Some of the arrested demonstrators were as young as ten years. Demonstrators and pickets under seventeen were to be escorted home and their parents summoned to appear in Juvenile Court the next day.

July 24   Four more demonstrators arrested in front of county jail when they refused to leave at the request of Sheriff L. O. Davis.

July 26   Two more Negro juveniles arrested for demonstrating.

More Sit-Ins

August 1   Nine Negroes found guilty under the Florida "Undesirable Guest" Act in connection with July 18 sit-ins and lying down in public places. Fines of $100 or 45 days in jail levied. Courtroom cleared after noisy protests.

August 22   Nine more persons arrested for trespassing on private property.

30

August 28   Five colored children enrolled in previously all white schools without incident. No national news or TV coverage.

August 31   Twelve persons arrested for disturbing the peace.

Sept. 3   Twenty-seven Negroes arrested on charges of holding a meeting in a public park without a permit. Two were charged with resisting arrest. Twelve others arrested for sit-ins at lunch counters.

209

Sept. 9   City Commission empowers City Manager Charles Barrier to ban indefinitely all parades, marches, demonstrations, and large open meetings, in the interest of public safety and welfare.

Sept. 18   Nine young colored persons, six of them girls, were found guilty of trespass when they refused to leave a drug store lunch counter on August 22, and fined $50 each.

The K.K.K. Arrives

Sept. 18   Dr. Robert Hayling and three colored companions were severely beaten when they tried to observe a Ku Klux Klan meeting 3 miles south of St. Augustine. Deputy sheriffs rescued the four Negroes and arrested four Jacksonville Klansmen. The *St. Augustine Record* reported
Sept. 18-19   this "the first open meeting of its kind in this area in recent years." A crowd of 400 attended the first night's session and well over 2,500 on the second night. Klansmen reported many new recruits.

Sept. 27   Five St. Augustine Negroes filed petition in U. S. District Court in Jacksonville, asking that the City of St. Augustine be restrained from interfering with peaceful racial demonstrations.

October 1   Seven Negroes arrested under Florida Trespass Act and disturbing the peace.

The First Death

October 25   A white youth, William David Kinard, age 24, was shot through the head while riding in a car on Central Avenue in the Negro neighborhood with three companions. Kinard was carrying a loaded shotgun with the barrel pointed at the floor when he was hit. There had been no gunfire from the car.

October 28   The murder of Kinard apparently touched off retaliatory firing when two Negro night clubs, a market, and two Negro homes were fired on by moving automobiles.

November 5   Goldie Eubanks, Sr., and his son of the same name arrested in connection with the fatal shooting of William David Kinard. Eubanks had been an active N.A.A.C.P. member. A neighbor, Chester Hamilton, was also arrested and charged with first degree murder.

November 15 U. S. District Judge William McRae, after long hearings in Jacksonville Federal Court, dismissed with prejudice the St. Augustine N.A.A.C.P. suit seeking to enjoin city officials from further arrests of integration pickets and demonstrators.

November 29 City Manager Charles Barrier announced lifting of city ban on marches and demonstrations.

The Strange Disappearance of Joyce Green

December 1   Sheriff L. O. Davis revealed that Joyce Green, a fifteen year old colored girl and material witness in the Kinard murder case had been miss-

210

32

ing since November 8, the day she had been picked up and questioned about the slaying. F.B.I. was asked to investigate the disappearance of this key witness.

Grand Jury Convenes

December 9   Grand Jury for St. Johns County convened to inquire into St. Augustine racial unrest. Two jurors are colored.

December 16   Grand Jury hands up presentment to Circuit Court Judge Robert Winfield blaming two militant elements, the Negro movement and the Ku Klux Klan, "which does not represent the majority view of the white citizens of St. Johns County."

December 20   Dr. Robert Hayling and Goldie Eubanks told United Press International that they had resigned from the local N.A.A.C.P. in the hopes that "less militant" Negro leaders perhaps could make more progress in restoring interracial harmony in St. Augustine.

1964

February 8   Four loads of buckshot were fired from an automobile into home of Dr. Robert Hayling at 1:25 A.M., killing a dog and causing considerable damage.

March 11   Dr. Robert Hayling, a Negro dentist and former head of the St. Augustine branch of the N.A.A.C.P., directed a letter to the Massachusetts Chapter of the Southern Christian Leadership Conference, urging northern college students who might be coming to Florida during spring vacations to stop off at St. Augustine to help "struggle for human rights." This was the beginning of the so-called "Florida Spring

211

33

Project" similar to the Mississippi Summer Project. Demonstrations were set for March 21 to April 4, 1964. (See Appendix 5.)

The "Spring Project" Begins

March 12   Between 150 and 175 newsmen, TV crews, and cameramen began arriving in St. Augustine from all over the United States presaging that some of "big news" story would soon break.

Mayor Shelly received long distance call from a St. Augustine student in a New England college warning of a mass invasion of civil rights demonstrators from that area.

A Boston radio commentator phoned Mayor Shelley that Mrs. Peabody, mother of the governor of Massachusetts, was coming to St. Augustine, and what would he do if she violated any local laws?

March 23   First contingent of some 30 New England students, chaplains, and faculty members arrived by bus to stage anti-segregation demonstrations. They said they would stage sit-ins, pray-ins, picketing, etc.

March 28   Twenty-six Negro and white demonstrators led by a Yale University chaplain arrested after warning for trespassing and conspiring to commit misdemeanor. Most of them white northerners.

Easter Sunday in St Augustine

March 29   Traditional Easter parade held without incident. Negro high school band loudly applauded by some 25,000 spectators. Mrs. Malcolm Peabody arrived late in the evening from Boston. Never contacted a single city official.

March 30   Ninety demonstrators, including Mrs. Peabody, arrested for trespass in connection with various sit-ins. Mrs. Peabody had previously told newsmen of her intention of getting arrested. A Communion service set for 10:00 A.M. at the Trinity Episcopal Church was cancelled when it was learned she intended to integrate the service. Bishop Hamilton West of Jacksonville had appealed to Mrs. Peabody's husband, Bishop Malcolm Peabody of Boston, to urge his wife not to disrupt church services. Mrs. Peabody refused bail and elected to remain in jail.   213

April 1   Eighty-four more demonstrators, 20 of them juveniles, arrested under trespass and conspiracy statutes. Mayor Shelley issued press statement alleging that some of his previous statements had been "misquoted and distorted by some of our national news wire services and broadcasters." He also deplored the fact that the mother of a governor came to another state with the open intention of flouting the law.

New York Attorney John Pratt filed petition in Federal Court in Jacksonville to take jurisdiction of all St. Johns County trespass cases on the grounds they could not get a fair trial in that county.

April 2   Federal Judge Bryan Simpson refused change of venue plea filed by attorneys John Pratt, Tobias Simon and William Kunstler in behalf of St. Augustine mass demonstrators.

April 3   Mrs. Peabody posts bond for $450 and departs by plane from Jacksonville. Some 128 other Negro and white demonstrators arrested during past hectic week in the Ancient City posted bonds and were released.

April 5   Hosea Williams visibly disappointed at mass meeting of over 200 when only 10 adults volunteered for a sit-in and probable arrest. Teen-agers and even children have made up majority of the Negro demonstrators. Williams quoted in press as warning: "If segregation barriers remain up in St. Augustine it will be because the people here (Negro) did not support the movement."

April 14　　Five Negroes attended services at Trinity Episcopal Church this Sunday without incident. North Florida diocese Bishop Hamilton West had ordered all churches in the diocese to admit anyone seeking to attend services.

April 17　　City Commission requested that NBC give Mayor Shelley equal time to appear with other St. Augustine officials on TV in order to "present true and correct" picture of just what happened in the city as rebuttal to biased and "misleading statements made on the 'Today' program of April 13, 1964."

April 23-28　　Total of 38 more demonstrators arrested for trespassing and conspiracy to commit misdemeanor in various sit-ins.

May 11　　Demonstrations resumed and 43 more arrested.

May 12　　Board of County Commissioners unanimously passed a resolution to back county and city officials seeking to block transfer of some 280 demonstration cases now pending in U. S. Federal Court from local jurisdiction.

May 18　　Martin Luther King arrived in St. Augustine and was quoted as charging that St. Augustine "was a small Birmingham." He left the following day promising to return at a later date and bring with him "our non-violent army" which he described as being made up of Negro and white "volunteers" from throughout the South who demonstrate for integration.

May 20　　Mayor Shelley and Earle W. Newton, executive director of the St. Augustine Historical

Restoration Commission appeared for fourteen minutes on NBC's "Today" show to refute charges Mrs. Peabody had previously made on the same show against St. Augustine. The mayor stated that Mrs. Peabody's intrusion into St. Augustine's racial problem had caused "irreparable harm" and that she had done a disservice not only to St. Augustine but to the nation as a whole.

Robert Hayling filed suit in the U. S. District Court to compel desegregation of the Flagler Memorial Hospital.

215

May 23   Federal District Judge Bryan Simpson, after a seven hour hearing, ordered cases of 53 racial demonstrators remanded to St. Johns County court.

May 25   Harry Boyte, white assistant to Martin Luther King and Andred Young, S.C.L.C. call on Mayor Shelley.

King Promises St. Augustine A "Long Hot Summer"

May 26   King returned to St. Augustine.

May 27   Martin Luther King promised St. Augustine "a long hot summer, but hopefully a long hot non-violent summer." He added that his "non-violent army" was being mobilized and was on the way.

May 28   All the King's men invaded America's oldest city. Some 300 marched on the misnamed "Old Slave Market," which is really a pavilion used by elderly whites to play checkers and cards. City police, county deputy sheriffs, and state highway patrolmen prevent clash between Negro demonstrators and large group of whites armed with clubs and tire irons. Cameramen attacked by young toughs; one injured. Mayor

Shelley issued warning against violence. (See Appendix 10.) Fourteen demonstrators arrested for trespassing, refused to make bond, beginning the "flood the jails" tactic.

May 29   Police Chief Virgil Stuart issued orders for demonstrators and counter demonstrators to stay away from the down town àrea as authorities did not have enough manpower to cope with possible outbreak of racial violence.

216

King, in California, wired President Johnson, requesting Federal protection for St. Augustine demonstrators.

"Flood the Jails"

May 30   Nearly 200 racial demonstrators defied police ban and began another march on the downtown area, but were turned back by helmeted police with police dogs. Fifteen more demonstrators arrested. Some elected to serve 10 to 12 days in jail rather than pay fines.

May 31   Five more demonstrators arrested and they also elect to stay in jail.

June 1   Nineteen more trespassers arrested; sentenced up to 10 days in jail.

City Commission adopted emergency measures prohibiting minors under 18 to be on the streets or in public places from 9:00 PM until 5:00 AM. Parking also banned on 42 streets downtown between the same hours in order to prevent large crowds from gathering in the center of the city.

County and city officials appeared in Federal Court in Jacksonville, where integrationist lawyers sought injunction to set aside police orders banning night marches.

A Federal Judge Takes Over

June 2   Injunction suit continued in Judge Simpson's court in Jacksonville. Simpson grilled Sheriff Davis as to whether he belonged to the K.K.K. and demanded production of list of all deputy sheriffs. Police Chief Stuart and St. Augustine *Record* general manager Tebault also testified.

Nine more demonstrators arrested. St. Augustine Lions Club adopts resolution calling upon Florida State Legislative Committee to conduct "full investigation of Martin Luther King as soon as possible." Marches postponed pending Judge Simpson's decision on plea for injunction.

June 3   Hearings before Judge Simpson concluded. Two more sit-in trespassers arrested.

June 5   City Commission in special meeting rescinded two ordinances setting a curfew for minors and prohibiting downtown parking. Rev. M. L. King returned to St. Augustine and denounced the city as the "most lawless he has ever visited." Also stated that President Johnson was watching racial developments in St. Augustine. More "non-violent marches" threatened.

June 8   Negroes hurl rocks and bottles at police car. King's cottage on the beach, which he never occupied, was vandalized and an attempt to set it afire apparently made.

Hearings started in Judge Simpson's court on complaint that detained demonstrators were being subjected to "unusual and cruel punishment" and held under excessive bail.

June 9   Sheriff L. O. Davis calls for law-abiding and responsible men between 21 and 55 to volun-

217

teer as special deputy sheriffs when called in emergencies. Three out-of-town Negroes report their car was fired on while driving through Vilano Beach, a suburb. Windows of a white owned store on Central Avenue smashed during the night.

Judge Simpson orders St. Augustine city officials to permit demonstrations at any time of the day or night. Demonstrations resumed that evening within a few hours of Simpson's order. M. L. King returned to St. Augustine promising "massive demonstrations" unless all integration demands are promptly met.

218

June 10

Demonstration marches resumed and racial tension mounted. King announced at news conference that he would go to the Monson Motor Lodge the next day and commit an "act of civil disobedience." Whole busloads of King's "non-violent army" began to arrive from other cities.

Governor Farris Bryant announced at Tallahassee that he would not hesitate to use every power at his command to preserve law and order in the Ancient City.

June 11

Eighteen more trespassers arrested and sentenced to jail terms up to ten days. King, Rev. Ralph Abernathy, and Rev. Robert England of Boston University were among the eighteen arrested. They were charged with disturbing the peace, trespassing, and conspiracy. Hearings set for July 7. King removed to Jacksonville jail next day as a safety precaution.

Harrassed news and TV cameramen hire bodyguards.

June 12

Whites begin counter-demonstrations, marching into Lincolnville or the colored neighborhood, citing Judge Simpson's order against police requests that they refrain from marching. Over 100 police, special deputies and state troopers accompanied the marchers. There were no incidents. March apparently inspired by Jesse B. Stoner of Atlanta.

Fifty-six demonstrators arrested, receiving up to fifteen days in jail.

Busloads of Negroes from other states began to arrive to reinforce King's non-violent army.

June 13   *New York Times* admitted that "Dr. King appealed for outside help to fill up the jails and put more people in the streets." Also that most St. Augustine Negroes "are not taking part in the movement."

219

June 14   King out of town to receive an honorary degree at Yale University. Fifty-one arrests for trespassing. Night marches simmer down. Andrew Young, a King Lieutenant, indicated marches would be resumed after new support was mustered from other states. Atlanta Klan attorney J. B. Stoner urged "Fire Negroes" campaign if out-of-town integrationists did not leave.

"Manucy's Raiders" subject of long by-line article in the Miami Herald.

June 16   Twenty-six more arrests for trespassing, interfering with church services, etc. Governor Bryant created special police force to cope with unrest and commotion in St. Augustine. Major John Jourdan placed in command. Grand jury continued hearings.

June 17   Twenty-seven arrests for trespassing and other law violations. Local businessmen met and adopted resolution requesting news media to point out to the world that "the great majority of law violations have been committed by outsiders who have invaded this community for selfish reasons of obtaining publicity.

June 18   Fifteen more arrests for trespassing and other violations, some individuals from as far away as Seattle and San Diego.

June 18   Grand jury returned presentment calling on King and all others to demonstrate good faith by calling off all demonstrations and "by removing their influences from this community for a period of thirty days." Grand jury also charged King with conducting one of his "noisiest demonstrations to divert public attention away from our good faith effort to reach accord in these matters."

Two whites and four Negroes invaded Monson Motor Lodge private pool for guests creating famous TV show. Northern rabbis invade St. Augustine. Tension again mounted higher.

June 19   King offers St. Augustine racial truce but Grand Jury refused to negotiate unless King first observed 30 day truce on all demonstrations, sit-ins, wade-in, pray-ins, etc.

June 20   State troopers hard pressed to head off packs of young white teenagers racing through narrow, dark streets trying to harrass integrationist marchers.

Governor Bryant issued first Executive Order prohibiting night marches in order to avoid possible bloodshed as situation assumed ugly proportions. Florida Attorney General calls Governor's order "iron clad."

"Wade-Ins" At Beaches

June 21   The battle shifted to the beaches as integrationists attempted wade-ins at white beaches.

More TV shows. Fourteen arrests for trespass, resisting officers, etc.

June 22

Judge Simpson, who twice before refused St. Augustine authorities the right to ban night marches, ordered Governor Bryant, Mayor Shelley, Police Chief Stuart, Sheriff L. O. Davis and Attorney General Kynes to appear in Federal Court and show cause why they should not be cited for contempt.

Twenty-one more arrests, mainly in connection with attacks by young whites on Negro and white integrationists continuing wade-ins at St. Augustine beach.

221

June 23

Sixteen more arrests for disturbing peace and other violations. More than 200 Negro marchers with few white integrationists attacked as young white hoodlums break through police lines. King returned to St. Augustine.

June 24

More wade-ins attempted, but menacing white mob standing in surf halted this attempt. Four arrests for disturbing the peace. Rabble-rousing speech by Connie Lynch of the National States Right Party sparks another white march into Negro section of city. Violence averted only because of massed police marching alongside white counter demonstrators.

Governor Bryant Stands Firm

June 24

Governor Bryant indicated he would ignore Federal Court order and stand on constitutional rights as governor of a sovereign state. Would send state's attorney general to represent him.

Twenty-eight arrests for disturbing the peace as wade-ins at St. Augustine Beach continue. King asks White House to send federal mediator to St. Augustine.

43

June 26   Governor Bryant flies to St. Augustine to confer with city officials and Adjutant General Henry W. McMillan. Major Jourdan of State Highway Patrol told Judge Simpson that St. Augustine situation was "dangerous and explosive." Twenty-one persons injured in what was described as the "wildest and most violent melee since Negro integrationists leaders started demonstrations over a year ago." Governor Bryant ordered 80 more state police officers to St. Augustine.

June 27   Governor Bryant appealed for citizens' help to quell civil riot and commotion in the Ancient City. Five arrests for disturbing the peace.

June 28   Tampa N.A.A.C.P. Negro attorney Francisco Rodriguez issued two and a half page statement condemning St. Augustine demonstrations as the handiwork of "one man who wants to become a super emancipator," presumably referring to Martin Luther King.

June 29   A 72 year old white fruit peddlar was pulled from his truck and severely beaten by a gang of teenage Negroes. A white Miami youth was pulled from his car and beaten by young white toughs when he expressed opinion that Lynch and Stoner meetings were "ridiculous."

June 29   More ocean beach wade-ins attempted under heavy police guard. Thirty arrested, half of them juveniles, for various law breaches, including carrying of concealed weapons.

                  Messrs. Frank Harrold and H. E. Wolfe, after first accepting, later decline to serve as "Federal Mediators" in the St. Augustine situation. Mr. Wolfe stated that he had been contacted by Senator Smathers "acting as liaison officer for the President of the United States."

July 1   King outlined rights law tests he will conduct. St. Augustine businessmen met and stated they would comply with new civil rights law. Governor Bryant stated he had named four man bi-racial committee for St. Augustine, but declined to identify the members. Martin Luther King called hurried press conference to announce a 12 to 15 day truce on all demonstrations. AP quoted King as stating "The purpose of our direct action was to create a crisis."

An integrated Miami church, First Unitarian, announced plans to send mixed group to St. Augustine to join demonstrations. Pastor John Papandrew stated that anyone was welcome to go along, provided they first completed CORE non-violent training course and promised to abide by Southern Christian Leadership Conference orders. Lynch and Stoner had apparently left St. Augustine.

223

July 2	President Johnson signed Civil Rights Bill. St. Augustine peaceful and quiet.
July 4	Some 200 robed Klansmen arrived to parade in the afternoon. No disorders reported.
	St. Augustine "Affiliate" of the Southern Christian Leadership Conference mailed "The Black Revolution" by Thomas Merton to St. Augustine businessmen.
July 5	Racial truce marred by gang of young white toughs who attacked six Negroes peacefully fishing off a bridge. Police later arrested 9, charging assault and battery.
July 6	S.C.L.C. leaders await return of Hosea Williams before making further plans.
July 7	Mayor Joseph A. Shelley issued statement on racial relations to all citizens urging restraint and respect for law and order.
July 9	"Testing" continued at some 29 motels and restaurants. Monson Lodge accepted five Negro guests.

July 10 White segregationist pickets appeared before integrated motels and restaurants.

July 12 St. Augustine Chapter S.C.L.C. sends out form letter to local Negro ministers asking that it be read at their church services. It urged Negroes to take their wives "out of the hot kitchen and treat her to dinner in the restaurant of your choice or take the kids out to the local drugstore for a soda."

224

July 13 H. B. Chitty, director of St. Augustine Chamber of Commerce, stated that St. Augustine's summer tourist trade was running $5 million below 1963 and might reach $8 million by the end of the year. Many motels faced bankruptcy.

July 14 New York lawyer Robert Preiskil and Harry Twine, local integrationist leader, claimed five men armed with iron bars had attacked them near a motel.

July 16 Chicago lawyer, David Halperin, filed suits against two motels, alleging violation of new Civil Rights Act.

White citizens Council picketing continued with restaurant owners complaining that they were far more effective in discouraging trade than former Negro pickets. Martin Luther King returned to St. Augustine, threatening more "massive demonstrations." After a two weeks absence, King also charged that "terror tactics" had resegregated most of the eating places and motels which had agreed to integrate. "We are determined to see this community fully integrated and the Ku Klux Klan driven out of positions of power," King stated.

July 18 Four Negroes beaten. Troopers returned to St. Augustine.

July 23 Federal Judge Simpson ordered two St. Augustine restaurants who had refused to serve

Negroes to comply with Civil Rights Act. Some 30 other motels and restaurants faced similar action after a week of S.C.L.C. "testing."

July 24   Two flaming "Molotov cocktails" hurled through front window of Monson Motor Lodge at 3:00 AM. Damage set at $3,000. Two suspects later arrested and turned over to FBI.

July 24   J. B. Stoner, "Connie" Lynch and three others arrested and charged with burning a KKK cross on private property without owner's permission.

225

July 28   Holstead "Hoss" Manucy took Fifth Amendment 33 times as a witness in U.S. Federal Court, Jacksonville, in injunction case against 15 St. Augustine restaurant and motel owners charged with failure to comply with 1964 Civil Rights Act.

July 30   Civil Rights case in Judge Simpson's court ended. St. Augustine businessmen who testified said they were "caught in the middle" and feared mob violence if they complied with law and served Negroes.

July 31   Florida Legislative Investigation Committee issued 15 page report charging that National States Rights Party had played a "key role" in exacerbating racial tension and violence in St. Augustine.

Dr. Robert Hayling, local head of the S.C.L.C. rejected Negro organizations moratorium on demonstrations until after November election. Criticized King as having no authority to speak for St. Augustine Negroes (AP and UPI)

August 1   St. Johns County Grand Jury convened.

August 2   Circuit Court Judge Horace D. Reigle declared St. Augustine city ordinance requiring permit to hold meeting on public property to be invalid.

August 5   Federal Judge Simpson ordered 17 St. Augustine motels and restaurants to desegrate forthwith and also enjoined a group of segregationists from further interference with such motels and other places.

August 5   St. Johns County Grand Jury hands down its presentment. King denounces the presentment as "impractical and immoral." There was nothing in it which Negroes could accept, he said, and it was "out of line with the mood of the age."

226

August 14   Federal Judge Simpson ordered Flagler Memorial Hospital to integrate within thirty days.

Judge Simpson Fires Deputy Sheriff Lance

August 19   Federal Judge Simpson found motel manager William Chew and Deputy Sheriff Charles Lance, Jr., in contempt of court for refusing to rent a motel room to Negroes and for following them in car. Simpson also ordered Lance to turn in his badge or resign his commission from the sheriff's force within twenty days.

Sheriff L. O. Davis had testified the day before that there "was not $5 left in St. Augustine" and that deputies could hardly be expected to protect integrationists with "glad hearts."

August 20   Senator Strom Thurmond in Washington, D. C. denounces Judge Simpson's action as "approaching judicial dictatorship."

August 26   A white integrationist and two Negroes swimming at St. Augustine Beach attacked by young white toughs later chased away by the police. Charles Allen Lingo, white field worker for S.C.L.C. treated at Flager hospital for cut over eye.

September 3   Charles Allen Lingo and Arthur Funderberk filed civil action for $20,000 damages against Sheriff L. O. Davis for failure to protect them from being beaten at St. Augustine Beach.

September 27 *St. Augustine Record* published long, half page summary on the summer's events entitled: "Law, Justice in County Feel Lash of Federal Court Power." (See Appendix 23)

227

October 14   Federal Judge Simpson ordered Holstead Manucy to produce within 15 days the "best list he can find" of the Ancient City Hunting Club. Manucy countered that he carried the list of 1476 names in his head and kept no records.

October 23   Federal Judge Bryan Simpson jailed Holstead Manucy and Jerome Godwin for up to 90 and 15 days respectively unless they produced the membership list of the Ancient City Gun Club. After an hour in a detention cell, Manucy told Simpson he had some names in the glove compartment of his car and was released to return to court with them on October 26.

November 16 N.A.A.C.P. executive secretary Roy Wilkins in concluding address at Florida state convention in Tallahassee, stated while his organization "would not mount a personal vendetta on Florida . . . the economic screws" should be tightened on St. Augustine because the nation's oldest city "had the oldest ideas on race relations in the United States."

Martin Luther King

Martin Luther King has been in the headlines for so many years that he hardly needed the Nobel Peace Prize, St. Augustine, Florida, Selma, Alabama, or F.B.I. Director J. Edgar Hoover's characterization of being the "most notorious liar in the country." While he was in jail in Atlanta on a parole violation charge in 1960, Mrs. King was pleasantly surprised to receive a long distance telephone call from presidential candidate John F. Kennedy asking whether there was anything he could do to be helpful. Just how many hundred thousand or more votes this brought the presidential aspirant from Negroes in critical states became a subject of debate among politicians of both parties.

In 1962 the *N. Y. Times* in a short biographic sketch of King stated that he and A. Philip Randolph had announced just prior to the national conventions of 1960 that they would lead 5,000 pickets at both the Democratic and Republican national conventions. These demonstrations would be held to force anti-segregation planks in the platforms of both parties.

King has authored several books setting forth his views on various questions. He has also been the subject of at least two favorable biographies. Despite all this publicity and nationwide attention, there nevertheless remains a considerable amount of information on King's background and activities not generally known to the public or to his numerous admirers and supporters. As King played such a leading role in the St. Augustine disorders during the "long, hot summer" of 1964 a summary of this information would seem in order in this report.

Michael Luther King was born in Atlanta, Georgia, in 1929, the son of a colored preacher. His name was changed to Martin Luther King some time during his childhood. He acquired degrees at Morehouse College, Crozier Theological Seminary, and Boston University. King also holds a number of honorary degrees. He was awarded the coveted Nobel Peace Prize in 1964.

According to the *New York Times,* December 22, 1957, King attended a four day seminar at the Highlander Folk School near Monteagle, Tennessee, from August 30 to September 2 of that year. It was both the 25th anniversary of the founding of the school and a workshop for civil rights workers in the South. The Highlander Folk School was the subject of an investigation by a joint committee of the Tennessee Legislature because of its long history of subversive activities and the disrepute it had acquired in the community as a hotbed of radicalism.

229

Following extensive hearings, the special legislative committee recommended court action for the revocation of its charter on what amounted to purely technical charges. The committee found that:

"A great deal of circumstantial evidence, which is competent, was unfolded before the committee in this direction, to the effect that the 'school' is a meeting place for Communists or fellow travelers."

A state circuit court subsequently ordered the Highlander Folk School's charter revoked and on April 1, 1961, the Tennessee Supreme Court upheld the lower court and the school was closed down later that year.

However, its director Myles Horton, transferred the school in effect to Knoxville, Tennessee under a new name, The Highlander Research and Education Center. Martin Luther King was listed as one of its sponsors. It was again closed down in 1963 by the sheriff of Blount County when a number of individuals were arrested for illegal possession of liquor, disturbing the peace, and contributing to the deliquency of a minor. (Letter to Senator Spessard Holland of Florida from the House Committee on Un-American Activities, August 10, 1964.)

The Georgia Commission on Education obtained a picture of the Highlander Folk School seminar in 1957 showing King seated next to Aubrey Williams, then president of the Southern Conference Educational Fund, and just behind Abner Green, a high-ranking Negro Communist from New York.

Both Green and Williams are now deceased. The Southern Conference Educational Fund has been extensively investigated by the Louisiana Joint Legislative Committee and made the subject of several reports by that committee. These reports contain a number of letters exchanged between King and known Communists or veteral Communist Party fronters.

The Louisiana Committee in Part 2 of its Report No. 5, April 13, 1964, made the following comment on Martin Luther King:

230

"The infiltration of the Communist Party into the so-called 'Civil Rights' movement through the S.C.E.F. is shocking and highly dangerous to this state, and the nation. We do not suggest, nor do we believe, that everyone connected with the civil rights movement is a Communist. There are many sincere and well-meaning people involved in this cause. We do suggest and the evidence before us is quite conclusive, that the civil rights movement has been grossly and solidly infiltrated by the Communist Party. Those persons in the civil rights movement who deny this deny overwhelming evidence that it is so. The evidence before us shows clearly that Martin Luther King has very closely connected his organization, the Southern Christian Leadership Conference with the S.C.E.F. and the Communist personalities managing the S.C.E.F. This had been going on for some four and a half years. By thus connecting himself with the Communists, Martin Luther King has cynically betrayed his responsibilities as a Christian minister and the political leader of a large number of people. It is the hope of the Committee that this report will enlighten his followers and supporters as to his true allegiance and purposes." (page 125)

In his own autobiography King states that he accepted his pastorate in 1955 in Montgomery, Alabama, shortly after securing a DD at Boston University. The famous year long Negro boycott of Montgomery buses began shortly after King's arrival in that city. A U. S. Supreme Court decision in December, 1956, ended the long dispute, not the King-led boycott as some of his admirers claim today.

In 1956, King became a member of the Advisory Committee of the Congress of Racial Equality, herinafter referred to as C.O.R.E., according to a letterhead of that year. His name was also carried on the masthead of *Liberation*, a radical pacifist monthly, for December 1956. Six years later *Liberation* still carried his name as a "contributor."

The Communist *Daily Worker*, December 2, 1957, listed a number of "notables" who had signed an open letter urging that the United States cancel all hydrogen bomb tests. King was one of the signers.

From about 1955 to 1960, Bayard Rustin was King's secretary. "The SCLC Story in Words and Pictures" published in 1964 by the Southern Christian Leadership Conference, traces the history of the early days and founding of this organization in 1957. "Bayard Rustin, who all along was the most sensitive to the situation, prepared 'working papers' for the group, spelling out themes on a broad front."

231

Rustin had been a member of the Young Communist League in 1936. He was sent to prison for draft evasion on March 7, 1944 and was not discharged until June 11, 1946. Rustin was arrested in 1953 by the Pasadena, California, police together with other men and charged with sexual perversion. He pleaded guilty and served a sixty day sentence. (See *Los Angeles Times*, January 22 and 23, 1953.) Ten years later he was the chief organizer of the "March on Washington." Rustin's criminal record as recorded by the F.B.I. may be found on pages 14030-37, *Congressional Record*, August 13, 1963. See also C.R. September 17, 1961, page A6444, for a long summary of Rustin's questionable background. Rustin visited India and Ghana, then still the Gold Coast, in 1947, to study civil disobedience tactics. After his return to the United States he became executive secretary of the War Resisters League, a non-Communist but radical pacifist organization. It has been alleged that Rustin first introduced King to Kwame Nkrumah, the iron-fisted dictator of Ghana. A Senate Sub-committee later termed Ghana a Soviet satillite and issued a report to that effect.

Rustin ostensibly departed from the S.C.L.C. and King some time in 1960. He apparently was replaced by one Hunter

Pitts O'Dell, sometimes known as Jack Odell. The Senate Internal Security Subcommittee called O'Dell as a witness in 1956, but he had little to say other than using the 5th Amendment to most questions. New Orleans police who searched his room had found documents identifying O'Dell as an important Communist Party functionary. A great deal of other incriminating evidence was found in his room at the same time. O'Dell was elected to the National Committee of the Communist Party, U.S.A., in 1961, a position never given to anyone but top-ranking Communists with at least five to ten years of party membership. O'Dell appears to have worked for King as recently as June, 1963, when he was in charge of the New York office of the S.C.L.C.

232

In addition to Rustin and O'Dell, Martin Luther King has been closely associated with or a supporter of Aubrey Williams, James Dombrowski, and Carl and Anne Braden, all identified as Communists before the Senate Internal Security Subcommittee. A complete compilation of all of King's affiliations with or activities in behalf of Communist fronts would make tedious reading and burdensome to this report.

King has signed several open letters in full page paid advertisements urging abolition of the House Committee on Un-American Activities. According to the *Worker*, May 14, 1961, he signed a clemency petition for Carl Braden, convicted of contempt of Congress and before that of sedition in Kentucky, a conviction which was later reversed by a higher court. In 1962 he also signed a petition urging executive clemency for convicted Communist Junius Scales.

All of King's activities have not been as "non-violent" as he likes to proclaim. The National Baptist Convention met in Kansas City in September, 1961. The Rev. Dr. Joseph H. Jackson of Chicago, was elected to his 8th consecutive term as president. At the opening session an "invasion" of the convention was attempted by followers of Martin Luther King, a vice president at large. A pushing contest ensued on the convention platform for control of the microphones and Rev. A. G. Wright fell or was shoved off the platform. He died the following day of head injuries and Dr. Jackson accused King as being responsible for masterminding the invasion which led to Wright's death. (*Washington Post*, September 10, 1961)

King professes to "hate Communism." In a sermon he once preached King called Communism "Christianity's most formidable rival" and said that "Communism and Christianity are fundamentally incompatible." King demonstrates a good fundamental grasp of the atheistic and evil nature of Communism in this sermon. Then he warns that "we must not engage in negative anti-Communism, but rather in a positive thrust for democracy, realizing that our greatest defense against Communism is to take offensive action in behalf of justice and righteousness." (*Strength To Love*, page 123, Pocket Books, Inc., 1964) Yet curiously enough the Communist press has never attacked or even mildly criticized King for any of his activities.

233

The Worker or *Sunday Worker* frequently gives King front page, large headline coverage. The December 6, 1964, *Worker* gave front page display to the story that Martin Luther King and five other top Negro leaders had urged President Johnson to leave the Congo alone and to halt all military support to Prime Minister Tshombe and to reverse present U. S. policy on Africa. "Christian minister" Martin Luther King had no Christian compassion for his fellow religionists, whites, being massacred by Congolese savages posing as "rebels." He also apparently was not too concerned about an estimated 5,000 Congolese blacks being butchered by the same rebels, armed and instigated by the Communists.

Martin Luther King has been called the "American Gandhi" by some of his more ardent admirers. King and the Hindu Mahatma never met but King did go to India about ten years after Gandhi's assassination to study Indian nonviolence direct action methods first hand. There actually is no similarity between the two men other than the fact that the American Negro leader has attempted to improvise on some of Gandhi's techniques and adapt them to American conditions.

Vast racial, religious, and cultural differences separate the Afro-American from the Hindu satyagrahis who followed

55

Mohandas K. Gandhi. Satyagraha literally translated means "insistence on truth." With five to six thousand years of ancient religious precepts and devotions to fortify his sufferings and sacrifices, the Hindu satyagrahis bore no relationship to the American Negro. Gandhi practiced and insisted that his followers also fast, engage in spiritual contemplation and exercises including self-purification. This is little evidence that Martin Luther King has ever imitated Gandhi in that respect. Gandhi was an ascetic who had learned to reject practically all the material comforts of life. There is no record that King ever started or even contemplated a "fast unto death" as Gandhi did on several occasions.

234

Gandhi faced the problem of driving a military conqueror out of his country with non-military means. The British, civilians and military, formed a minute percentage of the total Indian population. King's project is inciting an economically weak minority against the overwhelming white majority, dividing that majority, or at least neutralizing part of it, to win the maximum number of concessions possible before a strong counteraction sets in among the whites.

King outlined his general line of strategy on a number of occasions in speeches and writing. His letter from Birmingham Jail, dated April, 1963, is probably the most candid and succinct. Reproved by a group of eight Alabama clergy of all faiths for "actions as to incite hatred and violence, however technically peaceful those actions may be, have not contributed to the resolution of our local ·problems." The reverend clergy did not believe that "extreme measures were justified."

Imprisoned in Birmingham, King replied at great length in a letter later reprinted in "Why We Can't Wait."

"You may well ask, 'Why Direct action? Why sit-ins, marches, etc? Isn't negotiation a better path?' You are exactly right in your call for negotiation. Indeed, this is the purpose of direct action. Non-violent action seeks to create such a crisis and establish such a creative tension that a community which has constantly refused to negotiate is forced to confront the issue. It seeks so to dramatize the issue that it can no longer be ignored.

I just referred to the creation of tension as part of the work of the non-violent resister. This may sound rather shocking. But I must confess that I am not afraid of the word tension. I have earnestly worked and preached against violent tension, but there is a type of constructive non-violent tension that is necessary for growth. Just as Socrates felt that it was necessary to create a tension in the mind so that individuals could rise from the bondage of myths and half-truths to the unfettered realm of creative analysis and objective appraisal, we must see the need of having non-violent gadflies to create the kind of tension in society that will help men rise from the dark depths of prejudice and racism to the majestic heights of understanding and brotherhood. So the purpose of direct action is to create a situation so crisis-packed that it will inevitably open the door to negotiation."

235

It would seem difficult for King to be more honest and candid in openly proclaiming that the very purpose of non-violent direct action "is to create such a crisis and to establish such a creative tension" that a community is "forced to confront the issue." King might also have added just as the "blood of martyrs is the seed of the Church," so a death, particularly if that of a child or woman, is what all non-violent direct action organizers secretly hope and pray for in any demonstration to insure its success. It takes very little to convert a peaceful demonstration into a bloody riot. A serious riot can always lead to a full scale racial riot extending for days with hundreds of casualties as we have unfortunately learned in the past.

NOTE: A similar report on Stoner and Lynch, leaders of NSRP, may be found in a separate report of this committee.

Summary and Conclusions

A review of all available evidence deemed to be reliable on the disorders and commotion during the summers of 1963 and 1964 in St. Augustine leaves this committee with the following conclusions, not necessarily in order of importance or significance:

236

1. That the city of St. Augustine was deliberately selected by Martin Luther King and his associates as the most economically vulnerable target in Florida. This was borne out by the frank admission of one of King's lieutenants, Andrew Young, to Mayor Shelley that St. Augustine was "symbolic" because it was known to most Americans and that additionally it would be easier to get nationwide publicity in America's oldest city.

2. With a small police force of twenty-five men and an even smaller sheriff's force it would require only a few hundred demonstrators to get things out of hand quickly and easily. The managing editor of the *St. Augustine Record* pointed out that staging a similar demonstration in a larger city riotous enough to receive national attention would require several thousand "nonviolent direct actionists."

3. The Florida Memorial College (Negro) on the outskirts of St. Augustine assured the Southern Christian Leadership Conference of a ready and enthusiastic supply of pickets and demonstrators who already had gained considerable experience during the summer of 1963.

4. As Jacksonville was less than forty miles away another large reservoir of manpower was available in the evening after school and working hours.

5. There was also a considerable K.K.K. element in and around Jacksonville which could be trusted to be stimulated into counter demonstrations giving the national news and camera crews dramatic "action" demanded by sensation seeking news media.

6. King's tactic of "flooding the jails" and clogging the limited judicial facilities of a small county would be relatively simple in St. Augustine.

7. Such racial problems as faced the city very probably could have been amicably solved by the Negro and white citizens of St. Augustine had they been free from outside agitation. The intrusion of King and his trained army of provocateurs with ample financial resources destroyed inter-racial relations.

8. That some network TV cameramen and newsreel photographers, requiring "action" shots for sensationalism, connived with demonstrators on both sides to stage it. See Appendix No. 24.

237

9. Well-known bias in some of our news media slanted news reporting and editorials in certain large-circulation newspapers both in Florida and in the nation giving their readers an unfair and distorted picture of what was happening in St. Augustine. Factual reports reported by the more responsible and ethical press could not entirely counteract this mass enterprise in news-poisoning.

10. The physical attacks by white segregationists on integrationists played directly into the hands of Martin Luther King. They were inexcusable and a discredit to the good name of America's oldest city. That some of these attacks were provoked by imported young white girls strolling through the Plaza arm in arm with Negroes or imported white men escorting Negro women, in no way excused assault and battery. (See report by Police Chief Stuart, Appendix 25.)

11. The local police department and sheriff's office did not have the manpower to disperse and keep away from the center of the city several hundred segregationists and integrationists who were congregated there creating an atmosphere of tension. There was the additional thorny legal problem that under Judge Simpson's order and the First Amendment, whites had the same right to the streets as did the demonstrators. Nevertheless, a great deal of violence

could have been prevented had citizens of both Negro and white races stayed away from the demonstration area as requested on several occasions by Mayor Shelley and other officials.

12. The events of the summers of 1963 and 1964 in St. Augustine also demonstrated that thorough training in riot and mob control are now imperative for all Florida law enforcement officers, state as well as local. Highway patrolmen, Conservation Officers, and others whose primary duties and training have little or no relation to mob handling and provocative demonstrations, are little better than armed civilians hastily thrown into the line against trained professionals.

238

The State Highway Patrol now has a training film taken at St. Augustine and an excellent manual on crowd and riot control which should be circulated to every law enforcement officer in the state. As more and larger demonstrations may reasonably be expected this year as the result of additional so-called "civil rights" legislation, this committee is of the opinion that special training courses with police specialists from cities with effective riot control details should be established at an early date.

13. The Committee is of the firm belief that the laws of our land—local, state, and national—should and do apply to all people.

We feel that intentional violations of law to promote some special interest or cause are not in consonance with our best traditions and the American way of life, no matter how appealing or desirable such interests or objectives may appear to some element of our population.

We mutually share the grave concern that such displays of open contempt for our laws will in turn create greater lack of respect or regard for the law and its enforcement. Even though such open violations of law may accomplish some temporary gain, often more apparent than real. Increased disrespect for *some* laws cannot but possibly lead in time to greater disrespect for *all* laws with consequent threat to property, liberty, and eventually the very lives of our families.

Our country was built on and became great because of our traditional respect for law and order. Those who intentionally violate our laws merely because they do not happen to suit their whim or caprice or for the purpose of disrupting the peaceful existence in our cities are doing just as much damage to our social structure as the laws which they oppose. When laws are bad they should be respected but until repealed they are the law and are worthy of the same respect and obedience as all other laws. Every man who substitutes his own judgment as to what should be the law for that of established government endangers our democratic heritage which is based on a government of law and not of man.

239

14. Chapter 14, Florida Statutes, under which the Governor acted in dispatching special police forces to St. Augustine and by virtue of which he moved to ban night demonstrations will expire on July 1 of this year. Various meaures for revising and/or modifying this statute have been discussed by the Committee, with the conclusion reached that the best course of action would be its re-enactment in its present form. The Committee's proposals include a bill to re-enact this statute.

This statute provides discretionary power for Constitutional actions by the Governor, which, in the face of such situations as were manifested in St. Augustine, is desirable and necessary for the preservation of law and order in the state.

Appendix 1

The St. Augustine Record

Negro Leaders Here Say They Are Arming In The Event Of Race Trouble

By United Press International

Negro leaders in St. Augustine yesterday said they were arming themselves in case the battle for equal rights becomes violent.

"We are not going to die like Medgar Evers," said Dr. Robert Hayling, a dentist and civil rights leader.

"Passive resistance is no good in the face of violence," he said, adding that he and NAACP leaders had been threatened since taking their pleas to the City Commission recently.

"I and others of the NAACP have armed ourselves and we will shoot first and ask questions later," he said.

Hayling said Negroes are not satisfied with the progress of the civil rights movement here. He said meetings were scheduled with white leaders later this week.

Earlier in the week, Negroes urged President Kennedy to withhold a requested $350,000 grant from St. Augustine until the city was completely integrated.

The funds were asked for use in the city's planned 1965 celebration of its 400th birthday.

Negro youths in St. Petersburg, meanwhile, have announced that they are planning to test desegregation at local theaters.

The NAACP Youth Council said it would not be fair to plan mass demonstrations without giving the establishments a chance to show if they have integrated.

And in Jacksonville, Mayor Haydon Burns said Tuesday that city officials are willing to name a bi-racial committee to study the problems of Negroes after a group of local Negroes appeared before the City Commission to ask for such a group.

In Gainesville a bi-racial committee recommended Tuesday night that local motels be integrated immediately but called for "patience and tolerance" in cases where they were not.

The committee also asked for a meeting with city officials to discuss fair employment practices.

In recommending that motels be integrated, the committee said "because of economic and other problems involved, the committee further recommends that patience and tolerance also be the course of action in this matter."

Appendix 2

MRS. F. FULLERWOOD, PRESIDENT   **MRS. E. HAWTHRON, SECRETARY**

ST. AUGUSTINE BRANCH OF

THE NATIONAL ASSOCIATION FOR THE ADVANCEMENT OF

COLORED PEOPLE

P. O. BOX 682

ST. AUGUSTINE, FLORIDA

241

June 24, 1963

Mr. Charles Barrier, City Manager
City Building
St. Augustine, Florida

Dear Sir:

The St. Augustine Branch of The National Association For The Advancement of Colored People, would like to request a meeting with the City Commissioners on Friday night June 28th. It is our understanding that this meeting was arranged in the aborted meeting held Thursday afternoon June 20th. We would like to hear the proposals or measures the Mayor and City Commissioners are willing to take in order to achieve peaceful desegregation in the Nation's Oldest City.

In addition, we would like to discuss the following items with the Commission.

1. Fair employment in city government. All city civil service examinations for all positions will be open to all citizens regardless of race, creed or color.

2. Complete desegregation of all city owned facilities. (Clarification)

3. Assurance from the City Fathers that picketing within the code of the city will be allowed with adequate police protection.

4. A blanket statement from the Mayor and City Commission making their position known to all about desegregation.

5. The establishment of a bi-racial committee composed of responsible citizens and representing these organizations having an interst in the Civil Rights Struggle. The members of this committee should meet the approval of all involved. The findings and recommendations of the bi-racial committee should be binding on both sides.

6. We are asking the Commissioners to use their influence to get the White and Colored Religious Leaders of the City together so; that their Wisdom and Christian Training might be brought to bear in attempting to achieve racial harmony in the City of St. Augustine, Florida.

Yours for a more democratic St. Augustine,

242

Mrs. F. Fullerwood, President

Mrs. E. Hawthron, Secretary

CC:

John F. Kennedy, President of The United States of America
White House
Washington, D. C.

Vice President Lyndon B. Johnson
Washington, D. C.

Mr. Roy Wilkins, Executive Secretary, National Association For The Advancement of Colored People.
20 West 40th Street
New York 18, New York

Mr. James Farmer, National Director, Congress of Racial Equality, 38 Park Row, New York 38, New York

Mr. H. E. Wolfe, Exchange Bank Building and Mr. Frank Harrold, St. Aug. Nat. Bank

Appendix 3

Florida Advisory Committee
U. S. Commission on Civil Rights

The City of St. Augustine has previously stated its position on matters pertaining to civil rights. There are no City ordinances prohibiting the use of any municipally owned facility by any person regardless of race, creed or color.

243

Picketing has been permitted as long as it conforms to State and City laws. There are no City ordinances which prohibit any merchant from conducting his business in the manner which he deems necessary to continue a successful business.

The City Commission of St. Augustine will permit any group of citizens the right to appear before the Commission, provided they follow the proper procedure for making such appearance. This is provided for by making application to the City Manager not later than Wednesday preceding the regular City Commission meeting, when they will be given a regular place on the agenda.

The Police and Fire Departments are the only City departments which come under Civil Service. Any one desiring to take an examination for a position in either of these departments may do so when such examinations are held. Under the new city budget provision was made to employ three more police officers, one negro and two white. The negro selected for this position came with very high qualifications and was in the process of training to go on the city payroll. However, a group of colored citizens threatened this man with dire reprisals if he took the job, forcing him to decline this employment. This man had been employed at the East Coast Hospital, and is now without a job. We question the sincerity of some people who demand better employment opportunities for our negro citizens when they use tactics such as this to destroy an opportunity for one of their own race to gain a good job in the service of his community.

The population of St. Augustine, as reported by the 1960 Federal Census, is 14,734, with an estimated 76.7% white and 23.3% colored. The last City payroll showed a total of 156 employees, 127 white an 29 negro, which percentage-wise is very close to the population percentage.

244

The City Commission has not seen the necessity for forming a Bi-Racial Committee. These committees have not proven successful in many communities in our state and in some instances have forced the resignations of duly elected City officials. No recommendation by such a committee has any standing in law which would force a merchant to comply with its recommendations against his desires. This very issue is being debated in Congress at this time.

The colored citizens of St. Augustine have never been barred from registering to vote, and have even been encouraged to do so. Because of the foregoing facts, the City Commission of St. Augustine feels that racial tension in our city has been misrepresented, and the basis for such tension has been falsely propagandized out of proportion to its true significance. This, very briefly, summarizes what we feel is the true state of affairs in St. Augustine, Florida.

Very truly yours,

Joseph A. Shelley,
Mayor-Commissioner

Appendix 4

Youth Council

National Association For The Advancement of Colored People

P. O. BOX 758

ST. AUGUSTINE, FLORIDA

August 3, 1963

245

Lyndon B. Johnson, Vice President of the
    United States of America
United States Senate Building
Washington, D. C.

Dear Mr. Vice President:

At the March 11, 1963 banquet in your honor in St. Augustine, Florida, you asked to be kept abreast of the negotiations and developments in the N.A.A.C.P.'s efforts to desegregate the Nation's Oldest City. If you remember, our objection to your visit to St. Augustine was withdrawn when we received a letter from you dated March 7, 1963. Your letter stated, that, "no event in which I will participate in St. Augustine, will be segregated. I understand that Mr. Reedy has already called you and discussed some of the arrangements that have been made." To clear the records, only twelve tickets were made available to Negroes (though there was an unlimited supply available to the white public) and the Negroes were seated at two tables reserved for them only. The arrangements referred to by Mr. Reedy and Mr. Scotty Peeks (of Senator Smathers' Office) were understood by our group to include a meeting of N.A.A.C.P. Officials and the City Commission on the Tuesday morning following your visit.

To our dismay and disappointment, instead of meeting with the City Commission we met with the City Manager,

67

his tape recorder and his secretary. Mr. Reedy had stated as late as the night of the banquet that you would probably leave an observer from your office to be present at this meeting; namely Mr. Sinclair, but no one stayed from your office nor Senator Smathers' office.

All of the requests and suggestions of the Negro Delegation were published by the City Manager's Office under the pretence of being presented to the individual City Commissioners for study. We have not heard from the City Manager, Mayor nor Commission. Three other meetings have been held with the City Officials: the only thing that was accomplished was the statement that "the City has no laws against desegregation and no control over private business plus, all public facilities were opened to the public." Needless to say, we encountered difficulty when we tried to use the same. After our first closed meeting with the Commission, members received phone calls threatening their life.

The second meeting was arranged by Vice Mayor Harry Gutterman, at a time when he and several of the other Commissioners would have returned from a workshop to see how other cities in Florida had handled their racial problems. At this third meeting on Thursday, June 13, 1963, only two commissioners of the four in town at the time appeared, even though the State N.A.A.C.P. Field Secretary, Mr. Robert Saunders, and an attorney were on hand. This meeting was gaveled to an end in about five minutes because no quorum was present. There was a standing room only crowd present with three-fourths of the crowd being Negroes. The results of the third meeting was that Mayor Joseph Shelley issued the statement, "there is no racial tension in St. Augustine, just some trouble being stirred-up by racial agitators. I see no need for a bi-racial committee nor any other negotiation group."

Since that time race relations in this city have declined to its lowest ebb. The home of the advisor to the N.A.A.C.P. Youth Council was fired upon, with four youths being injured. One injury included a bullet through a member's shoe and his heel. A shot gun and rifle were found in the auto of the four white youths when they were apprehended.

The auto in which they were apprehended had the same license-tag number as reported by the Negro youths on the car from which the shooting was done. The four white youths were set free by County Judge Charles Mathis because of insufficient evidence.

The N.A.A.C.P. Youth Council began peaceful sit-ins and picketing at Woolworth, McCrory's, Rexall and Walgreen's. These demonstrations were begun after a period of time was allowed for replies from registered letters which were sent to the local managers, regional offices and main offices, asking them to desegregate their lunch counters and employ persons without regard to race, creed or color. We did not receive a single reply. The demonstrations were peaceful and orderly for about two weeks and then County Judge Mathis issued orders for arrest.

247

Sixteen were arrested one day, seven juveniles and nine young adults. The nine adults were charged with trespassing. All were convicted by Justice of the Peace Marvin Gier, July 28, 1963 and sentenced to 45 days in jail or $100.00 fine. The seven juveniles were found to be delinquents when their parents would not sign forms, presented to them by Judge, which stated, "that they would not allow their children to participate in racial demonstrations or picketing until the youths are at least twenty-one years of age." Since St. John's County has no Juvenile Detention Home for Negroes, we have had four youths, two girls and two boys, fourteen to sixteen years of age, confined in cells at the County Jail as any common prisoner would be. Moreover, six additional youths were arrested for passing out reprints of the enclosed editorial. In addition the Youth Council Advisor's automobile, in which they were riding, was impounded.

The two juveniles were released to their parents' custody, but the other four were found guilty and sentenced to 30 days in jail or $100.00 fines. Dr. R. B. Hayling, the Youth Council Advisor's automobile is still being retained by the city.

Mr. Vice President, as you can see from these facts presented herein there seems to be no level to which this city and county government will sink in their efforts to deprive the Negro citizen of his inherent American rights.

On June 21, 1963 a union shop steward (believed to be Mr. Barker) at Fairchild Aircraft Strato Corporation called all Negro workers together and told them, if they or any other member of their family participated in any of the demonstrations or picketing in this city they would not have a job because the union nor the company would allow it. This is a terrible indictment for this International Machinist Union branch and the AFL-CIO and CLC with which this union is affiliated.

Such other police-state tactics as numerous arrests and fines of Negroes for any trivial matter or open threats to heads-of household, and innumerable dismissals from jobs for either picketing or being in sympathy with the movement.

All of the white moderates, if there are any in this area, have chosen to remain silent on all issues. The white Ministerial Alliance has even been mute. The major discouraging factor is that this is the seat of the Northeast Florida Catholic Diocese and Archbishop Joseph Hurley has received numerous communications from us but has chosen not to even acknowledge a single communique.

Local City and County Officials have charged us with being Communist and trouble makers. We know and you know, nothing could be further from the truth. One of the fifteen year old youths in jail at this time is the son of a Purple Heart Winner, in World War II: almost all of our male members have served in the Armed Forces. Dr. R. B. Hayling, our Youth Council advisor is an Air Force Officer Candidate School graduate and served a four year tour of duty. He holds the rank of First Lieutenant, U. S. Air Force Reserve.

Mr. Vice President, this is a most urgent appeal to ask you to use your good office and personal friendship with Senator Smathers, Senator Holland, Governor Bryant, Mr. Herbert E. Wolfe, Mr. Frank Harrold, Archbishop Joseph Hurley and other State, County and City Officials to let Christian practices and principles prevail in achieving racial harmony in this community.

Our organization will await your advice and assistance in correcting these most evil conditions in our Nation's oldest city.

Yours for a more Democratic St. Augustine, Florida.

Mr. Gerald Eubanks,
Youth Council President

249

R. B. Hayling D.D.S.,
Advisor, Youth Council

CC: President John F. Kennedy
Washington, D.C.

Attorney General Robert Kennedy
Washington, D.C.

Senator Spessard Holland, United States Senate
Washington, D.C.

Senator George Smathers, United States Senate,
Washington, D.C.

Senator Jacob Javits, United States Senate,
Washington, D.C.

Senator Kenneath Keating, United States Senate,
Washington, D.C.

Appendix 5

March 11, 1964

The Massachusetts Chapter of
The Southern Christian Leadership Conference
41 Winthrop Street
Boston, Massachusetts

250

Dear Sir:

Spring Vacation is a time when college students from all over the nation head south to the sunny beaches of Florida. During the coming spring vacation, the Southern Christian Leadership Conference of St. Augustine, Florida, invites the Massachusetts Chapter of the SCLC and clergy and students from the colleges and universities of New England to join with it in its struggle for human rights in St. Augustine.

This call is issued because of the particularly intolerable conditions within the city of St. Augustine; it may well be that the oldest historic city in the United States is one in which the patterns of discrimination, hatred, and violence are most deeply entrenched. As this city prepares to celebrate its Quadricentennial, it asks the people of the nation for support through a congressional appropriation of $350,-000. It is plainly ludicrous to use a city, as an example to the world, of a free people in a free country, when that city daily denies freedom to its Negro citizens.

The Southern Christian Leadership Conference of St. Augustine hopes that clergymen and students from New England will act with it in bringing to light the tragic conditions existing for Negro citizens of this city and help in seeking a remedy for this moral blight which lays so heavily on the nation as well as on this community.

Sincerely,

Dr. R. B. Hayling, for the
St. Augustine Chapter of the SCLC

FLORIDA SPRING
PROJECT
SCM-SCLC

251

Sponsored by:

    STUDENT CHRISTIAN MOVEMENT and SOUTHERN CHRISTIAN LEADERSHIP CONFERENCE

    DEMONSTRATIONS in ST. AUGUSTINE FLORID/

        MARCH 21 to March 28

            and/or

        MARCH 29 to April 4

RACIAL AND CIVIL DISORDERS IN ST. AUGUSTINE

FACTS: St. Augustine, Florida, has one of the tightest segregation systems in the South, and yet is one of the most isolated and least publicized. Most public facilities are segregated, including hotels, restaurants, and the local hospital. The only instance of school integration was followed two weeks later by the burning of the family's house. No tenure or civil service status is granted to any Negro city employee. In adequate police protection has contributed to several shootings and beatings. Demonstrations have been curtailed the past five months by the city's use of 15 police dogs donated by the local Rotary Club. These conditions are not generally known because of rigid press control in the city.

St. Augustine, the oldest city in the United States, is about to celebrate the 400th anniversary of its founding. For this purpose, it is requesting a Federal grant of $350,000. Since the city is largely dependent on tourist trade, and will be particularly so in the coming year, local and regional Negro leaders feel that a great deal can be accomplished to weaken the segregation system by a short period of concentrated direct action.

WHAT ACTION ? In response to a request by the leadership of the local chapter of the Southern Christian Leadership Conference (SCLC), the Student Christian Movement of New England and the Massachusetts chapter of SCLC have committed their support in sending students and faculty from the New England area to be put at the disposal of local leadership. A number of different approaches are under consideration including demonstrations, visits to local public and private officials, speeches and visits within the Negro community, and training sessions. Large numbers of students and faculty, of both sexes, are needed to make this an effective protest.

WHAT IS INVOLVED? This is not a vacation, these are serious demonstrations. Arrests are not planned at this time, but students must be willing to accept it. Before demonstrations, participants will be trained and expected to follow non-violent action techniques. All participants must agree to a non-violent approach and to the rules which have been established by the SCLC for non-violent direct action.

The costs involved will be transportation plus $4 a day for meals and accomodations. It is hoped that it will be possible to stay with local families in St. Augustine. Students should previously secure a source of bail (up to $500) if at all possible.

It is hoped that participants can work out their own transportation. SCM plans to charter busses where practicable and necessary.

IN NEW HAVEN CONTACT:
FLORIDA SPRING PROJECT
404-A YALE STATION
NEW HAVEN, CONNECTICUT
624-8996

RACIAL AND CIVIL DISORDERS IN ST. AUGUSTINE

APPLICATION

Name (please print)_____

School address_____Phone_____

Home address_____Phone_____

Age_____   Sex_____   Race_____

Departure date_____From where?_____

Return date_____To where?_____

Do you have a car?_____Number of passengers_____
                                (excluding yourself)

[   ] I can secure $500 bail if necessary.

[   ] I can secure $_____ bail if necessary.

Previous participation in civil-rights work, if any:_____

_____

If possible, give this form to your area representative (see previous page).
If not, mail to Florida Easter Project, 404A Yale Station, New Haven,
Connecticut.

I agree to abide by SCLC rules of non-violent conduct, to obey instructions
of the local SCLC, and to stay in jail up to three days if asked to by
SCLC. I recognize an obligation for action in the North after returning
from this project.

_____   _____
       (Date)   (Signature)

253

MASSACHUSETTS UNIT OF THE SOUTHERN CHRISTIAN LEADERSHIP CONFERENCE

Visit to St. Augustine, Florida

GENERAL INFORMATION

Dates: Clergymen and students from the North will be in St. Augustine from March 21 through April 4. Anyone who goes should plan to spend a minimum of four days in the city.

Transportation: If enough people plan to go and return on the same dates, we will try to charter a bus. Otherwise, the wisest transportation is by Greyhound or by plane. Please coordinate all transportation plans with Bill England.

Costs: Each participant is asked to pay $5.00 dues to the Mass. unit of SCLC (for legal and administrative costs). Transportation costs will be as follows: Bus; $64.55, Plane $111.72 (from Boston). If a full bus could be chartered the cost could be reduced to $45. If private cars are to be used a savings might be enjoyed. In addition each participant must be prepared to contribute to board in homes or as the St. Augustine SCLC sees fit ($4 per day is an acceptable estimate). Legal costs are discussed below.

Legal matters: Mr. William A. Kunstler is our counsel. He will seek to have all cases tried in Federal District Courts where defendants need not appear. This may not be possible. Defendants should be prepared to return when and if they are called. This may go on for some years. Participants should be prepared to help raise money for their defense. Further information on bail procedure will be forthcoming within the next few days.

Press relations: All press coverage is handled by Mass. Unit of SCLC. A spokesman for the group will be appointed, and other participants should not deal with the press. This is quite important to maintain a unity

254

within the group. You could send us names and addresses of people or paper who want to receive press releases.

Clothing: Participants are asked to wear ties or clericals at all times in St. Augustine. Also they are asked to take sleeping bags.

General qualifications: Dr. Cox's article gives a picture of the tense situation in St. Augustine. Our coming will increase this. Many have sought to dissuade us with predictions of violence. No one denies this possibility. The advocate of non-violence does not deny violence. The existing conditions of injustice results in great violence to the lives of people there. Non-violent direct action is a means of speaking and acting in the midst of a violent world, in a way that seeks to convert the world. Anyone who is not committed to non-violence should not go to St. Augustine. Workshops will be held for all participants when they arrive. In St. Augustine each participant must be prepared to follow the authority of the designated leader. Each participant must be willing to go to jail.

255

Support from the North: Those who cannot go South are asked to participate in supporting actions in the North (for both Williamston, N.C. and St. Augustine). We will be asking those who will to join in a fast, beginning some time during Holy Week. Let us know if you want to be informed about this. Details will be available from the SCM office.

Contacts: The coordinator in the North is the Rev. William England of B.U. His number is CO 7-2100 (office ext. 512) and KE 6-3788 (home). Information is also available from the Rev. Sam Slie. (EL 4-6583). Mass. Unit of SCLC office is at 41 Winthrop St. (GA 7-2993). In St. Augustine Dr. Hayling's office number is 305-VA 9-3126.

All of the above can be changed without notice.

Appendix 6

STATEMENT OF JOSEPH A. SHELLEY

MAYOR-COMMISSIONER OF THE CITY OF

SAINT AUGUSTINE, FLORIDA, MARCH 22, 1964

The following statements are in answer to accusations contained in a folder being distributed on University Campuses of the New England States. This folder is sponsored by the Southern Christian Movement and Southern Christian Leadership Conference.

It states that most public facilities are segregated. This is totally false. There are no city ordinances requiring segregation. All publicly owned facilities have been desegregated. There are privately owned facilities that are segregated the same as in Washington, New York, Boston and Chicago. Hotels, Restaurants, and the only local hospital are privately owned. The City of St. Augustine has no authority over any of these properties.

It states the only instance of school integration was followed *two weeks* later by burning of the family's house. This is false in several respects. Three schools were desegregated in September of 1963 without incident of any kind. On February 7, 1964 the Robinson family home burned down under suspicious circumstances. This was six months after the schools were integrated. Oddly enough, the family bought this home in 1958 for approximately $2,200 and in October 1963 insured it for $11,500. The State Fire Marshall was called in to investigate this fire and his report confirmed the local fire Chief's report that the fire apparently started around an oil heater in direct contrast to statements issued by the family. Insurance companies are still investigating this fire. Furthermore, the Robinsons themselves issued a statement after the fire that they had been treated well at all school functions and P.T.A. meetings for six months prior to the fire.

78

The folder states that no tenure or civil service status is granted to any Negro City employee. This is false. The only departments of the City covered by civil service are the police and fire departments. There are no restrictions as to national origin, religion or color on who may take examinations for these two departments.

The folder states that inadequate police protection contributed to several beatings and shootings. This is false. The only floggings occurred about three miles outside the City of St. Augustine. The City refused to give the Ku Klux Klan a permit to parade and hold a meeting in the City. It was held in the country and the four Negroes who were beaten were attempting to spy on the meeting. The Klan's men arrested by the Sheriff's office were all from Jacksonville, Florida. The first shooting incident that occurred would have been prevented had certain Negro citizens cooperated with the police department. Under questioning a local leader of the N.A.A.C.P. admitted that he knew trouble was brewing but would not call the police because the police chief had insulted him.

The folder states that demonstrations have been curtailed for the past five months by the city's use of 15 police dogs donated by the local Rotary Club. This is a totally false statement. In October 1963 the N.A.A.C.P. initiated court proceedings against the Mayor and all City Commissioners, the Police Chief and the Sheriff of St. Johns County in which the City of St. Augustine is located. At the conclusion of this trial held before a Federal Judge in Jacksonville, Florida, the Court gave the City officials a 100% clean slate. He stated that there was no evidence of public discrimination by the City, that only private discrimination existed. The Court further severely criticized and reprimanded the leadership of the local N.A.A.C.P. for coming into Court with unclean hands. Demonstrations had stopped before, during and after this trial.

Now about the dogs. First, they were not donated by the local Rotary Club. The City Commission included in the 1964 budget funds sufficient to hire three new policemen, two white and one Negro patrolman. They were selected from

257

among candidates who passed their Civil Service exam and who received security clearance. They trained with the police department and on the night before they were to go on the force the Negro candidate came to the Chief and said that he had been threatened and coerced by the local N.A.A.C.P. until he felt it would be impossible to go on the force. After a discussion the City Commission determined that the money which would have paid his salary and clothing allowance would train, house and feed 15 police dogs. On September 9, 1963, *after* demonstrations had stopped, the dogs and their masters began an intensive course of training. They graduated and joined the police force on February 16, 1964. They have never been used on demonstrators or any other people to this date. They ride in patrol cars at night and thus release one patrolman from night duty. Prior to the use of these dogs two men patrolled at night. Incidentally, night prowlers and peeping tom complaints have been reduced by 70%. The record speaks for itself.

The folder speaks of rigid press controls which have kept its content from becoming generally known. Quite the contrary is true. As Mayor of St. Augustine I have never refused to talk to reporters, radio or magazine editors. The Miami Herald, The Daytona Beach News Journal and the St. Petersburg Times have repeatedly blasted the City of St. Augustine and accepted as truth practically all statements issued by the N.A.A.C.P. The New York Times sent Mrs. Phillips down here for one week and she wrote a fairly nice article. The Times Magazine sent a reporter to St. Augustine and after a 30 minute interview he apparently chose not to write anything about our City.

JOSEPH A. SHELLEY
MAYOR-COMMISSIONER
CITY OF ST. AUGUSTINE,
FLORIDA

258

Appendix 7

The three elderly and wealthy old ladies who acted as "dummy" owners of the Daily Worker were:

Anna M. W. Pennypacker of Philadelphia
Susan H. Woodruff
Fernandina W. Reed

259

Appendix 8

City of Saint Augustine

OFFICE OF
THE
CITY MANAGER

SAINT AUGUSTINE, FLORIDA
November 19, 1964

To Whom It May Concern:

Saint Augustine's racial disturbances began in the summer of 1963. These consisting primarily of sit-ins and lie-ins at restaurants and lunch counters located in the down town area. There was also picketing of the Chamber of Commerce, City Hall and a number of business establishments with lunch counters. These demonstrations were being supervised by two full time N. A. A. C. P. Field Directors, Willie Luden of Savannah and James Brown of Tifton, Georgia. The final demonstration was held in the down town plaza on Labor Day. This meeting was held without obtaining a permit from the City, thus resulted in the arrest of approximately 30 negroes. Permits had always been granted to any organization desiring to meet and requesting a permit. The City requires advance notice so proper police personnel could be on hand to handle traffic and crowds.

A few days after Labor Day the City Manager was informed by one of the N. A. A. C. P. Field Directors that they were pulling out of Saint Augustine because of the way Dr. Robert Hayling was acting. He and two other negroes had deliberately gone to a Ku Klux Klan meeting which was held several miles outside of the City of Saint Augustine, after being advised not to go by the N. A. A. C. P. Field Directors. To my knowledge this was the last time the N. A. A. C. P. was directly involved in the Saint Augustine demonstrations. In November, 1963 Dr. Hayling announced that he was resigning his position as Youth Director of the local N. A. A. C. P. Chapter. The local law enforcement agencies, Sheriff's Department and Saint Augustine Police Department, had no trouble handling the disturbances. The local people paid very little attention to the picketing and sit-ins, and went on about their business. Everything was very quiet until April, 1964 when we learned that

RACIAL AND CIVIL DISORDERS IN ST. AUGUSTINE

Dr. Hayling had invited students from Northern Colleges to spend their Easter vacations in Saint Augustine. Dr. Hayling had sent letters in March, 1964 to a number of these Colleges, giving false and misleading information about the conditions in Saint Augustine. Dr. Hayling had made this request in behalf of the Saint Augustine Chapter of theSouthern Christian Leadership Conference. This was when we learned that Dr. Hayling had joined forces with Martin Luther King's S. C. L. C.

It was through the Massachusetts Chapter of the S. C. L. C. that Mrs. Malcom Peabody, mother of the Governor of Massachusetts, came to Saint Augustine. Advance publicity was given out that she was coming, and immediately a large number of newsmen were sent to cover her arrival and planned arrest. Prior to her arrival a number of college students and professors had arrived and immediately attempted sit-ins and were arrested. These arrests were made after the property owners had requested them to leave their property and they refused. There was no demonstration during the Easter period that the local law enforcement was not able to handle.

After the arrest of Mrs. Peabody, Saint Augustine was the main topic for newsmen throughout the United States. It was very evident that Martin Luther King and the newsmen were working together in the demonstrations. Newsmen were notified of when, what and where everything was to happen. It was very easy for the local law enforcement officers to know where the demonstrations were to take place, because the news media would set up their equipment in advance.

There was a lull in the demonstrations after Easter until June, at which time Martin Luther King sent his personal staff of field workers to direct the Saint Augustine project. The demonstrations were very orderly as long as they were being held in the day time. The local people and tourists paid very little attention to the marching and sit-ins. Due to the lack of local support in the day time, the demonstrations were changed to late at night. The night demonstrations gave outsiders time enough to come to Saint Augustine after getting off work.

The local law enforcement officers had complete control of the demonstrations as long as they were held in the day time, but the night marches created a problem. This brought about an order from the City Manager and Chief of Police that there was to be no street marching after 8:00 P.M. Immediately, City officials and the County Sheriff were taken to Federal Court. Federal Judge Simpson, Jacksonville, ruled that the negroes could march anytime and any place they desired. This order tied the hands of the law enforcement officers, and turned the demonstrators loose to do as they pleased. The Court order further stated that the demonstrators were to be protected from anyone trying to interfere with them.

The Federal Court order created additional trouble. Outside white groups, led by Halstead Manucy, Saint Augustine; Connie Lynch, California; and J. B. Stoner, Atlanta began holding meetings and marches at the same time as the negro demonstrations were being held.

Governor Bryant had sent troopers to assist the Sheriff and City Police. When the negro and white groups began demonstrating at the same time, it was almost impossible to prevent minor outbreaks of disorder. These outbreaks of disorder were very quickly brought under control, and at no time did they last more than a couple of minutes. The press played up every incident, to make outsiders believe that there was just no law and order in St. Augustine.

262

There is no doubt in the minds of all local law enforcement officials, that the misleading press releases were causing the greatest trouble. The Governor, bowing to outside pressure, issued an Executive Order on June 15, 1964, establishing a Special Police force. This Special Police Force was to direct all law enforcement of the County. Instead of strengthening the law enforcement, it created friction between the different agencies which up to this time, had been working together.

The Special Police force began searching, and questioning only the white people and left negroes alone to do as they pleased. There were a number of incidents where the white people were arrested or pushed around for no reason at all. The Special Police force would not help the Chief of Police and Sheriff in enforcing valid State laws regarding trespassing of private property, when requested by the property owners. It seemed to us that this Special Police force had been given instructions to leave the negroes alone, but arrest all the white people they could. The local people became very upset about the way the outside law enforcement officers were acting.

When the Civil Rights Bill was passed, the merchants agreed to comply with all of it's requirements. This brought on another problem. The restaurants and motels that were complying with the law, found their places of business being picketed by white people. This continued until Federal Judge Simpson issued a restraining order against those picketing. Since that time everything has been very quiet and peaceful.

Charles P. Barrier

Charles P. Barrier,
City Manager

Appendix 9

The St. Augustine Record

PUBLISHED BY THE ST. AUGUSTINE RECORD, INC.

OLDEST NEWSPAPER IN THIS OLDEST CITY

ST. AUGUSTINE, FLORIDA
32084

263

January Seventh, 1965

Florida Legislative Investigation Committee,
Post Office Box 1044,
Tallahassee, Florida.

Attention Mr. R. O. Mitchell, Chairman.

Dear Mr. Mitchell:

As per the request of Mr. K. Baarslag, Special Consultant to your committee, for a statement of fact from our publication with regards to racial strife in St. Augustine during the period from April 1964 to the present time, I make the following statements.

During this period of time, it was our unfortunate task to cover a series of demonstrations and public altercations between groups of racist, both Negro and white. Using the files of our publication and examining their contents for a hindsight overall picture, it was quite easy to make the following conclusions.

#1. Racial demonstrations in St. Augustine were planned and implemented for one single reason—"National Publicity." Within a city of 500,000 population, it would have taken at least 10,000 demonstrators to make national headlines and in our small community, an imported group of 150, proved to be most successful.

85

#2. The stimulus to both sides of the racists view-point can easily be laid at the feet of the national news media: i.e. on several occasions I personally witnessed newsmen urging Negro demonstrators into action on a given date and the next day, urging white demonstrators in the same manner. The entire racial panorama was staged, using the Nation's Oldest City as the theatre and world-wide television and news media readers as the audience.

#3. The Federal Court appeared to be the most important single detriment to local and state law enforcement in the keeping of the peace: i.e. while racial agitators, both Negro and white were planning to parade the streets of St. Augustine, with full support of the Federal Court, Federal courts in New York and New Jersey prohibited same.

#4. It appears that the arrival of outside agitators, such as Mrs. Malcolm Peabody and Martin Luther King, served no useful purpose other than to play roles in the stage play scheduled by the Southern Leadership Conference and the National Council of Churches.

#5. I have furnished for Mr. Baarslag's use, four files of clippings with regards to numerous incidents occurring over a two year period, all of which were witnessed either by myself or by a staff member. I further offer to you and your committee, my own personal testimony, and that of any member of our staff, with the fervent hope that no other city in Florida will be offered on the racial altar as a publicity stunt to aid and abet the desires and plans of organizations such as the SCLS, NAACP, CORE, and the National Council of Churches.

With kind regards

Sincerely,

A. H. Tebault, Jr.

86

Appendix 10

Mayor Issues Statement On Seriousness Of Taking Part In Demonstrations

Mayor Joseph A. Shelley has issued the following statement to the citizens of St. Augustine and St. Johns County:

Spring is here and summer is just around the corner. With summer will come the end of the 1963-64 school year. I believe that this is an appropriate time to call to the attention of all our citizens something which I consider to be of the gravest importance.

Militant civil rights leaders in a number of different organizations have repeatedly stated that with the coming of summer they intend to continue their demonstrations in St. Augustine. What I am offering is not a warning, but rather it is a word of advice and a word of caution to all parents of young people of both races in St. Augustine. Soon these young people will be out of school. With the coming of the summer heat, it is a well known scientific fact that emotions and passions run deeper. Idle minds and idle hands are a fertile field for bad and evil thoughts and actions. Parents can not for one moment escape being held, to some degree, responsible for the actions of their children.

Police Department records all over the United States prove beyond doubt one definite fact. A high percentage of young people who are coerced, induced or otherwise appealed to by violent, radical civil rights leaders to go out and deliberately break civil laws of a state or community have become later involved in crimes of violence which place a criminal mark against their records. Once a young person has been induced to violate a civil law, and has gained some excitement from this adventure, it is but a simple step to become involved in criminal acts, such as burglary, breaking and entering, automobile stealing, assault and battery, and even murder and rape. I can only say that any parents who allow their children to become involved in so-called peaceful demonstrations which may later evolve into violation of state laws, are themselves involved in crimes against both God and man. Keep in mind that once a criminal act and conviction becomes part of the record of your child, that he or she may well find it impossible to gain useful employment for the rest of his or her life. Any person convicted of a felony can never enlist in the military services nor can they ever hold a Civil Service job. These black marks, once they are placed against a person's records, can be very difficult to erase.

For many years, the people of St. Augustine of both races have lived side by side in peace and tranquility. Many close and binding friendships have developed because of the serenity which has surrounded life in St. Augustine, but because of the demonstrations and violence which have occurred in the past year, relationships between long standing friends have become strained. The acts of innocent individuals in both races now become suspect. No matter what laws are passed in Washington, the damage which has been done to relationships between the races in St. Augustine and in practically every other community in the United States, will be a long time in healing. Do you want to contribute to this further disintegration of relationships between our people in St. Augustine? You have a choice. You have a full, free choice of your activities in the coming months ahead. If you consider yourselves to be responsible citizens, you will adhere to the laws which are in effect in the state today. These laws are designed to protect the rights and property of all citizens, and as long as they are valid, as long as they are not repealed by a constitutional amendment, or declared unconstitutional by court action, these laws will be enforced. The decision is yours.

Mayor Joseph A. Shelley

266

Appendix 11

Executive Department

Tallahassee

Executive Order Number One   267

Pursuant to the authority vested in me by Chapter 14, Florida Statutes, and in implementation of my Proclamation dated June 15, 1964, I hereby promulgate the following Order; and when the same is filed with the Secretary of State of Florida, it shall have the force and effect as law and shall remain in effect until revoked by my further order.

Section 1.1—There is hereby created a special law enforcement detail which shall be known and designated as "Special Police Force." The duty and purpose of the Special Police Force shall be to maintain peace and good order and to enforce all state laws and municipal ordinances applicable in St. Johns County, Florida. In the performance of any of the powers, duties, and functions authorized by law or by orders promulgated pursuant to the Proclamation issued by the Governor dated June 15, 1964, the members of the Special Police Force shall have the same protections and immunities afforded other peace officers, which shall be recognized by all courts having jurisdiction over offenses against the laws of this State. All officers temporarily assigned to the Special Police Force shall continue to receive all pay, allowances, and benefits from the appropriation of and in accordance with the laws governing their respective departments.

Section 1.2—The Special Police Force shall consist of each and every officer of the Florida Highway Patrol, State Board of Conservation, State Beverage Department, Florida Sheriffs Bureau, Game and Freshwater Fish Commission, and those investigators from the Governor's and Attorney General's offices as are designated and assigned by the Governor and the Attorney General, respectively.

Section 1.3—The number of officers temporarily assigned for duty in St. Johns County from each of the departments of the state government subject to this Order shall be designated by the Governor; and upon receiving from the Governor the number of men required to be temporarily assigned, the agency or department head shall notify the Commander of the Florida Highway Patrol of the names of the officers so temporarily assigned, after which time these officers shall be under the general supervision and direction of the Commander of the Florida Highway Patrol until relieved from this assignment by the Commander.

Section 1.4—The Commander of the Florida Highway Patrol shall designate one of its members as the Commanding Officer of the Special Police Force, and the officer so designated shall have direct supervision and control of all officers temporarily assigned for duty in St. Johns County. The Commanding Officer of the Force shall designate one of its members as Deputy Commanding Officer and shall make such other assignments and appointments as in his discretion seem proper.

Section 1.5—The officers of the Special Police Force are hereby declared to be police and peace officers with power to make arrest for violations of the laws of this State committed in St. Johns County, for violations of municipal ordinances of any municipality in said county including St. Augustine, and for violations of any rule or regulation promulgated by the Governor pursuant to his Proclamation of June 15, 1964.

Section 1.6—The officers of the Special Police Force shall have power and are hereby directed and ordered to investigate any violation of the law which may be reported to them or which may come to their attention and to accumulate all evidence necessary. The officers of this Force shall prefer charges against all persons they have reasonable grounds to believe have violated the law.

Section 1.7—The headquarters of the Special Police Force shall be the Florida National Guard Armory in St. Augustine, Florida; and the State Adjutant General is hereby order and directed to cooperate with the Force and to make available such space, equipment, secretarial assistance, and facilities as shall be necessary to perform the duties required.

Section 1.8—The Sheriffof St. Johns County, the Chiefs of Police of every municipality of St. Johns County, and each and every officer and deputy, special or regular, operating under their authority, jurisdiction, or control are hereby ordered and directed to fully enforce the laws of Florida, municipal ordinances of St. Augustine, Florida, and to promptly arrest and charge any person who violates the same and to do all lawful things necessary to maintain peace and good order.

Section 1.9—Each and every peace and police officer of the Special Police Force, the Sheriff of St. Johns County, the Chief of Police of St. Augustine are ordered and directed to submit a daily report to the Commanding Officer of the Special Police Force of all arrests made in St. Johns County during the previous 24-hour period. Among the information required to be submitted shall be the names, addresses, and ages of those so arrested, the formal charge made both by the arresting officer and by the court, the bonds set on each case, and the disposition of any previous charges which took place during the previous 24-hour period. To be included in said daily report shall be a descriptive report of all weapons seized or taken into custody, the names and addresses from whom taken, and an identification of those weapons, including serial numbers if available. All weapons taken into custody by state, county, or municipal officers, after being properly identified, shall be delivered to the custody of the Commanding Officer of the Special Police Force for transmittal to the crime laboratory of the Florida Sheriffs Bureau, Tallahassee, Florida, for such tests and identification as in his discretion seems proper.

Section 1.10—The Sheriff of St. Johns County, and the Chief of Police of St. Augustine as custodians of the county

269

91

and city jails, respectively, shall also make a daily report to the Commanding Officer of the Special Police Force of the names of all defendants delivered to his custody and the disposition of the charges placed against them during the previous 24-hour period.

Section 1.11—The Commanding Officer of the Special Police Force shall create an investigative division to make a thorough investigation of any circumstances which, in the Commanding Officer's discretion, shall be proper including any arrest or failure to arrest on the part of any state, county, or city officer. One of the duties of this investigative division shall be to maintain proper records of incidents, intelligence reports, arrests made in the county, the bond set on each of the charges preferred, the disposition of such case, a descriptive report of all weapons seized or taken into custody by any city, county or state officer, and the names and addresses from whom taken. These reports as prepared by this division shall be forwarded daily to the Governor, the Attorney General, and the Director of the Department of Public Safety.

Section 1.12—Any person, firm, corporation, association, officers or members of such firm, corporation, or association, or public official who shall interfere with or fail to comply with the provisions of any rule, regulation or order made pursuant to the Proclamation of the Governor dated June 15, 1964, shall be guilty of a misdemeanor and be punished as prescribed by law. Any officer failing to comply with the provisions of the Proclamation dated June 15, 1964, or any order promulgated pursuant thereto shall be guilty of malfeasance in office.

Section 1.13—The Attorney General of Florida or his designee shall provide such legal advice to the Special Police Force as from time to time shall be necessary in the performance of its duties; and in his absence the State Attorney of the Seventh Judicial Circuit shall consult with and render whatever legal assistance is necessary to the Special Police Force to effect the goals and objectives of said Special Police Force.

Section 1.14—This Order shall be liberally construed so that the greatest force and effect may be given to its provisions for the maintenance of peace and order under the state of emergency which presently exists in St. Johns County, Florida.

IN TESTIMONY WHEREOF, I have hereunto set my hand and caused the Great Seal of the State of Florida to be affixed at Tallahassee, the Capital, this 15th day of June, 1964, A.D.

SEAL

271

GOVERNOR

ATTEST:

SECRETARY OF STATE

Appendix 12

TO THE HONORABLE BRYAN SIMPSON
UNITED STATES DISTRICT JUDGE
JACKSONVILLE, FLORIDA:

272

We, the undersigned residents of the City of St. Augustine, Florida and residing on Central Avenue, Valencia Street, Cordova Street, Cuna Street, King Street, Markland Place and Menendez Avenue, respectfully petition Your Honor for relief from the annoyance of nightly negro marches.

We assure Your Honor that we are law abiding and non-participating in any racial demonstrations; however, we have been unduly disturbed by singing, clapping of hands and general noise of 200 to 300 marching negroes accompanied by police officers, sheriff's deputies, highway patrolmen and dogs and these demonstrations have continued until as late as 11 o'clock p.m., long after the average citizen has retired for the night.

We earnestly urge Your Honor to give us relief of your injunction which prevents the police officers from protecting us in our peace and quiet.

We also respectfully represent that the atmosphere occasioned by these night marches is detrimental to our children and harmful to the entire community.

NAME	ADDRESS
	102 King St
	Monson Motor Lodge
	46 Avenida Menendez
James Kalina	18 Bay St
	99 King St
Mrs. Robert N. Pattie	20 Valencia St
Ev Overby	6 Valencia St.
Mrs. M. B. Dalton	6 Valencia St
Wallace L. Lopez	#116 La Quinta Pl.

94

NAME   **ADDRESS**

[handwritten list of names and addresses, partly illegible]

F. Victor Grahic ?   12 - Fort Marin - line

Bernice Dinger   Cliff... by Dorothy   16 Bay St.

Mrs. Lola Erickson   16 Bay St.

Fred J. Erickson   Mgr. Monton...   16" "

Bill Hartigan   87 St. George St.

Oscar J. Stevens   21 Bay St.

Charles W. Adams   24 Bay St.   273

Norene Adams   24 Bay St.

Nicholas Prince

James Dart   Tanana Ships Bar

Eugene S. Wasson   King St.

Mrs. Eugene S. Wasson

Ben W. Adams   146 King

Mrs. Ben W. Adams   148 King St.

Mamie Andrew   134 King St.

Izora Blackwelder   4 Clark St.

Mrs. C.B. May — 121 King St.

D. D. Wells   27 Milton St.

C.R. Howe Jr. —   20 Central Ave.

J.H. Lanpher   11 Central Ave.

Mrs. J.H. Lanpher   11 Central Ave.

Theodore Mueller

Andrew Mumford, Jr.   86 Cedar 3 tree

Mrs. C.R. Howe, Jr.   20 Central

Jane S. Hetherington   22 Central

Tom Alyea   Sanford Street

Jim Alexander   Sanford Street

Mrs. Gordon Pacetty   24 Central

NAME   **ADDRESS**

274

[The following are handwritten names and addresses]

Sharpl M Perry - Marsha Perry
21 De Soto Pl.

Mrs. M.M. Evans
34 Central Ave.

Mrs. D.H. Gatlin - 58 Central Ave.
D.H. Gatlin " "

Mr & Mrs N.P. Stabel - 186 So Oneida St. City

Mrs. R.L. Stone - 30 De Soto Place

Emory L. Jenkins 27 De Soto place

Sons E.G. Jenkins 27 De Soto Pl.

Dora theresa - 27 De Soto Pl.

Herbert Davis 25 De Soto Pl, St. Augustine, Fla

Mr & Mrs Charles Pawlety 25 Desoto plc.

Kenneth A. Arreola - 11 Cordova St.

W.H. Forrester - 115 Cordova St.

W Forrester - 115 Bridge St

John Gunski 80 Cedar st

L H Boos 40 cedar st

Hathie L. Baas - 80 Cedar st

Thomas A. Warne 80 Cedar St

John Versaggi 48 Valencia

Arthur Spiller Jr. 38 Valencia St.

Clyde C. Hoey 45 Valencia St.

Marie von Eberstein 140 Markland Place

Mrs Vincent J Amato 41 Valencia st Aug Fla

Mr. V.J. Amato 41 Valencia St. St. Augustine. Fla

Miss S. Vowell 29 Valencia St. Augustine Fla

Mr. Joseph D. Colee 68 Cuna St. augustine fla

Mrs Joseph D. Colee 68 Cuna St. Augustine, Fla
34 Cordova st

Arnold J. Segui 36 Cordova St.

Emma K. Segui

Kathryn Tillett 14 Saragossa St.
32 Valencia St St augustine

H. Coughlan

Ray doom 42 Rhode ave.

Mrs. F.C. (Ruth) Bowman 20 Saragossa St St. Augustine Fla.

NAME	ADDRESS
Mrs. Gilbert Lopez	113 La Quinta Place
David C. Brock (mark)	111 La Quinta Place
John H. McGee	93 King St.
Henry J. Bingham	51 Cordova St.
Stuart Gray	20 Granada St.
Mrs. C. Adolw Killey	70 Cuna St.
Charles Keeley	70 Cuna St.
Paul Ray Jr.	218 Laguna
W. F. Clark	145 Blanco
S. Thompson	61 St. George
Mrs. John E. Cook, Jr.	23 Cuna Street
Mrs. Vera S. Harnage	75 Weeden Street
H. C. Jarvis	Marine St
D. L. Tylly	285 Cathedral Place
Olive Lawton	134 Marine Street
Melana Davelli	7 St. Lawrence Court
Marion Wilson Gray	103 South Tanlangan
Hazel McCormack	75 Ribena St.
Ed Lynam Faver	135 Marine St.
D. L. Bracett	16 M Jatial St.
G. P. Gibson	929 Leo Blvd.
R. E. Curtan	202 Oglethorpe
Robert Smith	Trade Winds

275

97

Appendix 13

STATE OF FLORIDA

EXECUTIVE DEPARTMENT

TALLAHASSEE

Executive Order Number Two

WHEREAS, the Governor of the State of Florida is authorized and empowered under the constitution, statutory law, and police power of the State to take such measures and to do all and every act and thing which he may deem necessary in order to prevent overt threats of violence or violence to the persons or property of citizens of the State and to maintain peace, tranquility, and good order of the State, and

WHEREAS, the Governor, under Article IV, Section 6 of the constitution of the State of Florida, is charged with the responsibility to take care that the laws be faithfully executed and has the dominant interest in protecting the people against violence, and in his capacity as the Supreme Executive power of the State as chief magistrate, and as natural guardian of the public is empowered under the general sovereign authority of the State to prevent violence and overt threats of violence, and

WHEREAS, because of the circumstances and conditions now existing in St. Augustine, St. Johns County, Florida, I make the following findings of fact:

1. On June 10, 1964, I ordered certain state law enforcement officers to St. Augustine, St. Johns County, Florida, in an effort to assist in maintaining peace and order therein under the circumstances created by certain demonstrations, counter-demonstrations, and protests being carried on in said county, and since that time violence has been prevented.

2. The government of Florida has recognized and is dedicated to the protection of the rights of its citizens to peace-

fully express and assert their views and protest as is guaranteed by the constitutions of the United States and the State of Florida, and I have exercised appropriate power and authority entrusted to me to provide protection for a lawful assertion of such protests and views.

3. On June 15, 1964, I invoked certain emergency powers available to me as Governor to make every reasonable effort to insure the maintenance of law and order and the protection of the rights of individuals existing in and being asserted in St. Augustine, St. Johns County, Florida, and assigned to this area an additional 150 state law enforcement officers, all vested with sufficient powers to effectively carry out reasonable objectives and to provide reasonable means of protection for those asserting their views and demonstrating their protest in said community. Every opportunity has been given for those so demonstrating their views and protests to do so in a reasonable, lawful, and peaceful fashion, but certain lawlessness and utter disregard for the laws of Florida exhibited by the demonstrators and counter-demonstrators such as an invasion of private property, disobedience of lawful orders of the officers, and disturbances of the public peace, have all caused the nighttime demonstrations being carried on nightly by white and negro groups in said area to create a danger to peace and order.

4. The physical layout of the routes used by these demonstrators consists of narrow streets bordered by shrubbed and wooded areas without sufficient lighting, and contrary to certain assurances that notice would be given and routes would be designated in advance, the demonstrators have purposely attempted to mislead the law enforcement officers as to their projected routes and to times of marches; and in addition to the predominantly negro demonstrations there have been counter-demonstrations of white groups taking place on or about the same time as the negroes, all causing an intolerable situation dangerous to the persons, property, and lives of the citizens in that area.

5. I find that the law enforcement has been strengthened to its maximum since June 9 and that additional law enforce-

277

ment sent into that area would not in any way alleviate the circumstances creating the danger to peace and order.

6. That on this Saturday afternoon, June 20, 1964, notwithstanding my vigorous and aggressive effort to strengthen law enforcement in St. Johns County, Florida, to the maximum, the situation has progressively worsened in spite of the presence of state law enforcement officers sent into St. Augustine on June 10, and has worsened since state law enforcement officers were strengthened on June 15, 1964.

7. That the Grand Jury of St. Johns County after having met and attempted to conscientiously find a solution to the problems giving rise to the circumstances now in existence made their presentation suggesting several possible avenues of solution, on which occasion I called upon those to whom it was directed to act in good faith and proceed in accordance with the suggestions of this arm of the Circuit Court in and for St. Johns County. There was no good faith effort on behalf of some to attempt to find a solution to the problems but to the contrary they continued the lawless course of interferring with the rights and property of others with utter disregard of the suggestions of the Grand Jury.

8. That the demonstrations first confined to public areas in the downtown section of St. Augustine have now, without warning or advance notice, been carried into the residential areas of St. Augustine, and the law-abiding citizens of that area have been disturbed by singing, hand clapping, and general noise. These demonstrations have continued until as late as 11:00 p.m., long after the average citizen has retired for the night.

WHEREAS, pursuant to my Proclamation of June 15, 1964, and the power derived therefrom, I hereby promulgate the following rules and regulations to be designated as Executive Order Number Two as follows:

2.1 For the period of the emergency presently existing in St. Johns County, Florida, and until my further order, it shall be unlawful for any person to use any public park, public building, public street, or public facility for the purpose

278

100

of participating in any demonstration, march, parade, mass meeting or assembly between the hours of 8:30 p.m. and sunrise in St. Johns County, Florida, and any person so using such public park, public building, public street, or public facility in St. Johns County, Florida, shall be deemed to be a person participating in an unlawful assembly as prohibited by Section 870.02, Florida Statutes.

2.2 The Special Police Force, established pursuant to Executive Order Number One dated June 15, 1964, is hereby ordered and directed to disperse any such unlawful assembly in accordance with the provision of Section 870.04, Florida Statutes.

2.3 Any person violating this Order may be prosecuted and punished in accordance with Section 870.02, Florida Statutes, providing a punishment by imprisonment not exceeding six months or by fine not exceeding five hundred dollars.

279

IN TESTIMONY WHEREOF, I have hereunto set my hand and caused the Great Seal of the State of Florida to be affixed at Tallahassee, the Capital, this 20th day of June, A.D. 1964.

SEAL

GOVERNOR

ATTEST:

SECRETARY OF STATE

Appendix 14

IN THE CIRCUIT COURT, SEVENTH
JUDICIAL CIRCUIT, IN AND FOR
ST. JOHNS COUNTY, FLORIDA.

IN RE: GRAND JURY, SPRING TERM,
1964

PRESENTMENT OF GRAND JURY

TO: THE HONORABLE HOWELL W. MELTON, Presiding Circuit Judge:

We, the Grand Jurors of St. Johns County, duly sworn and empaneled for the Spring Term, 1964, have the duty to make this further presentment of the results of our deliberations into the racial unrest in the County, of our findings and recommendations.

This Grand Jury has heretofore presented to this Court its interim report, wherein the Grand Jury pledged itself to a good faith effort to attempt to bring about a peaceful solution of the racial unrest in the County and to attempt to accomplish this through local representative governmental institutions, this Grand Jury being a part thereof.

In furtherance of this pledge, the Grand Jury has spent many hours inquiring of witnesses from a cross section of both races in a good faith effort to find a solution to the local racial unrest.

The local racial problem confronting the City of St. Augustine, is no greater a problem than that of many other communities throughout the entire nation. No one denies that it exists in St. Johns County; but certainly not to the extent that has been shown to the nation by sensational news reporting.

The solution of how to solve the problem has not been an easy one to agree upon, for the solutions suggested by the witnesses or offered by the members of this Grand Jury were almost as diverse as the number of witnesses called.

In attempting to answer the question of how to solve the problem, there repeatedly arose another equally perplexing and elusive question of why St. Augustine was picked in the first instance by Dr. Martin Luther King's SOUTHERN CHRISTIAN LEADERSHIP CONFERENCE. This, at first, seemed unimportant, but as will be later shown and because of the history of St. Augustine, and the lack of job opportunity available to any race, it has become an important question to the solution of the problem.

281

Because this will be recorded among the public records of St. Johns County, the Grand Jury felt it necessary to restate some little publicized, but true, facts of the modern day history of St. Augustine.

Since the advent of mass transportation, St. Augustine has been and still remains primarily a one economy community: Tourism.

In reviewing the past history of racial relations in this community, and in light of this economic setting, the question of why St. Augustine has been picked, takes on major importance, for the Grand Jury is of the considered opinion that this question must be first understood before the solution to the problem can be had.

Racial harmony has existed in the past. A solid foundation of mutual respect has been achieved among the majority of local citizens in this community.

Unlike many cities, negroes have not been excluded from jury duty. They have served on jurys, both petty and grand, for many years, including this Grand Jury.

Unlike many cities, no voter test is required nor has one ever been required to the knowledge of this Grand Jury. In fact, by looking at the registration card itself, no classification is made as to race, color or creed.

Unlike many cities, negro homes are now and always have been interspersed throughout the mainland portion of the City; and, the inhabitants have lived in harmony.

The 13 internationally known tourist attractions are integrated.

In law enforcement, negroes have served in the past, and are serving now in this capacity.

The City has desegregated all municipal owned facilities.

The county school system is integrated, and was integrated without incident.

At the present time, two, and perhaps, more, of the modern, luxurious motels have integrated.

Two downtown lunchrooms have integrated.

The City has revised its Code to eliminate racial restrictions against the hiring of negroes in civil service positions.

Opportunities for jobs available to all people are extremely limited. Many of the service facilities are small family owned and operated, with three of four full time employees.

In this economic setting, with a solid background of harmonious race relations, with a past history of non-discrimination in governmental affairs, and of the more recent progress made toward the integration of privately owned facilities, St. Augustine has been libeled as "the most segregated City in America." This is not true.

Why then was it picked? Could it be that St. Augustine, as the nation's oldest city, is merely a symbol for the Negro civil rights movement? That those who have picked St. Augustine, are not really interested in solving the problem, but merely desire to keep this symbol before the world. This Grand Jury trusts that is not the case.

Only those who picked it can truly answer this question but its answer must be had before the problem can be solved.

The important question now becomes whether Dr. Martin Luther King, and SOUTHERN CHRISTIAN LEADERSHIP

282

CONFERENCE truly desire the problem solved here in St. Augustine.

This Grand Jury has made a good faith effort to find a solution to the community problem: This Grand Jury now calls upon Dr. Martin Luther King and all others to demonstrate their good faith by removing their influences from this community for a period of 30 days, and to further demonstrate good faith by publicly urging a cessation for alike period of time of those activities which tend to create tension; upon the expiration of 30 days following the above suggested demonstration of good faith, this Grand Jury will reconvene to name a recommended by-racial committee, composed of ten members, five negroes and five whites, whose members have tentatively agreed to serve, and to offer to that committee the services of the Grand Jury as they may be needed.

283

This Grand Jury wishes to commend our local law enforcement officials who have carried the burden of this very explosive and trying situation, and especially Sheriff L. O. Davis and Chief Virgil Stuart, Sr.

The Grand Jury respectfully requests that copies hereof be distributed to all interested parties, including the Governor of the State of Florida, the Attorney General of the State of Florida, and Federal Judge Simpson.

This Grand Jury desires to be in recess until the occurance of the above, and respectfully requests your Honor for leave to re-convene upon the happening of the same without order of court.

Respectfully submitted this 18th day of June, A. D., 1964.

Attest:

Clerk   Foreman

Appendix 15

ANSWER TO PRESENTMENT OF GRAND JURY

Dated June 18, 1964

When the Grand Jury of St. John's County was convened a few days ago, we felt that at long last the St. Augustine community was making a positive step toward the solution of its racial problem. When the presentment was given by the Grand Jury yesterday, however, we discovered that we were the victims of a blasted hope. We are, therefore, greatly disappointed at what we consider an unwise, unfair, and unreasonable position taken by the Grand Jury. It completely fails to grasp the deep discontent, the haunting frustration and the seething despair in the Negro community as a result of the continued existence of segregation and discrimination. The presentment is based on the false assumption that St. Augustine had genuinely peaceful race relations until the Southern Christian Leadership Conference "picked" it as a symbol before the world. A more honest assessment of the situation would reveal that St. Augustine has never had peaceful race relations: it may have had a negative peace which was the absence of tension, but certainly not a positive peace which is the presence of justice.

True, St. Augustine has made progress in race relations, like numerous other cities, but one must realize that progress whets the appetite for greater progress. Moreover, it must be recognized that the progress made has not been nearly great enough to compensate for the centuries of injustice and oppression inflicted upon the Negro. One needs to catalogue the numerous unsolved shootings and bombings in Negro homes and automobiles, the sick toleration of Ku Klux Klan activity, the economic deprivation of the Negro, and the exclusion of Negroes from most places of public accommodation in St. Augustine to see that the progress made has been all too inadequate. St. Augustine can, of course, try to temporize, negotiate small, inadequate changes and prolong the timetable of freedom in the hope that the narcotics of delay will dull the pain of progress. But the fact remains that there will be neither peace nor tranquility in this community until the righteous demands of the Negro are fully met.

In the light of the foregoing, we cannot in good conscience, accept the proposal of the Grand Jury. For the Southern Christian Leadership Conference to be asked to leave St. Augustine and call off all demonstrations, without any concrete steps being made to rectify the situation for thirty days, is not only an impractical request, but an immoral one. It is asking the Negro community to give all, and the white community to give nothing. This is hardly a just or ethical way to deal with such an urgent problem.

285

But even in spite of our disappointment we still want it clearly known that we are deeply desirous of reaching a settlement. We are not demonstrating for demonstration sake. We are merely seeking to make ourselves heard so that the community will be compelled to deal with our just demands. We would be happy to bring about a cessation of demonstrations if we could see a good faith move to solve St. Augustine's racial problem. We would, therefore, propose that the Grand Jury be re-convened in the next few days and that the bi-racial committee mentioned in the presentment be appointed immediately. At the appointment and convening of said committee, we would be willing to halt demonstrations for a week in order to demonstrate good faith and allow the committee to deliberate without undue community tension. If, at the end of this period of good faith communication a reasonable attempt is made to comply with our request, we will gladly accept this as a settlement.

Let us say, in conclusion, that we are not seeking to disrupt the life of St. Augustine or humiliate its white citizens; we are merely seeking to achieve a moral balance that will make justice a reality in this community. We are not seeking a hollow victory, we are seeking reconciliation. We are not seeking to develop a community of fear; we are seeking to develop the beloved community where all men will respect the dignity and worth of human personality.

SOUTHERN CHRISTIAN LEADERSHIP
CONFERENCE
Dr. Robert B. Hayling

June 19, 1964.   Martin Luther King, Jr.

Appendix 16

S. Raymond Cafaro, M. D.
Frank J. LaRosa, M. D.
Doctors Building
St. Augustine, Florida

April 8, 1965

Honarable Richard O. Mitchell
Florida Legislative Investigation Committee
Tallahassee, Florida

Dear Mr. Mitchell:

In reference to disturbances in the community of St. Augustine, Florida during summer 1964. I wish to take this opportunity to let you know that I, like many other citizens living in my community, was victimized by State Highway Police Department.

On the evening of June 16, 1964 at approximate 11:00 P. M. I was driving from Davis Shores, St. Augustine over Bridge of Lions into city of St. Augustine, when traffic light changed from red to green. I proceeded westerly on Cathedral street where a State Highway Patrolman was slowly waving a dim flashlight. Understanding his signal to mean proceed with caution I passed him slowly, when suddenly I heard a whistle blow. Two other patrolman immediately stopped my vechicle, requested that I get out and then searched all seats and compartments of my car. At this time I inquired about what I did wrong. I was informed that I had committed a traffic violation and one patrolman wrote out a summon. I was then placed in a State Highway Patrol car and taken to County Jail, at that moment, I was concerned about my own vechicle, and also how to let my husband a physician in the community know what was happening to me at the County Jail. I was granted permission to notify him and he immediately came down and posted a bond before I was released.

The purpose of my trip at that hour of the evening was simply to take some medication to a personal friend who had phoned and said that she had the "Flu". I need not stress, the embarrassment caused me for the first time in my life, being taken to the County Jail and I write this letter, with the hope that similar eposides would not happen to another citizen in our community or elswhere.

Respectively yours

Mrs. Gladys M. LaRosa
53 Avista Cr.
St. Augustine, Fla. 32084

Sworn to and subscribed before me this the 8th day of April 1965

Notary Publiic, State of Florida at large
My Commission Expires April 3, 1966
Bonded by Connecticut Fire Insurance Co.

108

Appendix 17

TO WHOM IT MAY CONCERN:

The following is in reference to the arrest of St. Augustine Police Officer Chessley G. Smith, a member of the St. Augustine Police Department for seventeen years, on 17 June 1964 in the city of St. Augustine, Florida, St. Johns county, on a charge of carrying a concealed weapon by Florida Highway patrolman Moore, Badge number 193 and Florida State Conservation officer R. Pierce.

This arrest was made during the height of the racial demonstrations in St. Augustine while these officers were under Governor Farris Bryant's Special Order number one. The arrest was made at approximately 7 P.M. on 17 June 1964 approximately 100 feet north of Cathedral Place on the east side of St. George St. At that time, I, Officer Chessley G. Smith, was in the process of an investigation for McCrory's Five and Ten Cent Store and had been summoned there by the manager, Mr. Carter. Someone had placed a short length of pipe or steel bar approximately ten inches long beside his place of business on St. George St. and I was called to check the pipe for fingerprints. I had just completed recovery of the pipe and was heading south on St. George St. holding the pipe with two fingers by the tip end and in plain view of anyone, trying to avoid disturbing any fingerprints. At that time a Florida Highway Patrol car came up in back of me and Florida Highway Patrolman Moore jumped out and grabbed me from behind, threw me against the car and jerked the pipe away from me. I was searched and then arrested and placed in the car. I was not asked at any time for any identification or what I was doing with the pipe. They proceeded to the county jail with me and as we were going north on Ponce de Leon Boulevard I asked Florida Highway Patrolman Moore to take me by the Armory to see his superior which he refused to do stating that we were going to the county jail.

A Police car, driven by officer Ken Durling, pulled alongside of the Florida Highway Patrol car and I called to officer Durling and requested him to have Chief Stuart meet me at the county jail. Upon our arrival at the county jail I was taken inside where Deputy Tanner was on duty. He asked, "What do you have Smitty for?" The two officers did not answer him. I was seated at the desk and asked for identification. I produced a 1964, valid driver's license and officer Moore, in filling in his report, asked me if I was still a Police officer. I replied that I was and had been for seventeen years and that this could be verified by anyone in the room including Deputy Tanner and the others. Florida Highway Patrolman Moore proceeded to finish his report and Summons (Summons No. 132548) charging me with carrying a concealed weapon. I asked him how much Bond would be and he replied that I would have to get that information from Deputy Tanner. Deputy Tanner than asked him what the charge was against Smitty and he replied "carrying a concealed weapon." Deputy Tanner then stated, "if that is the charge his Bond will be $50.00." I was then taken upstairs and locked up.

Approximately twenty minutes later Mr. James Dart and Mr. Paul Eison were at the desk to post my Bond. Shortly thereafter Chief of Police Virgil Stuart in the company of Sheriff L. O. Davis, Major Jourdan and two of his lieutenants arrived and discussed the case. I was later released to the custody of the Sheriff to be arraigned at a later date.

Arraignment was on 19 June 1964 under a plea of not guilty and trial date was set for 14 July 1964 at which time I was tried in Judge Charles C. Mathis' court and represented by Attorney Robert Turner. Judge Mathis found me not guilty and I was discharged. During the trial officer Pierce and Florida Highway Patrolman Moore made numerous false statements on the witness stand as to my attempting to conceal the pipe and as to the degree of darkness and time of day. Mr. Carter, manager of McCrory's five and ten cent store, appeared in my behalf. I did not take the witness stand at any time during the trial.

Arrest Case No. was 73451 in the Sheriff's office and the case number in Judge Mathis' office was No. 506, Docket No.

25. Presiding Judge Charles C. Mathis, County Judge, St. Johns County, Florida.

                    Chessley G. Smith

Sworn to and subscribed before me this 29th day of November, 1964.

                    Notary Public

289

Commission expires:

Appendix 18

An Editorial: Front page St. Augustine Record, June 18, 1964

Two Sides To The Coin

Members of the special police force assigned to St. Johns County by the Governor protected and allowed around 300 Negro and white integration demonstrators to hold a prayer and singing demonstration on private property about 11:30 o'clock last night.

The demonstrators first marched through a peaceful residential section of the city late last night, before reaching the bayfront. There they were allowed by the protecting state police force to stop at the Monson Motor Lodge and demonstrate on private property at a late hour of night when paid motel guests were asleep.

The state police force apparently has assumed powers here which border on making the city a "police" state. Surely they had the authority to have kept the demonstrators marching instead of invading private property at this late hour of the night.

They have assumed the power to clear the Plaza, a public park, of citizens when the integrationists march and demonstrate at night and to stop and search automobiles and pedestrians without search warrants in order to protect the demonstrators. Yet, these same demonstrators were allowed to bring their threat of violence into a peaceful residential neighborhood and also to demonstrate upon private property late in the nighttime after a leader of the demonstrators had publicly declared that they were changing their tactics because there were not enough people in the downtown area—these citizens having heeded the appeals of authorities to stay out of the area to avoid adding to the threat of violence.

Citizens welcomed Governor Bryant's action in sending the state policemen here to maintain law and order and the community should be grateful for the protection afforded by them. But the rights of law abiding citizens should not be abridged in the process.

Appendix 19

St. Augustine Disorder

The following is an account of the St. Augustine civil rights disorder, between June 9th and July 4th, 1964.

St. Augustine is the nation's oldest city located on Florida's Northeast coast in St. Johns County, 38 miles South of Jacksonville. This ancient city of 15,000 population is one of the State's leading tourist attractions. Commercial fishing is an important industry here. Many St. Augustine families derive their livelihood from the Florida East Coast Railroad which has been involved in one of the longest strikes and labor disputes in the history of our nation.

At a time when Negroes throughout the South and across the nation have organized demonstrations and civil disorders to call attention to their demands for more civil rights, St. Augustine has had its share of conflicts.

In the summer of 1963, sit-in demonstrations and shooting incidents between white and Negro youths caused considerable tension in the city. In December, 1963, a St. Johns County grand jury deplored the racial unrest in the county which included a fatal shooting, beatings, rock throwing, and slashing of car tires, and blamed the violence on militant Negro leaders and the Ku-Klux Klan. The jury said that the difficulty centered around the desegregation of privately owned tourist accomodations and eating establishments. It pointed out that the conflict had adversely affected the morals, health and general welfare of the county, but it expressed the faith that harmony could be restored.

In the early spring of 1964, local Negroes began civil rights demonstrations with white and Negro sympathizers from the North participating. City and county officials arrested more than 250 persons, including Mrs. Malcolm Peabody, mother of the governor of Massachusetts.

By the end of May it was apparent that national Negro organizations had selected St. Augustine as a "target" city for racial demonstrations. A long, hot suummer was forecast by Negro leader Martin Luther King, head of the Southern Christian Leadership Conference, who came to St. Augustine to organize integration efforts along with accompanying civil disobedience demonstrations designed to focus national and world attention upon the oldest city in the New World.

As a means of demonstrating, large numbers of Negroes began marching through the downtown area at night. Reacting to this, large groups of white people gathered downtown where the situation became very tense.

292

Governor Bryant ordered the Florida Highway Patrol to send troopers to assist local enforcement agencies in the struggle. The troopers were on hand to back up the St. Augustine Police Department and the St. Johns County Sheriff's Office, where mobs were meeting in open conflict and where shots were being fired into homes and automobiles. News photographers became a target of white segregationists who attacked the photographers and smashed their equipment on several occasions.

The town's Old Slave Market became a focal point of the demonstrations as it apparently became a symbol of Negro efforts to integrate the nation's oldest city. Local enforcement officers used trained dogs to assist in crowd control. The dogs were effective in halting lines of marchers who would have otherwise been willing to press forward. It was estimated that one well-trained police dog could do the work equal to 10 or 12 police officers in crowd control.

On June 1st the City Commission adopted an ordinance to prevent parking on downtown streets at night and to prevent minors under 19 from being on the streets or in public places between 9:00 p.m. and 5:00 a.m. Throughout this time the highway patrol set up many vehicle check points in the area and took into custody a large number and variety of weapons including rifles, pistols, shotguns, machetes, night sticks, blackjacks, axe handles, hatchets and chains.

U. S. District Judge Bryan Simpson of Jacksonville, handed down an order which prohibited police forces from interfering with demonstrations following a petition by a Miami attorney on behalf of the Negroes.

Following this order, more trouble developed during a night march on June 9th, when more than 200 persons marched downtown to the Slave Market. Violence broke out when a small group of white men and youths began attacking the demonstrators singling out white demonstrators in the group of Negroes and photographers.

293

On June 10th, following this disorder, Florida Highway Patrol Major J. W. Jourdan, was sent to St. Augustine with additional troopers and officers from the Conservation Department and Beverage Department.

Martin Luther King returned to St. Augustine to lead what he called a "massive assault" against segregation. King and other Negro leaders organized demonstrations in attempts to obtain service in restaurants and motels. Meetings were held in Negro churches where integration leaders would incite their members to the task at hand. Prior to the demonstrations, these meetings would take place for at least one hour. At the end of the marches the participants would return to the churches for another lengthy session.

At the same time, three (3) white segregationists were taking the lead in organizing opposition to the demonstrations. These men were Halstead Richard Manucy, better known as Hoss Manucy, who was head of the Ancient City Hunting Club. Ku-Klux Klan Attorney J. B. Stoner of Atlanta, came to St. Augustine as an outsider. Stoner, who has long been a segregationist, joined with Hoss Manucy in leading marches of white segregationists into the Negro heart of town. The Reverend Connie Lynch came to St. Augustine from California. He spoke night after night to anywhere from 100 to 300 applauding segregationists gathered on the plaza in the heart of town. The white people who stood and listened to Lynch applauded and answered powers with Sheriff L. O. Davis and Police Chief Virgil Stuart to enforce

115

the law. This was the first time that any Florida Governor had invoked the special emergency police powers voted by a special session of the 1956 Legislature, and it had the effect of accomplishing with civil law officers the same thing that could have been done by sending the National Guard into St. Augustine.

This special police force, under the immediate command of Highway Patrol Major J. W. Jourdan, was given an initial strength of about 135 patrol troopers, beverage agents, state conservation agents, game and fish officers, division of corrections officers, and investigators from the governor's office, attorney general's office and sheriff's bureau. The special force could now make arrests for violations of city ordinances or violation of any regulation promulgated by the governor. The governor had said that just assigning large numbers of state law officers to the city was not enough because they lacked the power to do what was required. The governor made a personal appeal to the people of St. Augustine: "The thing that I want to say to the people of St. Augustine and Florida, in particular, is that we must maintain law and order. That, regardless of our feelings for or against certain people, for or against certain propositions, we have a task to perform, a society to maintain, and I anticipate that we will do it."

On June 17th, Negroes switched tactics by marching through a white residential section in the middle of the night. The march of 300 strong included a group of Jewish clergymen from nine other states who arrived to take part in the demonstrations. A heavy escort was given to the marchers but few white spectators watched as the marchers wound into the parking lot in front of Monson Motor Lodge, the major target in sit-in attempts. They held prayer service and returned to the church where the march began. On this same day 35 colored people staged a two-hour wade-in at St. Augustine Beach without incident, except that the white bathers left the area. This was the beginning of a series of daily conflicts on the beaches.

A St. Johns County grand jury recommended a 30-day truce in demonstrations so a bi-racial committee could be formed to study racial problems, but the recommendations were immediately rejected by Martin Luther King. A group of St. Augustine businessmen also issued a statement pledging to abide by present and future laws, including any Civil Rights Bill which would give Negroes the rights they are seeking and they expressed a willingness to sit down and discuss racial problems with a representative group of local citizens which would include Negroes. This was to no avail.

On June 20th, Governor Bryant issued an emergency order banning nighttime demonstrations. The special police force of troopers and other officers was directed to enforce the order to disperse any unlawful assembly. The executive order followed a night march in which bricks and bottles were thrown as whites attempted to break up an integrationist march. Previously, city authorities had banned night demonstrations on May 28th, but the curfew was knocked down by U. S. Judge Bryan Simpson. Governor Bryant's order could not be directly attacked in Federal or State courts. An attack would have to come in the form of a challenge of the constitutionality of the statute under which the powers are given to the state chief executive.

295

White and Negro demonstrations were carried on separately in marches through St. Augustine on June 21st and a group of whites attacked a racially mixed group of demonstrators at Atlantic Ocean Beach. It is often necessary for several officers to pursue and subdue a single attacker bent upon striking blows and escaping. Extreme care had to be used in the handling of the baton during these incidents. It was difficult to grasp the wet, bare arms of the attackers and these people often used grease on their bodies to give them an additional advantage in this regards. A Danish cameraman taking motion pictures of the violence was beaten by a shirtless white youth who fled down the beach. He was run down and apprehended several hundred yards away. The singing integrationists waded into the water and stayed for about 10 minutes. It was necessary for troopers to wade into the surf between the integrationists and whites on shore, and two Conservation boats were used to help keep the groups apart. Four members of the white group were arrested.

On June 23rd, Patrol Commander H. N. Kirkman sent Inspector H. Lee Simmons to relieve Major Jourdan and relief was given to other troopers who had been on the scene for some time.

On June 24th, whites turned away a group of about 30 Negroes who attempted a wade-in for the fourth straight day. The special police force escorted the Negroes from cars to the water's edge where the white group met them. The Negroes knelt on the sand and prayed for about 10 minutes before leaving. There were no arrests. Later, after hearing a fiery speech by segregationist Connie Lynch at the Old Slave Market, nearly 300 whites marched into the Negro area. The marchers were confronted by a large group of sign-carrying Negroes on Washington Street, but there were no overt incidents here. This situation became tense when the white marchers returned to the down town plaza to find Negroes marching on Cathedral Street. Officers and police dogs prevented the two groups from clashing. Several whites were arrested.

On Thursday, June 25th, the most serious rioting of the whole St. Augustine disorder occurred. In the afternoon violence erupted at St. Augustine Beach as a group of whites attacked about 75 integrationists during a wade-in demonstration. It is most important to act quickly to arrest those who engage in these fights. For the first time, State officers had to use their police batons. They broke up the action in less than a minute. About a dozen persons were injured and ten integrationists and ten segregationists were arrested. Those arrested were removed from the scene immediately. Usually two or more officers would control those arrested to minimize the force needed to place them in patrol cars for removal to jail.

In the evening, rioting broke out in downtown St. Augustine as about 500 angry whites crashed through police lines and attacked Negro demonstrators who marched through the area at the same time whites were holding a meeting. As the 200 Negro demonstrators marched into the downtown area shortly before 8:00 p.m., the whites smashed through the line of officers and disrupted the march. The Negroes were attacked for perhaps half a minute before the officers could halt the violence. The march continued around the plaza and the whites broke again through the lines on Cathedral Street in front of the Catholic church. As the officers tried to stop the attacking whites, the Negroes broke and ran. Some of them were overtaken and mauled before they could reach the safety of the Negro area. It is important to note that once this kind of action begins it quickly spreads to others. Some 20 persons were injured including a trooper shot by a pellet gun, a conservation officer's shoulder was broken and a beverage agent was severely beaten with fists and kicked. Other officers received several less severe injuries. About 15 persons were arrested, and a schedule of bonds for various offenses was considerably increased.

297

Following this outbreak on Thursday, Governor Bryant authorized a full strength of 235 state officers be made available.

After a relatively quiet weekend, on Monday, June 29th, troopers formed a wedge and a protective box around demonstrators to lead them into the water at St. Augustine Beach. This maneuver, while very hard on uniforms and equipment, was successful in preventing conflict by keeping opposing sides apart. The segregationists ran around the ring of officers, pointing and jeering, and they were joined by about a hundred spectators on the beach. Again the next day the demonstrators were permitted to swim in this way. After about 30 minutes in the surf, the integrationists left under protective guard. There were no incidents and no arrests on Monday and only one arrest on Tuesday.

On Tuesday night, June 30th, integrationist and segregationist groups called off further demonstrations after Governor Bryant appointed a biracial committee to study local racial problems. St. Augustine businessmen issued an announcement saying they would fully comply with the new pending Civil Rights Law which was expected to take effect later in the week.

As the truce was announced, most of the 235-man special police force was sent back to handle normal enforcement assignments around the State with the exception of about 25 troopers for a skeleton force. Since June 15th, 306 persons were arrested and this, along with an increase in bonds, were major reasons why whites agreed to the truce, it was reported.

To quote one segregation leader, "We just couldn't stand those bonds, particularly when they got as high as $1,500."

Governor Bryant made this statement:

298

"Several St. Augustine citizens have been named by me to serve their community in the re-establishment of communication between the races. They have been asked to serve until the Grand Jury names a permanent committee, as it moves to do in its presentment of June the 18th. During this period, it is my understanding that demonstrations will cease. The State will continue to assure law enforcement as necessary, but I anticipate that little assurance if any will be needed. Whether we agree with the Civil Rights Bill or not, and I of course do not, it is time to draw back from this problem and take a look down the long road at the end of which somehow we must find harborage. Upon one thing all mean can agree—we cannot solve this problem through violence. Violence is anarchy, and anarchy is the enemy of freedom."

Martin Luther King had this to say:

"In order to demonstrate our good faith, and reveal that we are not seeking to wreck St. Augustine, as some have mistakenly believed, we have further agreed to call off demonstrations, while the committee seeks to work out a settlement. This does not mean that the staff of S.C.L.C. will leave St. Augustine, nor does it mean that I or the President of S.C.L.C. will disassociate myself from this community. We have committed ourselves to staying here until there is a meaningful resolution of the problems facing this community. That is another warning signal. This move is not to be construed as a settlement. As the saying goes, every thousand mile journey begins with the first step. This development is merely the first step in a long journey toward freedom and justice in St. Augustine, but it is a creative and important first step, for it at least opens the channels of communication, something that St. Augustine has needed so long."

On July 4th, about 150 white people marched in a Ku-Klux Klan parade with about 75 of these wearing robes. There were few spectators and no incidents. The Klansmen had announced that they would have 5,000 members in the march.

Scattered incidents continued in St. Augustine, usually involving tests in restaurants of the new Civil Rights Law. Martin Luther King returned to the city again and declared "the Ku-Klux Klan is not going to take over St. Augustine even if we must offer our bodies as sacrifices."

299

It is apparent that the Florida Highway Patrol and other law enforcement agencies must be trained and prepared to cope with these disorders in the future.

H. LEE SIMMONS, Major   JOHNIE W. JOURDAN, Major
Inspector, FHP   Deputy Inspector, FHP

Appendix 20

ANDREW YOUNG,

Plaintiff,

300

vs.

No. 64-133-Civ-J

L. O. DAVIS, as Sheriff of
St. Johns County, Florida;
VIRGIL STUART, Chief of Police
of St. Augustine, a Municipal
corporation of St. Johns County,
Florida; and JOSEPH A. SHELLEY,
as Mayor of St. Augustine,
Florida, and STATE OF FLORIDA,

Defendants.

Order to Show Cause

In consideration of the matters set forth in the petition for rule to show cause filed herein this June 22, 1964, by the plaintiff, Andrew Young, it is

ORDERED:

1. That L. O. Davis, Sheriff of St. Johns County, Florida; Virgil Stuart, as Chief of Police of the City of St. Augustine, a municipal corporation of the State of Florida; Joseph A. Shelley, as Mayor of the City of St. Augustine, a municipal corporation of the State of Florida; Farris Bryant, as Governor of the State of Florida; James W. Kynes, as Attorney General of the State of Florida and Johnny W. Jourdan, Major, Florida Highway Patrol, and all persons acting under their direction, authority or control in connection

with the entry, the promulgation and any attempted enforcement (up to the hour of hearing fixed by this order) of the proclamation of the Respondent Farris Bryant, as Governor of the State of Florida of June 15, 1964, the Executive Order Number One of said Respondent Bryant of June 15, 1964, and the Executive Order Number Two of said Respondent Bryant of June 20, 1964, are directed to appear before this Court on Friday, June 26, 1964, at 9:30 O'clock A. M. and then and there show cause if any they have, why they should not be required to obey, conform to and abide by this Court's preliminary injunction entered in this cause June 9, 1964, and order entered June 15, 1964, denying the motion of the State of Florida (filed June 13, 1964) for modification of said preliminary injunction or, in the alternative, why they and each of them should not be held in contempt of this Court for failure to obey the lawful orders of this Court (said preliminary injunction and said order denying a motion of the State of Florida to modify same).

2. The United States Marshall for this district is directed to serve this order to show cause together with a copy of the petition for same upon each of respondents above named.

3. The Clerk of this Court is directed to mail copies to counsel—Bedell, Andreu, Kynes, Jacobs.

DONE and ORDERED in Jacksonville, Florida, this 22nd day of June, 1964.

/s/ Bryan Simpson
_____

Chief Judge
U.S. District Court
Middle District of Florida

Appendix 21

November 20, 1964

302

Statement

To the end that a record is made of the events that transpired in St. Augustine in the past couple of years, the following statement is made concerning the action by the County Judge of St. Johns County as Juvenile Judge and as Judge of the County Judge's Court.

This statement is to be confined as nearly as possible to the events having to do with the cases handled in the Court.

Juvenile Cases

One of the first events to occur that should have put the Court on Notice of an attack, was a planned and calculated effort to discredit the office and had to do with a group of children who had been turned over to the Juvenile Counselor. They were taken into custody, in company with some adults, on a charge of violating criminal laws of the State of Florida. The matter was investigated by the Juvenile Counselor, a petition was filed in the Juvenile Court, Notice was given the parents and other interested persons, and in due course, a hearing was held. A number of witnesses were examined; there was no doubt but that the children came within the statutory definition of delinquent children and were so adjudged by the Court. In as much as this was the first time that any of these children had been before the Juvenile Court and they had good school records, there was no thought but that the children be placed on probation and the first parent examined as to their willingness to accept the responsibility of probation agreed so to do. The next parent flatly refused to accept her child on probation and attempted an argument with the Juvenile Court in the presence of the children on the merits of the case; thereafter, the other parents, including the one who had first agreed to accept her child on probation refused so to accept the children and informed the Court that we could keep them. Under these circumstances, there being no other facility to take custody, we committed the children to the State Training Schools. There was no doubt but that these people had planned in advance to take such a united stand in the event the children were found delinquent in order that an attack might be made upon the procedures of the Juvenile Court. On the night following the hearing, an attorney called at the home of the County Judge to discuss the cases and the County Judge agreed to reconsider the commitment after he was assured by the attorney that the parents would accept the children on probation, but the following day when the parents called upon the County Judge four out of six parents refused to accept the children on probation and of the two that did accept, another attorney then present, made an obvious attempt to consult with such parents to dissuade them, but the parents refused to talk to the attorney. The children were held for several weeks awaiting acceptance by the Training School and when they were accepted, the parents descended upon the County Judge, accompanied by a number of other people, stating that they were going to "sit in this office until their children were released". Within a short while, a number of picketers appeared outside of the office and the halls of the Court House were filled with a number of colored people singing and otherwise creating a disturbance. The case was appealed to the District Court of Appeals. The first notice that the Juvenile Court had of a hearing on this Appeal was when an Order was issued out of the District Court of Appeals in which it appeared that the Attorney Generals office had entered into a Stipulation with the attorney by the appellants based upon a number of false statements. In its opinion, the District Court of Appeals while recognizing that the Juvenile Court after commitment to the State Training Schools lost jurisdiction over the Juvenile until it was discharged, yet suggested that the Juvenile Court request the Board of Commissioners of State Institutions to release said children.

303

Even though it was impossible to comply with the suggestion by the District Court of Appeals, it was obvious to the Juvenile Judge that the attorneys for the children did not desire the Juvenile Court to release said children; they wanted to bypass the Juvenile Court. After the decision of the District Court of Appeals, the attorneys for the children went to the Governor and the Board of State Institutions with a request that the children be released from the school. At the same time that this attorney had been arguing before the District Court of Appeals that the parents were now ready to accept the children on probation, the parents were giving an interview to a newspaper reporter which stated that they would not accept such children on probation, that they considered that the children were in school for a good cause. The Board of Commissioners for State Institutions eventually released the children to their parents and during succeeding weeks at least two of these children were again taken into custody for law violations.

In spite of the fact that these children have been released, that so far as his Appeal was concerned, the Attorney for the children was out of Court, the District Court of Appeals has re-opened the Appeal, has allowed the attorney additional time to file certain pleadings and has directed the Juvenile Court to resubmit the case, together with certain pleadings which said Court is directed to accept from said attorney.

The publicity in this case was handled in a masterful manner by an organized group then seeking the enactment of certain legislation in the Congress of the United States. By the use of half truths and outright falsehoods, much sympathy for the position of the children was generated, and we understand that large amounts of money were donated to the organized groups. The Juvenile Court, before these children were released, had control over the actions of the children of this community so far as their attendance in school, association of persons of ill repute and violations of the law were concerned. We had no problems with our colored children and we found them to be very truthful and cooperative when called upon by the Court, but after the children were released, we found the situation to be just the opposite. We

304

had little or no control over the children who decided to violate the law and the parents of the teenagers could exercise little control over them, and very few colored children had any respect for the Juvenile Court.

We are satisfied that the continued effort for the Appeal in the case of the four juveniles, that received so much publicity, is made with the hope of the attorney and the group that they can by "hook or crook" have this matter remanded to the Juvenile Court and by Motion there will have the cases transferred to the proper criminal court, and will file a Motion in the Federal Court to remove the case to the Federal District Court. The operation of this organized group in St. Augustine and St. Johns County impressed upon me that the Courts of a small county or of any one county with limited funds and personnel to handle only routine cases, is not equipped to combat a well planned and well financed attack by a force determined to obstruct, discredit or immobilize said Court willing to use any means possible to gain their end. As long as the State allows attacks to be made on any of its separate courts, one at a time, they could each be discredited starting with the lower courts and progressing from Court to Court to and through the Supreme Court.

305

In reporting on the Juvenile Cases I should mention that at the outset, after juveniles were being used in law violations with great frequency the attorneys for the group would demand of the Juvenile Court that they be furnished with the names of all juveniles taken in custody. The attorneys claimed to represent the children when they did not even know their names and were indignant when they were not furnished the information but instead were required to submit written authorization to represent children.

When the attorneys were successful in staying proceedings in the State Courts by filing motions to transfer to Federal Courts, the children and/or parents began to appear with a written designation of attorney which included a request that the case be transferred to the Criminal Court. At the hearing many of the parents repudiated the authorization, saying they did not know what they were signing.

COUNTY JUDGE'S COURT

The first persons arrested and tried in the County Judge's Court were charged with "Trespass after Warning", "Obstructing an Officer in the Performance of a Lawful Duty", etc., and the operation of the attorney for the defendants was revealing.

306

In one case the defendant did not appear for trial. His attorney informed the Judge that he did not know the whereabouts of the defendant who had been told to be present. The attorney made no objection when the Appearance Bond was Ordered Estreated. Within 30 days the Bondsman surrendered the defendant to the Sheriff and within the hour posted another Bond for the appearance of said defendant at the next term of Court. The Bondsman then came to the Court and demanded that the Estreature of the Bond be set aside because he had surrendered the defendant. If such procedures were allowed a defendant would never be tried as long as he could get a bondsman and a bondsman would never have to pay a bond as long as he could surrender the defendant within 30 days just long enough to write another bond.

The pattern in the cases tried was that the defendants made little or no defense but upon conviction they filed "Notice of Appeal" and posted a Supersedeas Bond. In many instances the appeals were not perfected according to the Rules of Practice and when the Appeals were dismissed on Motion, the defendant appealed the dismissal on technical grounds. In one case even though the Appeal had been dismissed, the Appeals Court reopened the case and ordered a new trial. The defendant then filed a Motion with the Federal District Court for removal and thus the lower Court has not been able to carry out the directions of the State Appeals Court. The Court cannot even take any action on the Supersedeas Bonds. It is interesting to note that the Federal Court will enjoin any effort to collect on any bonds posted and no such bonds have been paid, yet when the State Court shows some reluctance to accept surety bonds when the surety is in default or raises the amount of the bond, the Federal

Judge has defeated such action by very critical orders, the legality of which is doubtful.

It is a matter of common knowledge that the defendants in the criminal cases are really not the real party in interest. The real party in interest is the NAACP or the SCLC. These are the organizations that planned the operation, procured the persons to perform the acts for which the arrests were made, paid the premium on the bail bonds and secured the writing of the bonds. They retain counsel and through the paid trained organizers and field personnel keep the Movement going. After a number of arrests had been made in St. Johns County, upon complaint of property owners and other persons involved, the attorney for the defendants apparently secured permission from the Federal Court to file a Motion transferring a number of cases to the Federal Court in wholesale lots. The cases were not identified by date, charge or other specific information, only by the name of the defendant, and in many instances the name was incorrect. When the first case was filed, and incidentally, we are informed that costs of filing was waived, before any hearing could be had on the Motion, additional cases were transferred simply by furnishing the Clerk of the Federal Court with the names of defendants who had been taken into custody in the mean time. In all, four or five hundred cases have thus been held in suspense by the County Judge's Court. The Federal Judge initially remanded the first group, but his remand was stayed by a Federal Judge of the Appeals Court; thereafter, when the Motions were filed the Federal Judge has simply held up his ruling and although these cases are supposed to receive preference in the Federal Court, no ruling has been forth-coming for several months. The Federal Judge has been active in issuing injunctions in regard to the enforcement of municipal ordinances, in regard to acceptance of and amounts of bail bonds, and in other matters. In the hearings had before the Federal Judge, the attorneys for the organized groups were allowed great liberties, but the attorneys for the Court and County officials were barely heard. A number of suits have been filed against the County Judge, the County prosecuting attorney, Juvenile Counselor and Law Enforcement officers. In these

307

129

suits the Court and its personnel have been on trial. The suit is the first time, so far as I know, that a group of defendants in a number of criminal cases pending in a State Court have succeeded in putting the State Court on trial. The attorneys for the organized group called their motions up for arguments early in the week, serving Notice upon the County officials, and others, of from one hour to barely three days. The attorneys, of course, have had days to draft their pleadings, even to the point of having them mimeographed, but they are usually filed on the week end and the notice sets the matter down for hearing on the following Monday. Just recently the attorney for the organized group served notice of taking of deposition of the County Judge, County Prosecuting Attorney and Sheriff and the Chief of Police on Monday morning at 10AM without making any effort to see whether or not the Court had any matters scheduled at said time on said date, and on one occasion the County Judge and personnel of his Court were required to be in the Federal District Court on the first Tuesday in the month. The groups attorneys knew it to be the term day of said County Judge's Court for which a jury is summoned at least 10 days prior to said term. This all points up to the fact that these attorneys and the organized group have planned extensively and well to disrupt the local Court and keep it so bogged down in these cases as to render it ineffective.

The attacks upon the local Court, the Judge and officials thereof, were calculated to discredit them and at every hearing the Courtroom in the Post Office Building in Jacksonville was packed by negroes, many of them were defendants in cases pending before the County Judge's Court. Others were from out of the county, but were brought to Jacksonville in rental cars, some of which were from as far away as Dade County.

We believe that the organized group has been using St. Johns County, Marion County and Leon County in order to work out and try a method and procedure of attack upon the State Courts. They have been successful in establishing precedents that will make it very difficult for the State to defend other courts in other counties. The cases that have been transferred by Motion under the rule of the Federal Court, include such offences as "Aggravated Assault", "Parking on the Highway", "Possession of Concealed Weapons", etc. Just recently a case has been transferred out of the Circuit Court on such a Motion on a charge of "Murder". This case had been pending before the Circuit Court for about one year, and on the day scheduled for a hearing, one of the attorneys representing the organized group called the Clerk of the Circuit Court on the telephone and notified him that a Motion had just been filed in the Federal Court for transfer of the case. The Circuit Judge called the Clerk of the Federal Court and when told by the Clerk that such a motion had been filed, he continued the case. During the recent months of the agitation over the Civil Rights Issue, both before and after the enactment of the law a number of attorneys from out of State have been in St. Augustine advising the negroes engaged by the group. They have appeared in Court from time to time with these people but have insisted that they are not practicing law. They admit that they are not members of the Bar of the State of Florida. This matter was called to the attention of the Bar Association but nothing was done.

309

People in Florida from the Governor down who have not been directly affected by the activities of these organized groups have apparently wanted to "stay out of the mess", and this has been exactly what this group, or any subversive group, would desire. In this manner they can attack what ever portion of the populace they may select or think themselves capable of conquering and taking one group after another, gain such control that they may desire.

Appendix 22

MARTIN LUTHER KING, JR.,
et al.,

310

Plaintiffs,

vs.

No. 64-186-Civ-J

CHARLES C. MATHIS, et al.,
Defendants.

ORDER SETTING ASIDE CERTAIN ESTREATURES AND REINSTATING BONDS, AND FOR PRELIMINARY INJUNCTION

Upon Plaintiffs' application for a preliminary injunction and an Order setting aside certain estreatures of bonds and reinstating said bonds heard by and submitted to the Court, after notice, on August 6, 1964, upon the testimony and other proofs adduced by the Plaintiffs at the hearing, upon the argument and submission by counsel for the Plaintiffs, in the absence of Defendants Charles C. Mathis and Donald E. Buck, or their counsel, and in accordance with the Findings of Fact and Conclusions of Law this day filed by the Court herein, it is now by the Court

ORDERED:

1. That the estreature of the bonds of the Plaintiffs as set forth in the attached schedule, which is made a part of this Order, heretofore estreated by Judge Charles C. Mathis, be and the same are hereby set aside and rendered of no effect.

2. That, effective immediately, the bonds of the Plaintiffs, as set forth in the attached schedule, be and they are hereby

reinstated and rendered of the same force and effect as prior to the estreatures heretofore ordered by Judge Charles C. Mathis.

3. That, effective immediately and without the posting or filing of an injunctive bond by Plaintiffs, Defendants Charles C. Mathis and Donald E. Buck and all other persons to whose notice or knowledge the contents of this Order may come, are *restrained from taking any action,* including requirement of appearance, setting for trial, trial, arraignment, notice of trial, notice of arraignment, or estreature of bonds, or any other proceedings of any kind, *as to any criminal proceedings pending in the County Judge's Court* in and for *St. Johns County, Florida,* which have heretofore *or may hereafter be removed to this Court* and not subject to an effective Order of remand.

311

4. Since the Defendants Charles C. Mathis and Donald E. Buck are both members of the bar and responsible State officials, service of this injunctive Order by the U. S. Marshal is not deemed necessary. Service may be effected by the Clerk of this Court mailing certified copies of this Order, with the attached schedule, to said Defendants. The Clerk is directed to make similar service of certified copy upon the Defendant L. O. Davis, Jr., Sheriff of St. Johns County, Florida, St. Augustine, Florida.

DONE AND ORDERED at Jacksonville, Florida, within said District, this 7th day of August, 1964.

BRYAN SIMPSON

CHIEF JUDGE, U.S.
DISTRICT COURT

BONDS WRITTEN BY FLOYD BOATRIGHT

Plaintiff's Name	Bond Number
Baines, Geraldine B.	70820-21-22 K
Bancroft, Peter	70809-10-11 K
Fentress, Kathryn	72244-45-46 K
Fleming, Harry Jr.	72235-39 K
Harper, Elnora	72309-10-11 K
Johnson, John T.	70812-13-14 K
Riley, Beatrice	70841-42-43 K
Thomas, Audrey L.	72312-13-14 K
Thomas, Edna B.	72306-07-08 K
Clay, Joanne	72315-16-17 K
Sanders, Dorothy M.	70823-24-25 K
Brown, James C.	70337 K 72230 K
Lingo, Charles Allen Jr.	72304 K
Thomas, Julia Lee	70816-17-18 K
Vivian, C. T.	72303 K
Young, Andrew J.	72301 K

312

BONDS WRITTEN BY WILLIAM C. LEWIS

Boyle, Sarah Patton	70725-26-27 K
Chalmers, David	70719-20-21 K
Clarke, Benjamin Van	70722-23-24 K
Edwards, Audry Nell	75108-09-10 K
Fentress, Kathryn	70713-14-15 K
Halyard, James J.	70731 K
Jackson, Marva	70735-36-37 K
McNab, Brian	70728-29-30 K
Simpson, Robert	70732-33-34 K
Swan, Richard Dana	70738-39-40 K
Daniels, Carolyn	72601-02-03 K
Harris, William	72479-80-81 K
Jackson, Tyrone	72516-17-18 K
Taylor, Lavert	72879 K
Abney, Roland	70798-99-70800
Alexander, Barbara J.	72615-16-17
Brand, Francis C.	72461-62-63
Brown, Eddie	72844-45-46
Butler, Katherine	72581-83-84
Coley, Raymond	72930-31-32
Daniels, James	72857-58-59

BONDS WRITTEN BY WILLIAM C. LEWIS

Plaintiff's Name	Bond Number
Darten, Brenda	72683-85-86
Dorsey, Elouise	72860-61-62
Ford, Mamie N.	72488-89-90
Grant, Gertrude	72744-45-46
Hodges, Vina	72530-31-32
Johnson, John T.	72491-92-93
Jones, Danella	70792-93-94
Lingo, Charles Allen Jr.	72473-72472
Kendrick, Thelma	72863-64-65
Mathis, Johnnie D.	72838-39-40
McKenstrey, Frenetta	72738-39-40
Middleton, James C.	72452-53-54
Miller, Katherine Ann	72794-95-96
Mitchell, Joanne	72892-93-94
Mosley, Willie	72937-38-39
Phoenix, Harriet S.	72883-84-85
Reddick, William E.	72623-24-72639
Sanders, Deborah	72741-42-43
Sanders, Dorothy	72482-83-84
Shider, Jerome I.	72497-98-99
Shiras, G. Peter	72464-65
Tukes, John	72455-56-57
Utley, Sherman	72922-24-25
Victory, Solomon	72841-42-43
Vivian, C. T.	72450-51-52
Wallace, Barry J.	70795-96-97
Wells, Samuel B.	72940-41-42
Wiles, Nancy	72474-72458-59-60
Woods, Eugene E.	72853-54-55
Zellers, Isiah	72934-35-36

313

I certify the foregoing to be a true
and correct copy of the original.

Julian A. Blake, Clerk
United States District Court
Middle District of Florida

By:

Wesley R. This

Chief Deputy Clerk

135

Appendix 23

The St. Augustine Record

The St. Augustine Record, Sunday Morning, Sept. 27, 1964

314

Law, Justice In County Feel Lash Of Federal Court Power

St. Augustine has felt, perhaps, more than any other city, the lash of federal judicial infringement on the rights of citizens and the constitutional powers of local and state courts.

"We the jury find the defendent guilty or not guilty" . . are words that have meant the very foundation upon which justice for individuals and our judicial system has been built. Under our constitution every man has the right of trial by jury, if he so desires.

But, in these times when state's rights are looked upon as sort of a crack-pot belief by the federal government, the words of "We the jury . . ." as applied to justice in St. Johns County has been changed it seems, by the federal court judge to read: "I, Federal District Judge Bryan Simpson find . . ."

Proceedings in the federal district court for the past year show that the aging district judge sits indivisibly as judge, jury and prosecuting attorney whenever white citizens of the county are brought before him on petitions filed by integrationists.

He has established himself as the "law" in St. Johns County when the so-called question of civil rights is concerned.

Other judges, lawyers and persons familiar with the personal as well as property rights of individuals and judicial proceedings have expressed alarm over some of the court actions of Judge Simpson. These persons, for obvious reasons, prefer that their names not be mentioned.

During the past year over 500 cases involving misdemeanors by Negro and white civil rights advocates have been moved from our municipal, county and state courts to the federal district courts by the "snap of the finger," so to speak. These some 500 cases involve breaking of the laws of the municipality of St. Augustine, St. Johns County and the State of Florida.

In most incidents, the defendants publicly broke the law— some giving notice to the press ahead of time of their intention to do so.

Cases have been taken directly before Judge Simpson, or appealed directly to the federal court from the municipal, justice of the peace and circuit courts

136

without following the proper judicial course of law. Our state courts have been sidetracked.

There seems to have been a "hot line" between civil rights attorneys and Judge Simpson. Petitions by Negroes are granted quickly, and white defendants have been ordered to appear in the district court on short notice. In all cases against white defendants, rulings have been made.

But, over 500 cases against integrationists, some of them a year old, sit in the federal district court and the federal court of appeals. Some observers are inclined to believe that they will be there for a long time.

There have been so many petitions, appeals and counter-appeals that it is confusing as to the exact number of cases pending. But, Judge Chas. C. Mathis, Jr., has over 490 cases which have been transferred from his court to the federal court during the past year. There are over 150 more cases being held up by the County Judge's Court, pending federal court rulings of similar cases.

Usually there is a $25 fee to file cases in the federal court. It is understood that this fee in the some 500 cases has been waived, so it is not costing the integrationists anything. The legal staff, headed by Tobias Simon of Miami, is furnished the plaintiffs, and the bonds set in the cases have not been paid.

The grounds for petitioning that cases be transferred to the federal court is that the plaintiffs claim that they cannot obtain a fair trial in St. Johns County. This, of course, is an insult to the integrity of our city, county and state courts, and the people of St. Johns County.

As one observer said: "How do they know they can't get a fair trial? They never go to trial."

Judge Mathis, who has gained a reputation during his many years on the bench, as a fair judge without playing favorites, had this to say:

"The faith and confidence of the lawyers, laymen and law enforcement officers in the Federal Judiciary system has been shaken, if not destroyed, by the action of the Federal District Court in Jacksonville in cases entertained and considered as Civil Rights cases. The citizens of St. Johns County now see this court as a threat to their freedom rather than as a guardian of their rights."

Justice of the Peace G. Marvin Grier, from whose court some cases have been petitioned to the federal court commented: "I do not believe that recent decisions of Judge Simpson are in keeping with the best traditions and ethics of American jurisprudence.

"I do believe that failure to render prompt decisions on petitions to transfer local cases to the United States court is rendering impotent the municipal, county and state courts and is gradually breaking down all concepts of law and order."

When racial strife was at its height here, Judge Simpson made conditions worse by ruling that police could not place a ban on night demonstrations, and even issued an order requiring the governor of Florida to show cause why he should not be held in contempt of court when he ordered such a ban on night demonstrations to preserve law and order.

Such bans were granted and put into effect in many northern cities where Negro rioters ran amuck.

Chief of Police Virgil Stuart, in reviewing racial trouble which existed here, stresses that it is essential to law and order that demonstrations, mass meetings,

315

parades, public gathering, chanting, singing, etc. be regulated by city ordinance.

"By using this permit method the police department has heretofore always been able to regulate meetings, public gatherings and parades so that they would not conflict with other similar activities," the chief said.

But the federal courts issued a restraining order which in effect nullified the right of the police department and the City of St. Augustine to control the movements of large groups of people over the public streets and public parks.

"The results of the court order created mass confusion whereby large groups of people marched in the public streets at any time of the day and night. In our efforts to control and stop riots as provided under the city ordinance governing disorderly crowds we ordered the leaders to discontinue these mass demonstrations, parades, public meetings etc. upon public property. Again the court ruled against the City of St. Augustine and the police department stating that it had no right to issue such an order not withstanding the fact that many violations of laws occurred, including numerous juveniles and minors violating our curfew laws." Chief Stuart added.

Stressing that most of the trouble occurred at night, Chief of Police Stuart added that "the federal courts through their orders restraining the law enforcement agencies have caused police to almost completely lose control of the law enforcement in the city.

Mayor Joseph A. Shelley said: "Although I was personally treated with courtesy by Judge Simpson, it is my opinion that the judge deviated from normal court room procedure to such a degree as to make it difficult for defense attorneys to properly represent their clients. His actions indicated that he may have prejudiced a hearing before all the facts were presented."

City Commissioner James Lindsley said he felt that "Judge Simpson has greatly over-stepped his bounds as a federal magistrate, and has done St. Augustine a terrible disservice, both to the white and colored citizens."

Commissioner Harry Gutterman stated: That the federal court by failing to render prompt decisions on the many petitions before it is "rendering impotence to the municipal, county and state courts," and is contributing to breaking down law and order in the city and county.

Willard Howatt, attorney for the board of county commissioners, commented: "This continual infringement upon the states rights is slowly and surely depriving the people of this county of all their constitutional rights and leading to a dictatorship."

Chairman Dan Mickler and other members of the board of county commissioners have openly condemned rulings by Judge Simpson in regard to law enforcement and court actions in the county.

Sheriff L. O. Davis, who has been a constant visitor before the federal court in Jacksonville, is now being sued by a white and a Negro integrationist for $20,000 for allegedly not providing them with protection while they were swimming with a group of Negroes at St. Augustine Beach.

Sheriff Davis said he was attempting to "get the trial of the suits in another court for there is no way for a white person from St. Johns County to get a fair trial before Judge Simpson."

Those attending the numerous federal court sessions say that white witnesses and defendants were often brow-beaten by civil rights attorneys, and their statements under oath often questioned by Judge Simpson.

Attorneys for plaintiff had the "run of the court," while attorneys for the defense were often muffed from the bench.

Next to challenging the authority of the governor and the State of Florida, and ruling that demonstrators could demonstrate at any time at night they choose, the next most controversial decision was Judge Simpson's ruling holding Deputy Sheriff Charles Lance Jr. in contempt of court for allegedly harrassing Negro integrationists, whom Lance swore under oath he was protecting instead, and the judge's ruling that Lance must resign as a deputy sheriff.

Lance was ordered to pay $200 toward the fee of attorneys for the Negroes. Tobias Simon, the principal attorney for the plaintiffs, announced to newsmen that the money would be contributed to the NAACP legal defense fund.

In ordering the bonded deputy sheriff to resign, Judge Simpson was quoted by the Associated Press as admitting that "I have no authority to do that, but this is a special case, since he is a non-paid special deputy."

However, Lance is not a special deputy but a bonded deputy with all of the powers of a deputy sheriff.

The judge's ruling is under appeal to the United States (circuit) court of appeals, 5th circuit.

Judge Simpson has held one motel operator in contempt of court and ordered 17 other business places to conform to the civil rights law. In Judge Simpson's behalf, it must be said that he refused a petition by attorneys for the Negro plaintiffs that

the operators of these 17 places of business be ordered to pay $1,000 each toward their attorney's fees.

Donald E. Buck, county prosecuting attorney, had this to say about the actions of the federal court:

"The United States Federal Court Judges are appointed by the President, confirmed by the Senate and serve for life. The appointments to the Federal bench are usually political payments doled out by the party in office. The people have no voice in selection of the Judges and the people have no power to remove them. Under the present court structure it is virtually impossible to remove a Federal Court Judge for any reason, including incompetency, senility, indolence, etc."

"Aristotle, famous Greek, once wrote "That Judges of important causes should hold office for life is not a good thing for the mind grows old as well as the body."

"Senator Sam J. Ervin Jr. of North Carolina said in August 1964: 'It is a tragic hour in our history when Federal laws and Federal Court rulings are designed to give demonstrators an immunity from prosecution for their offenses."

"Insofar as State Courts of the United States are concerned today the Federal Judge sits invisibly in the State Trial Court behind the State Judge, State Prosecutor and State Jury with an absolute despotic power at any time to stop the trial of a criminal defendant with the threat of a jail term to everyone involved in the State trial EXCEPT the criminal defendant."

CONCLUSION: The purpose and intent of the above report on recent activities of the federal judiciary has been compiled in an endeavor to enlighten others con-

317

cerning recent. rulings by Judge Bryan Simpson concerning civil rights cases in St. Augustine.

The report in no way is meant to bring personal ridicule to any man, but rather to point out what is felt to be the injustice of a particular system. We have discussed at length recent actions of the federal court with many lawyers and judges. Not one lawyer could inform us on what legal basis cases in local courts had been granted appeals to the Federal Courts. Not one lawyer could explain under what laws the Federal Court had the power to usurp the constituted responsibilities of county and state courts.

We must conclude that if Judge Simpson is acting under the law of the land . . . then the "Law of the Land" has ceased to be the "Law of the People."

We suggest that every citizen who feels that the power of the federal judiciary is infringing the rights of state courts, write their senator and congressman and request that they take immediate steps to correct any laws that grant such power to the federal courts.

318

Appendix 24

Investigators of the Committee on several occasions witnessed representatives of the major television news organizations make public contributions of funds to Conrad Lynch and J. B. Stoner. Reports furnished the Committee by representatives of the Special Police Forces assigned to St. Augustine reflect that similar contributions were made by the same individuals to representatives of the Southern Christian Leadership Conference during public meetings held by that organization in St. Augustine.

Reports submitted by the Committee's staff reflect that on at least one occasion during the week of June 21, J. B. Stoner, Conrad Lynch and Halstead Manucey left the Slave Market after receiving a contribution of cash from a TV network representative and went with that representative to his motel where they participated in a filmed interview which was later shown nationally and which presented a distorted view of conditions then prevalent in St. Augustine.

Appendix 25

Date: 17 March 1965

From: Virgil Stuart, Chief of Police, City of St. Augustine, St. Augustine, Fla.

To: Florida Legislative Committee

320

Subject: Brief Comments On The Racial Agitation in St. Augustine, Florida For The Past Two (2) Years.

Records in the St. Augustine Police Department record the beginning of the Racial disturbance in the City of St. Augustine, Florida, as of 23 February 1963. In the beginning the demands were received mostly from the National Association For The Advancement of Colored People, Local Chapter, making demands that the Quadracentennial Commission be denied federal funds for this project. Strong protests were received when President Lyndon Johnson, who at that time was Vice President of the United States, was scheduled to make an address in St. Augustine, Florida to dedicate one of the older buildings.

The local representative of the National Association For The Advancement of Colored People began to make demands upon the City to fire or discharge city employees and replace them with negro employees. Some of the demands were for the de-segregation of all public facilities such as rest rooms, ball parks, golf links, etc. During the next several weeks all of these demands for total de-segregation of public facilities were met. The St. Augustine Police Department was one of the first cities in the State of Florida to start using negro police officers. We have been using them continuously for some thirty (30) years. We had a vacancy in the police department for a negro officer at the time of this racial disturbance. One was selected and cleared with the Civil Service Board, passed his physical examination and was given his appointment, but, did not show up for work. Later on being questioned the applicant stated that he was told by the

142

leaders of the local National Association For The Advancement of Colored People that if he took the job that they would kill him, as they had another man picked for the job. The police department did not hire the other man. He had not passed Civil Service Requirements.

Numerous negroes began to picket local places of business such as lunch counters during the months of May, June, July and August, 1963. Most of the picketing was done in the day time without any major incidents, however, violence did break out at times on the street especially at night time between bands of white and negro teen-agers. There were other incidents that occurred within the city and outside the city such as Dr. Robert Hayling, who headed a group of young negro trouble makers, who laid seige to the St. Johns County Jail on one (1) or two (2) occasions, and, groups of pickets also made an attempt to invade the City Police Headquarters with a large group of so-called pickets. Many juvenile and adult arrests were made for so-called sit-ins, lie-ins and trespassing on private property. After several months of this racial agitation things quieted down after leading citizens more or less disowned Dr. Hayling and some ten (10) to fifteen (15) of his young hoodlum followers.

321

In the Spring of 1964, starting in late March, the City was invaded by numerous so-called ministers, chaplains, white students, etc., sponsored by the National Council of Churches, mostly from the New England States. This group came at the invitation of DR. ROBERT HAYLING, an admitted *"ATHEIST,"* and local head of the Southern *"CHRISTIAN"* Leadership Conference. This group was sponsored by the Southern Christian Leadership Conference headed by Rev. Martin Luther King. A large group of young teen-agers, white girls and a few white male college students, came to the city enmasse and to live with negro families throughout the city. The young teen-age white girls began to show up dating and mixing socially with negro male students from the local negro college, (Florida Memorial College). The fact that the young college students mixed socially, white girls going with negro boys and white male students going with negro female students on a social basis, created resentment on the part of the local young white population and this resulted in extreme bitterness between the two (2) groups.

One of the better known participants in this invasion was Mrs. Mary Elizabeth Peabody, (Mrs. Malcolm Peabody) mother of the Governor of the State of Massachusetts. Just prior to her arrival, which had been well publicized by the news media, some one hundred fifty (150) or more newspaper reporters, still cameramen, TV cameramen and other press men necessary to cover a so-called "Hollywood Production" came in to the City. This group was large enough to fill up some two (2) or three (3) large local motels, some of whom established direct telephone and wire services from their motel rooms back to large Northern cities. Local law enforcement officers could tell each morning where the "Show" was going to be staged that day by watching where the TV cameramen set up their props, lights, etc. Shortly after these props were set up the "Show" would start. The participants who appeared in the "Show" were well trained and rehearsed. Mrs. Peabody had in her party a mixed group of whites and negroes who would deliberately go into local hotel dining rooms, motel dining rooms and restaurants demanding to be served knowing full well in advance that it was not the policy or practice of these places of business to serve food and/or drinks to these people. After several days of this agitation Mrs. Peabody and several other people forced an arrest by the local officers and were confined in the St. Johns County Jail. There never was any question in the minds of the St. Augustine Police Department that these demonstrators, agitators and other mixed groups were working hand in glove with members of the press, cameramen and other news coverage.

After the so-called Easter invasion, which ended about the middle of April 1964, things quieted down until about the middle of June 1964, when a plot was uncovered that Martin Luther King had instigated a plan to bring thousands of participants from other states by busses to force the local officers to arrest them therefore flooding the jails with thousands of people which would result in severely crowded conditions and that there would be a break-down in Law and

Order in the City of St. Augustine, Fla. We uncovered this plot through informants and gave advance publicity of the plan, which, we think resulted in *only* hundreds coming here instead of thousands. The project did result in hundreds being placed in the county jail, which was many times the capacity of the jail, and resulted in an extremely heavy burden being placed on the local community to feed so many outside agitators.

These demonstrators threw up large pickets in front of lunch counters, dining rooms, tourist information headquarters at the Chamber of Commerce building carrying signs asking tourists not to visit St. Augustine, Fla. No one appeared to pay any attention to these pickets during the day light hours. The local police had no trouble at any time controlling these pickets and maintaining law and order. In addition to this picketing and demonstrating St. Augustine is headquarters for the Florida East Coast Railroad, who had numerous pickets on duty at their buildings without any major incidents. In addition some seventy-five (75) of the so-called Peace Marchers from Quebec, Canada to Guantanamo, Cuba arrived in the city to spend from ten (10) days to two (2) weeks picketing, demonstrating, marching etc. without any major incidents. At all times the local police were able to control the demonstrations which were held in the day time.

The Southern Christian Leadership Conference leaders did not appear to be satisfied with this type of picketing so they started so-called night marches into the downtown area. These marches were conducted by several hundred participants without any permit or advance notice to the police on routes to be used, destination or any other information. These marchers were mixed groups of people; young teen-age white girls marched holding hands with negro males. White males marched in the group holding hands with negro females. Cat calls and obscene remarks were passed back and forth from marchers to spectators and from spectators to marchers. Bottles, bricks, sticks were tossed back and forth. Potash and battery acid were used, mostly by participants in the marchers against police officers, with hypodermic syringes and plastic containers, such as cleaning fluid, liquid

323

sun tan lotion, etc. come in. Some officers were hit in the face with this acid. When the marches resulted in injury to participants and spectators alike, including police officers, orders were issued by the Police Department that they would not permit any more night marches or demonstrations. This order was issued about the end of May 1964 or the first part of June 1964.

Lawyers, who the press stated were paid for by the National Council of Churches, started legal proceedings in the Federal Court in Jacksonville, Florida against the law enforcement agencies in St. Augustine, Florida, which resulted in a Federal Court Order permitting the demonstrations to continue using any streets at any time of the day or night. This resulted in riots which necessitated the Governor of the State of Florida sending in several hundred additional law enforcement officers. Generally speaking the officers worked very well together until the Governor issued an executive order about the middle of June 1964 establishing a Special Police Force, which resulted in the Local Police Department and the Sheriff's Department being isolated as law enforcement agencies. The Special Police Force was placed in charge of all law enforcement agencies, which resulted in Semi-Official Martial Law. Several incidents occured causing friction between law enforcement agencies involved including the actual arrest of a City Police Officer for no good reason and placing him in the County Jail.

INVASION OF THE BEACHES:

The bathing beaches in St. Johns County and in front of St. Augustine are outside the city limits of St. Augustine and, therefore, beyond the jurisdiction of the Municipal Police Department, and, is over FORTY MILES long. A "Hollywood Production" was staged at the St. Augustine Beach. This was reported to be a knock-out blow from a publicity standpoint, just before the passage of the Federal Civil Rights Bill in Washington, D.C. The stage was set up in a space less than a quarter of a mile wide, which, for generations had been used as a public bathing beach by the white people. On each side of this space was miles of open beaches that could have been used by any person, white or colored.

146

In fact a short distance south of this area is a section of the beach known as Butler's Beach, (Florida State Park), for the exclusive use of negro citizens. This section had been used for generations for bathing by negro citizens without incident.

BUT Martin Luther King's Southern Christian Leadership Conference selected the small space, used by the white bathers for many generations, to use for wading and so-called bathing by negroes and other mixed groups. As usual TV cameramen, Newspaper reporters, etc., which at times outnumbered the participants, set up props to cover this "Hollywood Production" for publicity purposes. The officers in charge of the Special Police Force, consisting of Highway Patrolmen, Conservation Agents and other State Officers, formed a flying wedge, in full uniform wading into the water, forcing the white bathers aside so that the negroes could wade in for their so-called demonstrations. This, naturally, caused strong feelings against the negro group, as well as against the State Officers, for this unnecessary use of force in chasing the white people out of their bathing beach area. This was especially true in view of the fact that a short distance down the beach the negroes could have bathed and waded unmolested. The Florida State Park (Butler's Beach) has been in use by negroes for over one hundred years (100) without any molestation by local persons or outsiders. These so-called demonstrations went on for days and, of course, resulted in some violence.

325

Outside invaders and race agitators left St. Augustine about the first of August 1964 and local officers have been able to control law enforcement again.

There are approximately seven hundred (700) cases against negro people, both adult and juveniles, pending in local courts. However, the attorneys representing the negroes arrested have appealed to the Federal Court to take jurisdiction. All of these cases are now in the hands of the Federal Court which includes sit-ins, lie-ins, trespassing, disorderly conduct, assault and even some charged with first degree murder. Needless to say this tends to demoralize the local law enforcement officers.

DAVID R. COLBURN

THE SAINT AUGUSTINE BUSINESS COMMUNITY

DESEGREGATION, 1963–1964

With the conclusion of World War II the United States entered into an age which would see a fundamental change in the social and economic condition of its people. No region remained isolated from this metamorphosis, especially the South. Southerners left the farms in record numbers to enjoy the economic opportunities offered by their cities. Northern industry flocked into the South seeking to take advantage of tax incentives, cheap labor, and expanding markets. Northerners frequently joined their departing industries. Socially, the South gradually abolished the accouterments of a segregated society. By 1971 public schools were integrated, and blacks voted in party primaries and held public office.[1]

The dramatic socioeconomic changes that have occurred in the South since World War II have yet to be fully explained or understood. In particular, the reasons for the evolution in the South's racial traditions are not altogether clear. Did the changes result, for example, primarily from pressures exerted on the South by the federal government and the federal courts? Or

1 For an elaboration of these social, economic, and political developments see Kirkpatrick Sale, *Power Shift: The Rise of the Southern Rim and Its Challenge to the Eastern Establishment* (New York: Random House, 1975).

were the changes effected by forces at work within the southern communities? This essay examines one community in the South, Saint Augustine, Florida, and the response of its businessmen to the pressures for change occasioned by the civil rights movement.

In analyzing a 1963 racial disturbance in Cambridge, Maryland, reporter Claude Sitton of the New York *Times* observed that although political, social, and moral considerations entered into the controversy's resolution, "the effective pressure to end the crisis came from within the business community." Sitton was personally convinced that similar developments had occurred in Little Rock, Birmingham, Atlanta, and several other southern communities. He concluded that "economic self-interest frequently leads to racial change in situations where other factors seemingly have little influence."[2]

Sitton's findings were endorsed three years later by Reed Sarratt, who observed that in Little Rock and New Orleans, "when controversy developed into public disorder and violence," businessmen "began to act in their accustomed role as community leaders." He also found that in Dallas and Atlanta "businessmen successfully exerted their influence to prevent disorder before it developed."[3]

On the surface, the racial attitudes and economic desires of the businessmen in Saint Augustine appeared little different from those found elsewhere in the South. They joined with their white neighbors in supporting the segregation barriers which had been erected in the city during the 1890s. Unlike most southern communities, however, Saint Augustine was a city that depended heavily on tourism for its economic vitality. Over 85 percent of its income was generated by tourism with the vast majority of visitors coming from the Northeast and Midwest. In this economic setting, the business community down-played racial extremism to avoid alienating their northern guests. As one historian and former resident commented, the business community consistently sought "to keep social order and peace" and avoid exciting passions.[4]

---

2   Quoted in Kenneth K. Bailey, *Southern White Protestantism in the Twentieth Century* (New York: Harper and Row, 1964), 148.
3   Reed Sarratt, *The Ordeal of Segregation: The First Decade* (New York: Harper and Row, 1966), 285, 286.
4   Interview with Michael V. Gannon by the author, May 3, 1977; interviews

During the post-World War II period Saint Augustine remained a relatively stable society in a state that was experienc-
ing rapid socioeconomic changes. Prosperity accelerated due to
a resurgent tourist trade but otherwise the community seemed
little changed from the prewar era. The leadership still came
from the oldest and most respected families and tended to be
lawyers, bankers, or businessmen, most of whom were involved
only indirectly in the tourist industry. The majority of newcom-
ers who arrived seemed to come chiefly to retire. According to
local observers, they generally accepted the prevailing values of
the community without dissent. "It was still a small town and
everybody knew everybody," a local clergyman commented. It
was also a society "not terribly interested in change," the same
man noted, and "not terribly interested in being disturbed." Despite the cosmopolitanism fostered by tourism, racial traditions
remained remarkably unchanged throughout the twentieth
century. In contrast to the conditions James Silver found in Mississippi, however, there was no constant beating of the drums
on behalf of white supremacy in Saint Augustine. Supremacist
views were much more subtly presented but nonetheless firmly
believed.[5]

Living in the nation's oldest city, Saint Augustinians were
especially conscious of their past. According to one historian
who spent several years studying the city's early history, the
postwar white leadership exhibited a craze "for genealogy." Several Saint Augustinians took pride in tracing their ancestry
back to the period of British and even Spanish occupation.[6]
These people lived in particular neighborhoods in the city where
they practiced very formal social customs modeled upon those

329

with Frank Upchurch, Hamilton Upchurch, and Douglas Hartley by the author,
January 27, 1978; *Wall Street Journal*, June 19, 1964, p. 1.
5   Interviews with Gannon, Hamilton Upchurch, Frank Upchurch, and Hartley; U.S. Bureau of the Census, *Census of the Population: 1950, Vol. II, Characteristics of the Population, Part 10, Florida* (Washington, D.C.: Government
Printing Office, 1952), 10–28; U.S. Bureau of the Census, *Census of the Population: 1960, Vol. I, Characteristics of the Population, Part 11, Florida* (Washington, D.C.: Government Printing Office, 1963), 11–29; interview with the Reverend Stanley Bullock by the author, January 17, 1978; interview with the
Reverend Charles Seymour by the author, August 16, 1978; New York *Times*,
July 5, 1964, Sec. 6, p. 30. See also James W. Silver, *Mississippi: The Closed
Society* (New York: Harcourt, Brace and World, 1964).
6   New York *Times*, July 5, 1964, Sec. 6, p. 30; Gannon interview; Bullock interview.

conducted by the very rich from New York and New England who had visited Saint Augustine during the late nineteenth and early twentieth centuries. Here then was a very stable, personally close, and structured society with strong ties to the past on the verge of being confronted by a civil rights crisis of considerable magnitude.

In this oldest of American societies, black citizens, who constituted 21 percent of the population, held a distinctly subservient role. Census data disclosed that black economic activity clearly meant waiting upon whites and the tourist trade reinforced this subservient status. A total of 60 percent of all black female employees were engaged in domestic or service work and 80 percent of all male employees worked in service or blue-collar positions. The black family median income stood at $3,500 in 1960, $1,500 less than white family income. The future seemed to offer faint promise to black children as they averaged only 7.4 years of schooling compared to 11.2 years for white children.[7]

Despite the pervasiveness of segregation and their economically inferior status, blacks generally "thought things were good" in Saint Augustine. While blacks were expected to defer to whites, relations between the races were cordial and, in many cases, friendly. No social interchange took place, but blacks and whites exchanged pleasantries on the street and often sat in discussion on the park benches in the plaza. Blacks were allowed to register and vote in the Democratic primary following *Smith* v. *Allwright* (1944) although only a small minority of black residents exercised this privilege. Black citizens also served on grand juries but this occurred very infrequently.[8]

Outside observers who visited Saint Augustine for extended periods of time considered race relations there to be "above the average." "Less segregation, less animosity" existed there, ac-

---

7 Bureau of the Census, *Census of the Population: 1950, Vol. II*, 10–28, 58, 67; Bureau of the Census, *Census of the Population: 1960, Vol. I*, 11–29, 127, 129, 204, 210.

8 Interview with Henry Twine, president of the Saint Augustine Branch of the NAACP, by the author, September 19, 1977; interview with Clyde Jenkins by the author, September 19, 1977; interview with John D. Bailey by the author, August 11, 1977; "Presentment of the Grand Jury, Fall Term—1963, in the Circuit Court, Seventh Judicial Circuit of Florida, In and For St. Johns County," in folder labeled "Governor's Statements, Legal Matters, St. Augustine," Governor Farris Bryant Papers, Florida State Archives, Tallahassee.

cording to reporter and native Floridian Hank Drane, "than in many communities in Florida." Historian David Chalmers noted in a similar vein that Saint Augustine permitted a greater degree of racial intermingling than "hundreds of other Southern towns." Even local blacks observed, "You really weren't too conscious at that time of the difference that existed." Black Assistant Superintendent of Schools Otis Mason portrayed it as "an harmonious thing."[9]

But all was not racial bliss in this southern town, and some leaders envisioned difficulty for black citizens should they seek to improve their lot. "Racially, there was no concern on the part of most of the white people there as to the black," the Episcopal minister commented. "They were servants. They were kept in this position and there was no attempt . . . to help them except . . . to the extent that you would keep them in their place."[10]

Following the *Brown* decision in 1954 and the efforts of a few local citizens, two of whom had just moved to the city, black Saint Augustine began to assert itself. Under the leadership of the Reverend Thomas Wright, blacks requested that the city commission provide additional recreational facilities and funding for a community library in the late 1950s. Since neither request threatened the maintenance of a segregated society, both were approved. The commitment of white Saint Augustinians to segregation, however, was apparent for any who wished to challenge it. In the summer of 1961 a young black student from Howard University, Henry Thomas, who had just returned home from a workshop on sit-ins, decided to seek service at Woolworth's lunch counter. Thomas was quickly carried off to jail once the waitress realized what he was attempting to do. The police transferred Thomas to the hospital during the night, seeking to have him ruled insane and committed to a mental institution. Only Thomas' screams for help and his reputation in the community, as well as the apparent reluctance of the doctors, prevented police from having him locked away.[11]

331

9   Jenkins interview; interview with Hank Drane by the author, January 31, 1978; interview with Otis Mason by the author, June 13, 1978; David Chalmers, *Hooded Americanism: The First Century of the Ku Klux Klan* (Chicago: Quadrangle, 1968), 378.
10   Seymour interview.
11   Interview with the Reverend Thomas Wright by the author, October 6, 1977; Twine interview.

Thomas' personal example and that of the North Carolina A & T students in Greensboro encouraged local black teenagers and students at Florida Memorial College, a black school in the city, to conduct additional sit-ins. Sporadic demonstrations began in 1962 under the direction of Wright and continued until Dr. Robert Hayling, a recently arrived black dentist in the community, took over the leadership of the Youth Council of the local National Association for the Advancement of Colored People in 1963. Hayling developed a Youth Council agenda and coordinated daily demonstrations during that summer aimed at ending segregation in places of public accommodation. Civil rights forces relied heavily on young people in Saint Augustine apparently because many old people were either afraid or satisfied with the way things were. Claude Sitton noted in the New York *Times* that "the Negro community here is generally poor, apathetic over the civil rights drive."[12]

The struggle proved to be difficult for Hayling and his young assistants. Hayling was waylaid at a Ku Klux Klan meeting and severely beaten. His home was also shot into several times and the family's dog was killed while sitting in the living room. Four black teenagers (two boys and two girls), who took part in the demonstrations, were placed in state reform schools for over four months by the county judge when their parents refused to keep them from participating in future sit-ins. They remained in jail until January when the state Correctional Institutions Board released them.[13]

During these early days of the desegregation drive, the civil rights forces achieved a few breakthroughs, persuading Howard Johnson's, Woolworth's and McCrory's, three national concerns, and Del Monico's Restaurant to desegregate. But these gains did not represent a trend in the business community. Indeed, they would be the only victories by the civil rights forces in Saint Augustine until the passage of the Civil Rights Act in July, 1964.[14]

The more typical response by the business leadership came in July, 1963, when three black men were fired from their jobs

12   Wright interview; New York *Times*, May 31, 1964, p. 50.
13   St. Augustine *Record*, February 9, 1964, p. 1; *Florida Times-Union* (Jacksonville), July 30, 1963, p. 20; Pittsburgh *Courier*, January 25, 1964, p. 1.
14   *Florida Star News* (Jacksonville), October 12, 1963, p. 1; "Along the NAACP Battlefront: Florida Breakthrough," *Crisis*, LXX (November, 1963), 553.

for participating in the demonstrations. Shortly after these firings the shop steward at the Fairchild Stratos Corporation, an aircraft manufacturing plant, called a meeting of all black workers and, with the apparent support of company officials, threatened them with the loss of their jobs if they took part in the sit-ins. Women and wives of men who were involved in the civil protests, and who worked in motels or as domestics, were also intimidated by employers. The business community seemed determined to stop the demonstrations before they spread further. No conspiracy existed among white businessmen to intimidate black residents. Segregationist attitudes were sufficiently widespread, however, that business leaders responded almost uniformly to civil rights demonstrations. This economic retaliation continued into 1964.[15]

The opposition of the businessmen to racial accommodation reflected their personal prejudices as well as those of their friends in the community. Typifying the views of many businessmen in Saint Augustine, Herbert E. Wolfe, president of the town's major bank and generally recognized as the most influential man in the community, regarded blacks as racial inferiors and opposed any equality between the races. A story he occasionally recounted to close friends reflected his personal prejudices: As a young man he was preparing his father's land for planting when an old black man, who was whiling away his time on a fence overlooking the land, told young Wolfe he was doing the plowing all wrong. The old-timer then proceeded to tell him how to do it correctly. Wolfe listened for a moment then dropped the plow and walked off, deciding he would never do anything again "that a nigger could do better."[16]

Businessmen were encouraged to resist the pressures to de-

333

15   Local Chapter of the Southern Christian Leadership Conference to Dr. William Sanders, Organization of American States, n.d., 7, in private papers of Professor David Chalmers, University of Florida, Gainesville; *Florida Star News* (Jacksonville), July 13, 1963, p. 1; *Andrew Young* v. *L. O. Davis, et al.*, #64-133–Civ–J, and pamphlet entitled "St. Augustine, Florida: 400 Years of Bigotry and Hate," 4, both in Judge Bryan J. Simpson Papers, P. K. Yonge Library of Florida History, University of Florida, Gainesville; interviews with Gannon, Hamilton Upchurch, Bullock, and Seymour.
16   Gannon interview. David K. Bartholomew in "An Analysis of Change in Power System and Decision-Making Process in a Selected County" (Ed.D., University of Florida, 1971), 42, ranked Wolfe as one of the two most influential men in the county.

segregate by the recently established John Birch Society. In fact, a large segment of the business community either belonged to or sympathized with the Birch Society. According to state senator Verle Pope from Saint Johns County: "There was a very active group who might be said to be of a John Birch variety, who were very prominent and very strong. They were the leaders in the Kiwanis Club and Rotary Club. They were on the vestries in the churches. Wherever you turned it was the same group of people who were in power in the various organizations." They also "tended to associate socially."[17]

334

Saint Augustine maintained a very active right-wing chapter called the Saint Johns Chapter of the Florida Coalition of Patriotic Societies. The organization brought together the community's right-wing organizations and maintained an office and reading room on Saint George Street in the heart of the old Spanish quarter. The chapter, headed by prominent local physician Dr. Hardgrove Norris, sponsored weekly lectures by right-wing speakers. The women who kept the room told a reporter that "the Communists are behind all this integration business." The anticommunist appeal of the Birch Society received widespread support from civil rights opponents in the community who perceived the civil rights movement as part of the Communist menace. Norris' views were shared by his many prominent friends in the community, including Mayor Joseph Shelley, Herbert Wolfe, newspaper editor A. H. Tebault, county school superintendent Douglas Hartley, city attorney Robert Andreu, police chief Virgil Stuart, county sheriff L. O. Davis, and county judge Charles Mathis.[18]

The support the John Birch Society received from the community made it very difficult, if not impossible, for those who wanted to compromise with the demonstrators in 1963 and 1964. Hamilton Upchurch, president of the Chamber of Commerce in 1965, noted: "Anything you proposed even . . . at a

17   Robert W. Hartley, "A Long, Hot Summer: The St. Augustine Racial Disorders of 1964" (M.A. thesis, Stetson University, 1972), 93; interview with Judge Richard O. Watson by the author, January 9, 1977; Hamilton Upchurch interview; Gannon interview; Bartholomew, "An Analysis of Change in Power System," 63, 64. The Birch Society regarded the civil rights movement as having "been deliberately and almost wholly created by the Communists." St. Augustine Record, August 22, 1965, p. 7A.

18   New York Times, June 14, 1964, p. 50; anonymous source; interviews with Bullock, Gannon, and Hartley.

cocktail party that was in any way conciliatory . . . you were ostracized by this extreme right wing. They said this thing is bigger than your pocketbook." Businessmen were also reluctant to take an independent position because the community was relatively small and close-knit. Upchurch observed that "every job had a name and a face."[19]

With progress at a standstill during the summer of 1963, leaders of the local NAACP, including Dr. Hayling, asked the city commission to establish a biracial committee. Mayor Shelley, a physician, and his fellow commissioners, all businessmen, opposed the idea. Shelly declared: "We have no biracial committee here because it could do nothing we have not already done." Dr. Norris, head of the local John Birch Society, opposed the creation of a biracial committee because "the negotiating table has been the chosen battleground by the Communist conspiracy for world conquest." Shelley was in great sympathy with this view. He pointed out that integration existed in all city-operated facilities. He was not being entirely truthful since the city's library was still closed to blacks. Shelley also contended that the commission "has no legal or moral right to tell any merchant how to operate his business."[20]

335

Local leaders argued that they had gone more than halfway in meeting the NAACP demands. Shelley noted repeatedly that the county school system had agreed voluntarily to desegregate its schools by admitting six black children to previously all-white schools. This was done, however, under the Florida Pupil Placement Law which had been designed to circumvent the Supreme Court's decision of 1954. While Saint Johns County had integrated its schools of its own accord, a suit by the NAACP was pending in federal district court asking for complete integration of the county schools. County school officials appear to have taken this first step to demonstrate some compliance with the *Brown* decision and thereby avoid massive court-ordered integration. In short, the school integration could not be said to demonstrate the city or county's racial progressivism as suggested by Shelley.[21]

19   Hamilton Upchurch interview.
20   St. Augustine *Record*, July 7, 1963, p. 1B.; interview with Dr. Joseph Shelley by the author, September 6, 1977; New York *Times*, July 3, 1964, p. 8.
21   Minutes of the Saint Augustine City Commission, June 28, 1963, pp. 4410–11, in City Hall, Saint Augustine; St. Augustine *Record*, May 10, 1963, p. 1,

336

Business leaders found additional support for maintaining the status quo in race relations from Governor Farris Bryant. Bryant had expressed his opposition to the civil rights bill while appearing before the United States Senate Commerce Committee. He argued that a motel owner, for example, should have the right to refuse service: "That's simple justice. The wonder is really that it can be questioned."[22]

The business community in Saint Augustine was thus under no pressure from the political leaders at the state or local level to ease the racial barriers that existed. In addition, the demonstrations had not caused any economic difficulties; tourism figures for the summer were above those for 1962. As a consequence, only the national chain stores which feared problems elsewhere modified their stance against serving blacks at lunch counters. The remaining members of the business community experienced no such pressures in this direction and opted instead to maintain racial barriers.[23]

In mid-August, 1963, the Florida Advisory Committee to the United States Commission on Civil Rights, which had been visiting several strife-ridden cities in the state, arrived in Saint Augustine. During the one day the committee received testimony on race relations in the community, not one member of the city commission, county commission, or any of the "invited business leaders" appeared as witnesses. White leaders stayed away from the meeting in the belief that the committee was not an impartial body and would only stir up more racial problems in the community. Many whites also felt that the problems in Saint Augustine were not the concern of any outside group. The committee noted that "in none of the other cities [in Florida] . . . has there been such a boycott." After hearing the testimony of several black leaders, their report concluded that "St. Augustine was a segregated super-bomb aimed at the heart of Florida's economic prosperity and political integrity, and the fuse is short."[24]

September 3, 1963, p. 1. Saint Augustine was not in the forefront of school desegregation in Florida; nearly two thousand black students attended white schools in Florida in 1964. Joseph Aaron Tomberlin, "The Negro and Florida's System of Education: The Aftermath of the *Brown Case*" (Ph.D. dissertation, Florida State University, 1967), 199.

22   *Florida Times-Union* (Jacksonville), July 30, 1963, p. 1.

23   New York *Times*, July 29, 1963, p. 9.

24   Florida Advisory Committee to the United States Commission on Civil Dis-

In December, 1963, a grand jury, which had been meeting for several weeks in an effort to head off the growing violence in the city—one white man was killed in the fall and several blacks beaten and their homes damaged—warned local leaders that unless they sat down and discussed black demands 1964 would see additional acts of racial violence.[25]

City leaders chose to ignore the warning of both groups and refused to negotiate with black leaders. Instead they laid the blame for Saint Augustine's racial difficulties on "outsiders," the Klan, and black militants. One leader commented, businessmen "attributed their problem [in 1963] to a pushy nigger [Hayling]." As a consequence, the city council, supported by the business community, refused to meet with black leaders. State Attorney Dan Warren from Daytona Beach viewed this decision by the white community as crucial for the future of race relations in Saint Augustine. In his eyes, by ignoring the grand jury's suggestion "the only remaining voice of moderation was smothered."[26]

337

During the late fall of 1963, after being approached by Dr. Hayling and other black leaders from Saint Augustine, the Southern Christian Leadership Conference decided to commit its resources to the desegregation drive in the city. The decision by the SCLC seems to have been based in part on the conditions in Saint Augustine and in part on its own needs and concerns. SCLC felt it needed publicity in 1964 to pressure Congress into passing the civil rights bill, to combat the growing militancy among blacks in America, and to raise money for its other campaigns. Since Saint Augustine was on the eve of its four hundredth anniversary, making it the oldest community in America and already the object of considerable nationwide interest, it had

---

orders, "Report on the Opening Meeting in St. Augustine, Florida, August 16, 1963," p. 3, and *Young* v. *Davis, et al.*, both in Simpson Papers; anonymous source; Hamilton Upchurch interview.

25 Reprint of article in Daytona Beach *Sunday News Journal*, February 21, 1965, in Simpson Papers.

26 Upchurch interview. Arrest records for 1963 and 1964 show rather clearly, however, that the majority of those arrested were Saint Augustinians and not outsiders. *Young* v. *Davis*, in Simpson Papers. The white attitude toward the demonstrators in 1963 was an old one—"These are our niggers—we can handle them." Pat Watters, *Down to Now: Reflections on the Southern Civil Rights Movement* (New York: Random House, 1971), 97; reprint from Daytona Beach *Sunday News Journal*, February 21, 1965, in Simpson Papers.

symbolic as well as practical value as a target. In addition to the desegregation of public accommodations, the SCLC also sought the employment of black policemen, firemen, and office workers by the city; establishment of a biracial committee; dropping of charges against demonstrators; and employment of people in the business community on the basis of merit, not race.[27]

The first wave of demonstrators arrived during Easter week, 1964. Led by Mrs. Malcolm Peabody, mother of the governor of Massachusetts, and accompanied by several prominent women and clergymen from the Boston area and a retinue of college students, the demonstrators transformed the situation in Saint Augustine from a rather insignificant local racial disturbance into a national civil rights crusade. In the process, the white community was further alienated. Mayor Shelley, speaking for many whites, declared that the trouble in the city was due to northern "scalawags" and that matters were well in hand until northerners "came down here with the idea of getting in jail."[28]

The intervention of northerners generated a deep-seated hostility among white Saint Augustinians who were personally insulted by these northern "do-gooders," especially the white college hippie and the "uppity" northern "nigger." Now the struggle took on the added appearance of a clash between cultures, and white southerners in Saint Augustine, very proud of their heritage, refused to accept criticism of their cultural traditions. Of additional concern to local residents was the view spread by the Birch Society that the Communist-led civil rights movement threatened the basic fabric of Saint Augustine society.[29]

27   Twine interview. Twine was a member of the Saint Augustine delegation that first approached the SCLC. Interview with the Reverend Fred Shuttlesworth by the author, September 13, 1978. See also John Herbers, *The Lost Priority: What Happened to the Civil Rights Movement in America?* (New York: Funk and Wagnalls, 1970), 68.
28   St. Augustine *Record*, March 29, 1964, p. 1. A variation of this view was expressed in 1963 by a businessman who told a northern correspondent: "Why don't you stay up North where you are really having trouble with Negroes." New York *Times*, July 29, 1963, p. 9.
29   For an elaboration of this point see Watters, *Down to Now*, 97. Interviews with Gannon and Shelley; interview with Dr. Hardgrove Norris by the author, September 15, 1978.

The Easter demonstrations were the highly publicized phase of the movement, designed to draw national attention to the problems in this historic city. In that they were very successful. Now, in late May, 1964, there began the second phase of the movement led by Dr. Martin Luther King, Jr., and aimed at bringing an end to segregation in Saint Augustine.

To facilitate this phase of the struggle, black leaders called for an economic boycott. Because the community was so economically dependent on tourism, civil rights leaders were confident that they could force the business community to abandon segregation. As Harry Boyte, a top King aide, pointed out: "This is the first time we've been able to put things on such a firm economic basis. In Birmingham the downtown merchants were hurt but we couldn't shut down U.S. Steel. Here it's a total community effort." A major part of this effort involved demonstrations to keep the city's problems on the front page of the nation's newspapers and on the evening television news. The daily sit-ins followed by the evening marches and the ocean wade-ins kept the press's attention, particularly when white mobs, spurred on by the rhetoric of J. B. Stoner of the Ku Klux Klan and the Reverend Connie Lynch, assaulted the demonstrators.[30]

The demonstrations were carefully planned in advance. Local black leader Henry Twine noted that strategy meetings were held every night to determine "whitey's reaction." One reporter observed that the demonstrators "always came up with something new that would cause the whites to trigger some violence and so it would get the headlines." The goal of SCLC was to keep the nation's attention riveted on Saint Augustine and in this manner to bring outside pressure to bear on the community as well as to point out the need for the civil rights bill.

Commenting on the movement in Saint Augustine, King observed, "Even if we do not get all we should, movements such as this tend more and more to give a Negro the sense of self-respect that he needs. It tends to generate courage in Negroes outside the movement. It brings intangible results outside the community where it is carried out. There is a hardening of attitudes in situations like this. But other cities see and say, 'We don't want to be another Albany [Georgia] or Birmingham,' and they make

30   *Wall Street Journal*, June 19, 1964, p. 1.

339

changes. Some communities, like this one, had to bear the cross."[31]

The use of the boycott seemed to make business leaders only more adamant in their opposition to desegregation, however. When Harry Boyte approached Herbert Wolfe and asked him to use his influence to stop the mounting violence, Wolfe refused. He told Boyte he saw nothing wrong with the status of Negroes in Saint Augustine. Wolfe said he agreed with a local editorial which accused King of being a troublemaker who was turning the city into a battleground. Two other business leaders who opposed any compromise argued that "the sole reason for this movement is that local public officials will not force owners of private businesses to integrate their facilities in direct opposition to the 13th Amendment to the United States Constitution which outlaws involuntary servitude."[32]

The motel and restaurant owners, who bore the brunt of the demonstrations, followed the lead of James Brock, manager of the Monson Motor Lodge and president of the state and past president of the local hotel and motel managers association. Brock refused to serve any blacks unless "a federal court orders us to." But, significantly, Brock was not unyielding in his position, for he later declared, "If a representative group of St. Augustine citizens appeals to us, in the interests of community welfare, we might consider it [integration]."[33]

Brock and his colleagues in the motel, restaurant, and tourist trade were desperately looking for help from other community leaders. Tourism had fallen off dramatically by the early weeks of June. One motel owner complained, "I've gotten as many cancellations as reservations this week. I just want all this to end." James A. Kalivas of Chimes Restaurant claimed his business was off 60 percent. Capt. Francis F. Usina, who ran a sightseeing vessel, grumbled that business was running 50 percent behind a year ago. "If Martin Luther King doesn't stay away, the whole summer will be lost," he said. Perhaps the most accurate barometer of the tourist trade was the daily attendance record kept by the Castillo de San Marcos, an old Spanish fort

31   Interviews with Twine and Drane; Herbers, *The Lost Priority*, 70.
32   Pittsburgh *Courier*, June 6, 1964, p. 4; New York *Times*, June 7, 1964, p. 48; *Florida Times-Union* (Jacksonville), June 14, 1964, p. 22.
33   Miami *Herald*, June 5, 1964, p. 8A; New York *Times*, June 7, 1964, p. 48.

340

administered by the National Park Service, whose attendance had fallen a full 30 percent behind the previous year's total. The fort's historian commented: "If it keeps up, there's no doubt the decline will get bigger."[34]

The business leaders who were only indirectly tied to the tourist trade and the professional leaders appeared largely unmoved by the growing problems of the tourist economy, however. Racial traditions, pressures from friends in the Birch Society, and the belief that the community was being used by outside forces for other purposes, made these business and civic leaders resistant to change or compromise. The sense of being beleaguered and embattled also created a "fortress mentality" in which the leadership turned increasingly inward. A reporter, who had covered the city since 1959, observed that "all of a sudden it became leaderless."[35]

341

The unwillingness of the business community, the most influential group in the city at this time, to assume the mantle of leadership enabled the Klan and local white militants to become spokesmen for the community. It also allowed city police chief Virgil Stuart and Saint Johns County sheriff L. O. Davis, both of whom opposed the efforts of the civil rights movement, to enforce the law selectively. Davis was generally recognized to be in league with the white militants. Hoss Manucy, their spokesman, maintained his office on a chair in front of the sheriff's office and appeared to have free access to the sheriff's office. Chief Stuart was alleged to be an "extreme right winger" who not only thought there was "a communist behind every bush . . . he saw one."[36]

The SCLC was clearly surprised by the unbending attitude of the community leaders and the violence it encountered on the street. Many members of the SCLC, including Dr. King and Andrew Young, had thought that a great deal could be accomplished in Saint Augustine since it had widespread residential integration and was so dependent on tourism. They now realized in mid-June that they were in for a long fight which would

---

34 *Wall Street Journal*, June 19, 1964, p. 1; New York *Times*, June 7, 1964, p. 48.
35 Drane interview.
36 *Ibid.*; interview with Judge Bryan Simpson by the author, June 24, 1964; Upchurch interview.

be every bit as arduous as the Birmingham struggle. King was moved by the hostility of business and civic leaders and the mounting violence in Saint Augustine as well as by a desire to elicit federal assistance to say that "we have never worked in . . . [a city] as lawless as this."

The night marches and the wade-ins by the civil rights forces generated the most violence. Whites responded by throwing bricks, acid, firecrackers and physically assaulting any black or white they could get their hands on. Cameramen who tried to film these events were also badly beaten and their cameras broken. After a few weeks of this violence, several cameramen and reporters asked for new assignments.[37]

By the third week in June as the violence continued unabated and business continued to fall off, the motel owners met, with Edward Mussallem, owner of the Caravan Motel, acting as chairman. The assembly also included representatives from the Chamber of Commerce, the Florida East Coast Railroad, Wolfe, and owners of restaurants and entertainment facilities. But rather than suggesting a compromise, the businessmen, through their spokesman state senator Verle Pope, denounced the role of outsiders for desecrating Saint Augustine "for some unknown reason." They only agreed "to continue to operate their businesses in accordance with present and future laws." The implication was that they would abide by the civil rights bill when it was passed by Congress.[38]

Without offering a concrete proposal, the merchants did announce that they were interested in a peaceful settlement of the crisis. They refused, however, to meet with Dr. Robert Hayling. The Reverend Fred Shuttlesworth of the SCLC characterized the statement as "segregationist" and declared that it did "not show much evolution." He promised "to keep up our present program."[39]

But SCLC was tiring of the violence and the cost of the struggle, and, with the passage of the civil rights bill imminent,

37 Drane interview. See also Miami *Herald* and New York *Times*, May 28–June 4, 1964. The residential desegregation was misleading. It was a result of geographic limitations as well as a carry-over from antebellum days when slaves lived in the rear quarters of their master's residence. New York *Times*, June 6, 1964, p. 10.
38 New York *Times*, June 18, 1964, p. 25; Tampa *Tribune*, June 18, 1964, p. 8A.
39 New York *Times*, June 18, 1964, p. 25.

decided to keep the lines of communication with the business community open. Dr. King said he would consider the necessity of including Hayling at such meetings. To add encouragement to the voices of moderation in the business community, he observed that he had heard that several business leaders were willing to desegregate, hire blacks, and drop charges against the demonstrators if a compromise could be arranged. Adding to King's initiatives, a special grand jury had just completed its hearings and was expected to recommend a cooling-off period of thirty days during which time a biracial committee would attempt to alleviate the crisis. Moreover, Herbert Wolfe had privately initiated discussions with civic and business leaders in an attempt to effect a compromise.[40]

343

Just when it appeared a settlement might be possible, the SCLC staged its most spectacular demonstration. Seven demonstrators jumped into the swimming pool at the Monson Motor Lodge. Brock, the manager of the motel and a moderating force in the community up to that time, lost his composure. Shouting at the swimmers to get out, Brock told them he was pouring acid into the pool (it turned out to be muriatic acid, a harmless cleaning detergent for the pool).[41]

This incident was followed by a series of marches, sit-ins, and wade-ins at the ocean which further alienated the white community and ended efforts to bring about a compromise. Verle Pope told reporters: "Well, we are through. We can't understand why they hit us like this when we were working sincerely on this thing. The jury was working on a really worthwhile report. Now it's all gone."[42]

Despite the improved chances for peace, SCLC had decided to continue the demonstrations because Dr. King and his aides felt the white leadership had not developed an adequate desegregation plan. King also believed the grand jury's thirty-day cooling-off period was much too long and would cripple the desegregation drive. It was back to the barricades for the organization.[43]

40   *Ibid.*, June 25, 1964, p. 19; Miami *Herald*, June 18, 1964, p. 1A, June 28, 1964, pp. 1A–2A; *Young* v. *Davis, et al.*, and notes of Judge Bryan Simpson, Box 1, both in Simpson Papers.
41   *Florida Times-Union* (Jacksonville), June 21, 1964, p. 22.
42   Miami *Herald*, June 28, 1964, pp. 1A–2A.
43   *Ibid.*

At the end of June, Florida Senator George Smathers informed his close friend and former campaign finance chairman, Herbert Wolfe, that President Lyndon Johnson was anxious for a cessation of the crisis before he signed the civil rights bill into law. Smathers asked Wolfe to see if he could establish a biracial committee to ease tensions and satisfy one of King's demands. Wolfe called together twenty-five civic and business leaders and informed them of the president's wishes. Mayor Shelley immediately expressed his opposition to the idea telling Wolfe, "You're going to sell the community out and give Martin Luther King a victory." The others agreed completely with Shelley and called Governor Bryant, who had also been contacted by Smathers and the president, to inform him of their decision.[44]

To the chagrin of these men, Bryant announced to the press on the following day, June 30, the formation of a biracial commission in Saint Augustine to end the crisis. Shelley called Bryant and asked him what had happened. Bryant replied that the "truth of it is, I haven't formed a committee in Saint Augustine." Bryant, who was under considerable pressure from President Johnson, decided to go ahead with his announcement as a concession to the president. King called off further demonstrations, praising Bryant and white leaders for taking "a first important step" toward peace, although he surely must have known that the commission was a fraud. Nevertheless, King also realized that the governor's proposal placed the state on the side of the civil rights movement and when combined with the signing of the Civil Rights Act on July 2 assured SCLC of achieving most of its goals in Saint Augustine.[45]

The crisis appeared to be at an end. At a meeting in which eighty of the town's one hundred businessmen were present, a vote was rendered to comply with the public accommodation sections of the new law. James Brock commented that his col-

344

44   Shelley interview.
45   *Ibid.*; St. Augustine *Record*, July 1, 1964, p. 1. Federal pressure was not confined to Governor Bryant. Hamilton Upchurch noted that he represented a group of men in 1964 who were trying to obtain a federal charter to establish a savings and loan association. The charter was rejected. Upchurch was informed some years later by the federal hearing officer that "St. Augustine could not have gotten the Red Cross if they had been wiped off the map in 1964." Upchurch interview.

leagues unanimously opposed the measure in principle but, with only "a few dissenters," agreed to abide by it.[46]

The racial problems were not over yet, however. No one had taken into consideration the response of the Klan members and their sympathizers. Allowed to assume a leadership position in the community when a power vacuum was created by the unwillingness of business and civic leaders to deal with the racial crisis, these elements were not now ready to step aside and permit the community to comply with this hated law. Carrying picket signs proclaiming DELICIOUS FOOD—EAT WITH NIGGERS HERE, NIGGERS SLEEP HERE—WOULD YOU, and CIVIL RIGHTS HAS TO GO, white militants paraded in front of the desegregated establishments. One businessman complained: "We have been caught in a dilemma." Under federal law "we are forced to serve Negroes although it hurts our business. If we serve them, then white pickets run the rest of the business away."[47]

The activities of the Klan and their supporters were not confined to demonstrations alone. When restaurant and motel owners continued to serve blacks, they began receiving telephone calls threatening their lives and their businesses. On the evening of July 24 two whites threw a molotov cocktail into Brock's restaurant, badly damaging the interior. The following day, those businessmen who had not begun turning blacks away now did.[48]

State Attorney General James Kynes, who viewed most of the crisis from Tallahassee but was periodically sent to Saint Augustine at the request of the governor, had little sympathy for the plight of the business community. Kynes felt the restaurant and motel owners wanted to have it both ways. When Negroes were conducting sit-ins, he observed, merchants allowed young white toughs to set the mood of the town with little or no resis-

345

46   Florida Times-Union (Jacksonville), July 2, 1964, p. 18; Lucille Plummer, et al. v. James E. Brock, et al., #64–187–Civ–J, and Simpson's Notes, both in Simpson Papers.
47   St. Augustine Record, July 16, 1964, p. 1.
48   Testimony of James E. Brock, Lucille Plummer, et al. v. James E. Brock, et al., #64–187–Civ–J, p. 56, in Record Group 21, Accession No. 73A377, FRC No. 1E15823, Agency Box 13, Federal Records Center, East Point, Georgia; St. Augustine Record, July 24, 1964, p. 1. Louis Connell of Santa Maria Restaurant told Judge Simpson, "I was scared; I don't mind admitting it." New York Times, July 23, 1964, p. 15.

tance to this takeover. Now, Kynes declared, the businessmen found they could not take back control when it no longer suited their purpose to have gangs of whites roaming the streets.[49]

Perhaps more significantly, a number of businessmen, who were angered by having to accept new racial patterns, hoped these militants might yet resurrect segregation. This attitude was further reflected during an abortive effort to establish a genuine biracial committee. In early August, 1964, a grand jury nominated several members to such a committee to head off the renewed violence. Only one of the white members appointed to the committee agreed to serve. Andrew McGhin, president of the Chamber of Commerce, said he could not serve "due to pre-existing business and a community commitment." Three of the remaining four whites named also spoke of more pressing concerns. The grand jury had erred in naming the committee without first informing these individuals. Nevertheless, after these four whites declined to serve, no other white leaders in the community could be found to replace them. Another opportunity to bring the community together had been consciously rejected by the white leadership.[50]

While SCLC leaders received little support from businessmen, they found a powerful ally in Federal Judge Bryan Simpson of the district court of appeals in Jacksonville. Simpson ordered the police department to enforce the laws equitably and made the businessmen abide by the new Civil Rights Act. In a series of decisions he blocked the resegregation of motel and restaurant facilities and forbade the segregationists from threatening or coercing owners. Furthermore, when he ordered a deputy sheriff to turn in his badge for intimidating a local black citizen, he made it demonstrably clear that he would not allow race relations to return to their pre-1963 state.[51]

Simpson's intervention was critical, for it led to the removal of outside militants from the community and enabled the more moderate forces to reestablish political control. This did not

346

50   Newspaper Scrapbook on the Saint Augustine Civil Rights Movement, August 7, 1964, Saint Augustine Historical Society, Saint Augustine; St. Augustine *Record*, August 14, 1964, p. 15B.
51   St. Augustine *Record*, July 20, 1964, p. 1, August 5, 1964, p. 1; New York *Times*, August 6, 1964, p. 16; *Plummer, et al.* v. *Brock, et al.*, Transcript of Oral Findings, August 19, 1964, p. 10, in Simpson Papers.

bring about an immediate reconciliation between the races nor a permanent end to the violence. Many white businessmen were still incensed over the intervention of outside forces into "their peaceful community." The restaurant association, for example, adopted a resolution reluctantly agreeing to integrate but also deploring "the action of the Congress and the Courts in enforcing integration" and stating "that integration of places of accommodation is obnoxious to us." Several restaurant owners put signs above their cash register stating that all money spent by integrationists in their establishments would be used to aid Barry Goldwater's 1964 presidential campaign. In a speech before a local civic group, Harold Colee, head of the state Chamber of Commerce and a native Saint Augustinian, reflected the views of many when he remarked derisively how the recent racial crisis could be marketed to attract more tourists: "You may interestingly point out just where a certain prominent New England lady—a professional bleeding heart—was standing when she posed for cameramen of the national news media, working from a prepared script, in the year 1964."[52]

347

By the middle of 1965, blacks were still unsure about their place in Saint Augustine and few were willing to dine in white restaurants or register at white motels. One black citizen who could afford to eat at such restaurants commented: "You can be pretty sure that if you eat at a white restaurant and they know who you are, your boss will be told that you're trying to stir up trouble. If they don't know you, you might be arrested after you leave so they can find out about you." Sporadic violence continued through the fall of 1964 and winter of 1965, as blacks were assaulted often for no apparent reason.[53]

Despite such circumstances, the business community had substantially altered its racial policies if not its racial attitudes by the spring of 1965. The impact of the racial crisis on the tourist industry in Saint Augustine had gradually awakened business leaders to the economic consequences of their actions during the past year. By the end of 1964 tourism was off by 40 to 60 percent from the 1963 levels in virtually all businesses. No

52 St. Augustine *Record*, August 11, 1964, p. 1; Pittsburgh *Courier*, September 26, 1964, p. 4.
53 *Wall Street Journal*, August 6, 1965, p. 1; *Florida Star News* (Jacksonville), September 18, 1964, p. 1, April 17, 1965, p. 1; St. Augustine *Record*, August 26, 1964, p. 6, July 21, 1965, p. 1.

one in the community, not even those whose businesses were only indirectly tied to the tourist trade, could afford a repetition of the economic decline experienced in 1964.[54]

With the four hundredth anniversary about to be celebrated in September, 1965, and the SCLC promising renewed demonstrations if the violence did not cease, businessmen organized to block further resistance. When racial incidents recurred in the spring of 1965, City Manager Charles Barrier, at the urging of Wolfe, and business leaders deplored the violence. In a front-page story in the city's newspaper, Barrier warned whites who committed such acts that they would be arrested and vigorously prosecuted. In a similar statement a few days earlier, Sheriff Davis let it be known that his department would not permit the fighting and rock throwing of last year. Reporter Hank Drane of the *Florida Times-Union* observed that "once the community decided they wanted to get rid of it [the Klan], it was amazing how speedily . . . they got the Klan out."[55]

If this decision to alter the racial policies of the past was not sufficient, Judge Bryan Simpson stood in the background having made it apparent to all that Saint Augustinians must abide by the Civil Rights Act of 1964 and accept a biracial society. Leon Friedman called Simpson "one district judge who has excelled all others in his speed in enforcing the law and in his willingness to embark on new legal territory to protect Negro rights." The community thus no longer had recourse even to southern justice.[56]

Finally, recently elected Governor Haydon Burns refused to challenge the judicial findings of Judge Simpson as Governor Farris Bryant had done on one occasion. If Saint Augustinians wanted to continue the struggle to preserve their segregationist society, they would have to do so alone. This they were unwilling to do.[57]

54   St. Augustine *Record*, January 22, 1965, p. 5. Chamber of Commerce manager H. B. Chitty estimated the economic loss at from eight to ten million dollars of the city's annual tourist income of twenty-two million dollars. Atlanta *Journal and Constitution*, July 5, 1964, p. 80.

55   St. Augustine *Record*, July 23, 1965, p. 1, July 21, 1965, p. 1; Drane interview. Blacks were also given token representation on all quadricentennial committees and encouraged to participate in all activities.

56   Leon Friedman, *Southern Justice* (New York: Random House, 1965), 193.

57   Bryant attempted to stop the night marches by the civil rights forces. Simpson ruled against Bryant's position and then threatened him with contempt

In many respects the business community's response to the racial crisis in Saint Augustine had a great deal in common with that found in such "'Old South' cities as Charleston [and] New Orleans." Numan Bartley observed that "tradition, respect for old wealth, concern for the style of social life, and an elitist outlook acted as barriers to changes in social and ideological outlook." While this observation appears applicable to the Saint Augustine experience, a distinctly non–Old South organization, the John Birch Society, added a new variable to the racial picture in this community making it much more difficult for civil rights leaders to change racial traditions. An Episcopal clergyman found the businessmen in the city to be "independently minded" and "sufficiently committed to what they believed . . . to jeopardize their businesses." The pressures of an influential John Birch organization and a relatively small, interpersonal society whose leaders shared the anti-Communist views of the Birch Society thus tended to suppress dissent and discourage moderation as the community rallied to ward off the civil rights movement's frontal assault.[58]

349

The businessmen in Saint Augustine had to be forced to abandon the racial traditions of the past by civil rights forces, the federal courts, and the federal government. Only when the business leaders realized there was no turning back, and their economic viability and the celebration of the town's four hundredth anniversary were tied to the amelioration of the crisis did they oppose the reemergence of racial violence.

In marked contrast to the era of Reconstruction, the federal pressure to desegregate Saint Augustine remained unwavering throughout the 1960s. Responding to the moral suasion and

---

when the governor indicated he would ignore the decision. Bryant then reversed his position. St. Augustine *Record*, June 10, 1964, p. 1. The business committee seems to have opposed completely Judge Simpson's decision overturning Governor Bryant's ban on the night marches. Businessmen felt these marches were largely responsible for the violence. The testimony before Judge Simpson clearly revealed, however, that the violence was fostered not by the marchers but by the white onlookers. Transcript of Hearing, June 13, 1964, *Andrew Young* v. *L. O. Davis, et al.*, #64–133–Civ–J, Record Group 21, Accession No. 73A377, FRC No. 1E15887, Agency Box 9, Federal Records Center. See also Arguments of Tobias Simon and William Kunstler in same location.

58   Numan V. Bartley, *The Rise of Massive Resistance: Race and Politics in the South During the 1950's* (Baton Rouge: Louisiana State University Press, 1969), 313; Bullock interview.

activism of the civil rights movement, the federal government abolished racial discrimination in public accommodations, schools, and voting. A social revolution did occur in Saint Augustine, but it did not emanate from the white leadership in the community as suggested by Claude Sitton and Reed Sarratt. Time, a dogmatic civil rights leadership, the constant threat of federal intervention, and a decline in influence of the Birch Society gradually brought about an acceptance of a biracial society by the city's businessmen in the 1970s. If Saint Augustine's response is typical of other tradition-bound, Birch-influenced southern communities, then such places did not willingly accept the racial developments of the 1950s. On the contrary, a federal government, encouraged to act by the courts, civil rights groups, and a sympathetic North, mandated these social changes.

Significantly, the change in white attitudes and in the political and social condition of black Saint Augustinians had very little impact on black economic standing. Because of the heavy tourist orientation of the economy, black residents continued to work in largely unskilled, service-oriented positions during the 1970s. The closing of the Fairchild-Hiller aircraft plant in 1972 further reduced employment opportunities for blacks outside the tourist industry. One black leader described the job opportunities as basically "pick and shovel." Hamilton Upchurch observed in 1978 that there were still "no blacks in responsible jobs." Black parents were particularly concerned about the departure of their children to other cities where greater employment opportunities existed.[59]

Jobs which offered more than menial wages and limited opportunity for advancement thus became the major concern of black leaders in the decade of the 1970s and into the 1980s. They have focused their demands on the city, seeking more jobs in government, especially in the police department and fire department. Presently, only one black is employed by the police department, where Virgil Stuart still serves as police chief, and none are employed by the fire department. Black employment has increased steadily in city government during the 1970s, but the jobs have been almost exclusively in the blue-collar and sec-

350

[59] Twine interview; Hamilton Upchurch interview; interview with Mrs. Catherine Twine by the author, September 19, 1977.

retarial ranks. Only in the school system have blacks been able to obtain white-collar positions in large numbers.[60]

Businessmen largely removed themselves from the civil rights debate after 1965. The rapid decline of the civil rights movement with the final departure of SCLC and the decision by Dr. Hayling to move to south Florida in 1967 facilitated the withdrawal of business leaders from racial deliberations. With the racial crisis at an end, businessmen readily returned to their chief concern, their own enterprises.

In recent years, businessmen have avoided becoming involved in civil rights developments. Black leaders have concentrated their efforts against the city in an effort to improve job opportunities and public services for black neighborhoods. Never anxious to be in the limelight on social issues which did not directly affect their economic enterprises, businessmen have been content to stay in the background and ignore recent racial concerns. Without the involvement of this most influential group, however, real economic opportunity for black Saint Augustinians has not been possible and black gains since 1965 have been largely limited to the social and political arenas.

351

60   Henry Twine interview.

About the Authors

David R. Colburn is Professor of History at the University of Florida. He has published widely, including his 1985 book, *Racial Change and Community Crisis: St. Augustine, Florida, 1877-1980* (Columbia University Press).

Robert W. Hartley has been a college administrator, college teacher, and businessman since he completed his Masters degree. He is originally from St. Augustine, lived through the "long hot summer" of 1964, and has now returned to live there, where he teaches in the public school system.

Edward W. Kallal received his law degree from Duke University in 1979 and is a partner in the Atlanta firm of Sutherland, Asbill and Brennan.

Bibliographical Information

and

Acknowledgements

1. *A Long Hot Summer: The St. Augustine Racial Disorders of 1964*, by Robert W. Hartley was originally written as an M. A. thesis at Stetson University in 1972. It has been edited for publication here, but otherwise is presented as written. It is published by arrangement with the author.

2. *St. Augustine and the Ku Klux Klan: 1963 and 1964*, by Edward W. Kallal, Jr. was originally written as a Senior Honors Thesis in the Department of History at the University of Florida in 1976. It has been edited for publication, but otherwise is presented as written. It is published by arrangement with the author.

3. *Racial and Civil Disorders in St. Augustine*, Report of the Florida Legislative Investigation Committee, was published by the State of Florida in February of 1965.

4. *The Saint Augustine Business Community: Desegregation, 1963-1964*, by David R. Colburn was originally published in *Southern Businessmen and Desegregation*, edited by Elizabeth Jacoway and David R. Colburn and published by Louisiana State University Press, Baton Rouge, Louisiana, in 1982. It is published here by permission of the Press.

Index

TITLES IN THE SERIES

Martin Luther King, Jr.

and the

Civil Rights Movement

DAVID J. GARROW, EDITOR

14. *Conscience of a Troubled South: The Southern Conference Educational Fund, 1946-1966*, by Irwin Klibaner

15. *Direct Action and Desegregation, 1960-1962: Toward a Theory of the Rationalization of Protest*, by James H. Laue

16. *The Sit-In Movement of 1960*, by Martin Oppenheimer

17. *The Student Nonviolent Coordinating Committee: The Growth of Radicalism in a Civil Rights Organization*, by Emily Stoper

18. *The Social Vision of Martin Luther King, Jr.*, by Ira G. Zepp, Jr.